The American Liberals and the Russian Revolution

THE
American Liberals and the Russian Revolution

BY CHRISTOPHER LASCH

Columbia University Press

NEW YORK AND LONDON

1962

THE author wishes to thank the following people and publishers for permission to quote material to which they hold the literary rights:

Lisa von Borowsky, for permission to quote from the papers of Raymond Robins; Mrs. Raymond Clapper, for permission to quote from the papers of Raymond Clapper; John O. Crane, for permission to quote from the papers of Charles R. Crane; Mrs. George W. Overton and Dr. Paul V. Harper, for permission to quote from the papers of Samuel N. Harper; Mrs. Amos Pinchot, for permission to quote from the papers of Amos Pinchot; Norman Thomas, for permission to quote from his papers in the New York Public Library; David R. Watkins, for permission to quote from the papers of William C. Bullitt; Nathaniel Weyl, for permission to quote from the papers of Walter Weyl; Ella Winter, for permission to quote from the papers of Lincoln Steffens; Doubleday & Co., Methuen & Co., the Macmillan Co. of Canada, and Mrs. George Bambridge, for permission to quote from Rudyard Kipling's "Gunga Din," from his *Barrack Room Ballads;* Farrar, Strauss & Cudahy and Hamish Hamilton Ltd., for permission to quote from the autobiography of Norman Angell, *After All* (1951); Harcourt, Brace & World, for permission to quote from *The Letters of Lincoln Steffens,* edited by Ella Winter and Granville Hicks (1938); Houghton Mifflin Co., for permission to quote from *The Intimate Papers of Colonel House,* by Charles Seymour (1926–1928); *Political Science Quarterly,* for permission to reprint portions of the author's article, "American Intervention in Siberia."

Library of Congress Catalog Card Number: 62-18617
Manufactured in the United States of America

To My Mother and

Father

Foreword

THE term "liberal" is surely one of the most baffling in political discourse. It can mean almost anything, from a belief in rugged individualism to a belief in the welfare state. It can be used so as to take in almost everybody or so as to take in nobody but a few intellectuals. All Americans are liberals, by virtue of the fact that they have no feudal past against which to rebel; but Americans at the same time are conservative in their liberalism, as Europeans keep reminding us, and as we ourselves have now begun to realize. One finally despairs of investing the term with any meaning at all. But efforts to find a substitute are equally unavailing. "Progressive" is not much better, although it is the term usually applied to the reform movement of the period embraced by this study—applied, indeed, to the period itself. I have stuck to "liberal" because I wanted to emphasize the continuity between the liberalism of 1917 and that of 1962, to show that the difficulties we face in attempting to understand the Soviet Union, to reconcile our uneasiness in the face of the "permanent revolution" with our belief in "self-determination," are by no means new.

Liberalism, then as now, was less a set of attitudes toward specific issues than a set of assumptions about human affairs. The liberal of 1900–1920 was an optimist; he believed in the moral progress of the human spirit; he believed that human reason could ultimately order the world so as to eliminate poverty, disease, discomfort and war. He did not think man had to be coerced into sociable behavior; that is why he was for self-determination, the removal of external restraints, in every area of human activity—for the self-determination of nations, of municipalities ("home rule"), of the individual ("self-reliance"). He believed, in short, that it would be possible in the not too distant future to substitute the rule of reason for the rule of force in the relations among men, in international as well as in domestic affairs. In domestic politics the issue between the liberal and the conservative was sometimes obscured; but the outbreak of the war in Europe in 1914 brought the deeper issues to the surface. No liberal could contemplate the war, the triumph of force over reason, without misgivings, or accept the necessity of American intervention without reservations—reservations the exact nature of which Wilson's Fourteen Points were to make clear.

But the war, if it pointed up the difference between liberals and conservatives, also brought to light a cleavage within liberalism itself, with which I shall be constantly concerned in the following narrative. It drove a wedge between those who, while critical of their own country in peacetime, eagerly closed ranks in time of war, and those who continued to doubt, throughout the war, that any nation or group of nations could be regarded as the repository of all political virtue. Not that the former of these, in their zeal for the war, became indistinguishable from conservatives, or that the latter renounced the war altogether. The more warlike liberal, William Allen White or Charles R. Crane or William English Walling or Woodrow Wilson himself, still sought to reconcile his support of the war with his liberalism, accepting the war only when he had convinced himself that it was a "war to end war"; while the true conservative was suspicious of all such programs for the redemption of mankind. The conservative held that the use of force in international affairs was not only necessary but desirable; the liberal, even the pro-war liberal, apologized for it. It was just his attempt to reconcile his support of the war—and his opposition to the Russian revolution—with the precepts of liberalism, which involved him in some of the difficulties explored in these pages.

If the "war liberals," as I have called them, did not go so far in their support of the war as to embrace a frankly conservative point of view, neither did the others go so far in their opposition to the war as to embrace pacifism. The pacifists were always a minority within a minority. But a number of liberals, such men as Walter Lippmann, Lincoln Steffens, Amos Pinchot, Frederic C. Howe, Oswald Garrison Villard and Walter Weyl, became what I have chosen to call, perhaps rather clumsily, "anti-imperialists." Their reservations about the war were more specific and a good deal more articulate than those of the war liberals, who felt only a vague need to reiterate, from time to time and in very general terms, the high moral purpose of the conflict. The anti-imperialists were not satisfied with rhetoric alone; they wanted the aims of the war as embodied in the secret treaties among the Allies to be formally redefined so as to preclude a punitive, vindictive, imperialistic peace. The revision of these treaties thus became the price which they demanded for their support of the war. Because President Wilson failed to bring about such a revision of war aims, the anti-imperialists eventually deserted him and campaigned against ratification of the Treaty of Versailles. But the war liberals stuck with Wilson to the end.

I am aware that the term "anti-imperialists" is an unfortunate choice, insofar as it suggests a parallel with the group of men who opposed acquisition of the Philippine Islands in 1898–1900. Such a parallel would be quite misleading. The earlier anti-imperialists were mugwumps. They held very conservative views on domestic politics, as is shown by their reluctance to support William Jennings Bryan in 1900 when he ran on a platform denouncing "imperialism." [1] The anti-imperialists of 1917–1919, on the other hand, were progressives. They supported domestic reforms, many of them of a sweeping nature, even though some of these men—the example of Oswald Garrison Villard comes to mind—sprang from a mugwump tradition; and even though progressivism as a whole owed a great deal to mugwumpery, as Richard Hofstadter makes clear in *The Age of Reform*.[2] The fact remains, however, that the leaders of the anti-imperialist movement of 1898—those who were still active twenty years later—became in 1917 "war liberals" of the most outspoken sort.

Why then have I used the term "anti-imperialists" at all? I have been obliged to use it for lack of a better term; but also because after all it describes as accurately as any other term the position of one particular group of liberals with regard to the war. They supported American intervention, these "anti-imperialists," only on condition that the war should not be used to further the interests of British and French imperialism, as embodied in the secret treaties. But the term "imperialism" came to have for them a broader meaning even than that. By 1917, everything about the prevailing social order which these liberals deplored, everything they were trying to reform, could be summed up in the single word "imperialism." Their own writings make the point again and again. The choice of the word "anti-imperialists" seems therefore not only appropriate but inevitable.

There is yet another difficulty raised by the categorization employed here. Although one can isolate a body of liberal opinion which can be called "anti-imperialist" and another body of opinion, the adherents to which can be called "war liberals," and although it is possible, moreover, to say at any given point what people belonged to which group, it is difficult over a longer period of time to speak of clear-cut groups at all, because the alignment of opinion tended, quite naturally under such circumstances, to fluctuate. Some liberals, the editors of the *New Republic*, for instance, stuck to an anti-imperialist position throughout the war. Others, of whom the war socialists are the best example (William English Walling, John Spargo, Charles Edward Russell and others), maintained with equal consistency the view that the war in Europe was from the beginning a conflict between democracy and autocracy, not, as the anti-imperialists argued, a conflict of competing imperialisms. But other liberals are more difficult to classify. Readers may notice, for instance, that in this study such papers as the Springfield *Republican*, the New York *Evening Post* and the Des Moines *Register* are sometimes referred to as "anti-imperialist" and sometimes as "war liberal" papers. This exasperating but unavoidable shifting of labels leads one to wonder whether it is not more accurate to think of "anti-imperialism" and "war liberalism" as opposite poles toward which liberal opinion gravitated, rather than as terms describing two clearly defined groups of men. Sometimes, of course, they do define groups of men as well as poles of opinion; the fact that they do not always do so simply reflects the uncertainty of liberal opinion in a time of crisis.

Why not simply say, then, that liberals were confused, and be done with it? The answer is that it is precisely the purpose of this study to define the nature of the confusion and to explain its implications. Nothing would be gained by giving up at the outset the effort to distinguish between two different kinds of liberal response to the war, encumbered as the effort is with all sorts of difficulties. We can distinguish between two attitudes, to one or the other of which liberals tended to adhere, and that is at least a beginning.

It is an indispensable beginning, in fact, if we want to understand liberal attitudes toward the Russian revolution; for the controversy over the revolution, in its earlier stages, was merely an aspect of the debate on war aims. The alignment of opinion on the revolution makes that immediately clear. It was the anti-imperialists who from the beginning insisted that the revolution would prove to be a blessing to the world. It was the war liberals who (together with conservatives) deplored the revolution as a menace to civilization—that is, to the successful prosecution of the war against Germany. Those who opposed a formal restatement of war aims when it was proposed by Allied anti-imperialists opposed such a program with even greater vehemence when it was proposed by the Provisional Government; those who advocated American intervention in France in 1917 also advocated, or at least acquiesced in, Allied intervention in Russia in 1918. If the question of the war split American liberalism into opposing factions, the question of the revolution widened the breach, until in many cases it became impossible for men who had once worked side by side in the cause of social and political reform to discover any common ground at all—or so it appeared in the violent emotional atmosphere of the immediate postwar period.

So deep, indeed, did the division within liberalism itself become that the division between liberals and conservatives seems at times, to the student of these events, to become insignificant. But whatever their differences, liberals were trying to work out a solution to the problems raised by the revolution within the context of certain assumptions which conservatives did not share. All of them looked with horror on the suggestion that Bolshevism be crushed by force—a policy advocated by Roosevelt and Henry Cabot Lodge and William Howard Taft in America and by Winston Churchill and others in England. All of them could find a common denominator of agreement in the eighth of Wilson's Fourteen Points, with its promise of forbearance, if not of sympathy, for the revolution. Conservatives, on the other hand, derided the Fourteen Points as hopelessly visionary. If I have ignored the conservative side of the debate, it is because I am convinced that most Americans who thought about these matters at all were unable, in the end, to accept such a position. The conservatives themselves were conscious of being in the minority. "I am not in sympathy with the bulk of my fellow countrymen," wrote Theodore Roosevelt to his son early in 1918. Even among the Republicans, he said, "there are any number of pacifists and shortsighted reactionary materialists [*i.e.*, people who hoped for an early peace]; and I see very evident, altho furtive, tendencies to deal with the pro-Germans . . . Probably," he concluded, "I am too extreme." [3]

On the other side there was another set of extremists. I was repeatedly asked, in discussing this project with people when it was under way, what I intended to say about men like John Reed and Max Eastman; and I still find a certain dissatisfaction, among some of those who have been kind enough to read the manuscript, at my failure to deal with them. Reference to the impact of the Russian revolution on American liberalism seems inevitably to call up the names of our greatest champions of the revolution. It may also call up a series of picturesque associations, associations which have become part of the folklore of American radicalism—the Masses trial, the hunger strikes, Reed dying in Russia, Eastman following Trotsky into spiritual exile. But I have not dealt with the radicals for the simple reason that they were not liberals. Radicals, by definition, had already given up on liberalism, even before the Russian revolution broke out. Hence it came as no surprise to them that the revolution turned out to be a revolution directed against liberal democracy as well as against autocracy. It was not only not surprising, it was a matter for rejoicing, since liberalism was, after all, a snare and a delusion, the opiate of the intellectuals. Later, of course, one by one, the radicals changed their minds about the revolution, though not always about liberalism; thus it has not been uncommon for disillusioned radicals to veer to the extreme Right. There is consistency in the career of a Whittaker Chambers; it begins and ends in a rejection of liberalism.

This is a study of ideas more than of men and movements. I have not attempted to assess the impact of the Russian revolution on American reform movements, to trace specific developments in the history of these movements to the influence of the revolution. It may be that the Russian revolution attracted some people to socialism and frightened others away; it may be that it had some effect on the labor movement—on the strikes at Seattle, say, in 1919; it may be that it tells us something about the Plumb Plan. But I have not attempted to explore the connection. And since my chief concern is not what happened, as a result of the revolution, to the Progressive party or to the careers of men like Walter Lippmann or William Allen White, I have made no effort to cover all of the important liberals of the period. I have been content, in a study of ideas, to rely on representative samples of opinion.

I am not in the following pages chiefly concerned even with the growing rift within the liberal ranks, which I referred to above. Nevertheless I have placed a good deal of stress on it, because unless one distinguishes between "war liberals" and "anti-imperialists" it is impossible to understand precisely what the revolution did to the idea which all liberals shared: the belief in the inevitable spread of democracy throughout the world, by orderly change or by revolution, as circumstances might dictate. What happened to that idea is the subject of the present study: not the influence of the revolution but the terrible question it raised. Liberals, themselves the heirs of a revolutionary tradition, had been brought up to believe in the efficacy of revolution. Yet the very first act of the revolutionists in Russia in 1917, to break relations with Russia's Western allies, was enough to raise doubts as to whether this particular revolution could be regarded as simply another stage in the long struggle against tyranny. Thus the history of the whole twentieth century was foreshadowed in the events of a few months in 1917.

The attempt of American liberals to understand the implication of this paradox is the theme of this study, which becomes, therefore, a chronicle of failure; for they did not succeed in the attempt. Rather they resolved the paradox for themselves in one of two ways. Either they denied, with the anti-imperialists, that the Bolsheviks and their immediate predecessors were in fact aiding the Germans by their actions; or, going to the opposite extreme, they not only maintained that the Bolsheviks were aiding the Germans but insisted that in fact they were the Kaiser's secret allies, hence not revolutionists at all. These opposite positions had in common that both served to resolve the paradox; both made it possible for liberals to continue to believe in progress through revolution.

This refusal, under the greatest imaginable stress, to give up the optimism on which liberalism rested, I have come to regard as the central fact of the period; and I have tried to show that even the "disillusionment" which followed the war brought about no real questioning of basic assumptions, no real loss of illusions. By pushing the study further into the thirties and forties, one could show, I think, that the depression, the New Deal, the rise of Nazism in Europe and the Second World War all brought about still a further postponement of the day of reckoning. The depression and the New Deal, by making the issue of economic inequality a matter of general concern, gave weight to the argument that the Bolshevik revolution was primarily an experiment in social justice; the rise of the Nazis made the Bolsheviks seem innocuous by comparison; and the war brought the United States into outright alliance with communism. Thus the full significance of the revolution, already made explicit under Stalin, went largely unnoticed in this country until the late 1940s. But even then it was difficult for Americans to believe that the revolution was not only a bad thing for liberalism but that, equally important, it was here to stay. On the contrary, Americans persuaded themselves that the communist dictatorship would topple of its own weight (providing the West stood firm). So autocratic a form of government, they thought, was inherently unstable. Even Mr. George

F. Kennan, who otherwise did so much to make Americans aware of the nature of the Soviet system, insisted that the only hope of the West lay in an eventual liberalizing of the system. Thus it may still be questioned whether Americans ever resigned themselves to coexistence with evil.

There were those, of course, who maintained that the Russian threat should be regarded not only as a threat but as a challenge to liberalism to prove itself. But the mere fact that such a challenge had appeared was enough, for most people, to prove that liberalism had already failed. For liberalism in America, no less than communism in Russia, has always been a messianic creed, which staked everything on the ultimate triumph of liberalism throughout the world. What else did progress mean? It was impossible to accept coexistence, therefore, without questioning progress itself. To live in a world half of which is dominated by one's enemies is something which the negroes or the Jews or the French of the Resistance might know how to manage; but it is not something that comes easily to Americans brought up in the benevolent assumptions of the eighteenth-century Enlightenment.

Contents

The American Liberals and the Russian Revolution

"There is some subtle mystery about Russia which makes discussion of its affairs passionately bitter. We are able to disagree about France or Fiume without losing our temper. But difference of opinion about Russia distils a peculiar venom.

"This was very noticeable to me [in Russia]. . . . But since I have returned to America I find it just as noticeable here. The subject of Russia turns dinner-table discussions into brawls, turns old friendships into feuds."

Arthur Bullard, *The Russian Pendulum,* p. vii.

I

The Russian Menace and the War for Democracy

AT the beginning of this century people in the West took it as a matter of course that they lived in a civilization surpassing any which history had been able to record. They assumed that their own particular customs, institutions and ideas had universal validity; that having showered their blessings upon the countries of western Europe and North America, those institutions were destined to be carried to the furthest reaches of the earth, bringing light to those still living in darkness. Not only the present ascendancy but the continuing progress and expansion of Western technology, Western culture, and Western standards of political behavior were taken for granted. Indeed if the people of the Atlantic countries had any fear about themselves it was that they were too civilized. The fear of "over-civilization" pervaded art, letters, music, even politics. It produced, among other things, the cult of the primitive which was so characteristic of the *fin de siècle.*

> Tho' I've belted you an' flayed you,
> By the livin' Gawd that made you,
> You're a better man than I am, Gunga Din!

It was difficult for a people dazzled by the vision of material progress to remember that other societies in some respects rivaled their own. The use of the word "civilized" where we should say "Western" was second nature. A German, an Englishman, even an American, was civilized; other people were less than civilized. That civilization had flourished elsewhere—in the Orient, for example—was not unknown, but it was a fact which could not be taken seriously. What fascinated Westerners about the Orient was precisely what was exotic and bizarre, what they thought of as primitive.

In theory the disappearance of the primitive was, of course, to be deplored. But since they were convinced that its disappearance was inevitable, Westerners did not hesitate to root it up and replace it with something more up-to-date. Destiny decreed that men wear shoes and worship at the Methodist Episcopal Church. One might regret the march of civilization, but one could not arrest it. Nor did one in fact regret it for very long. It was not easy to believe in the accomplishments of Africans and Asians (which Westerners sometimes professed to admire) when these people proved unable to defend them against the onslaught of the West. The term "Chinese," referring to a people utterly submissive in the face of invaders, became a term of contempt; to accuse a Western statesman of following a "Chinese policy" was an insult hard to forgive. The very weakness of non-Western peoples finally became the proof of their primitive condition.

Japan in 1905 proved an exception to the rule of Oriental submission by defeating Russia; but Russia was herself an exception. In any scheme of things Russia was difficult to classify. She was both Eastern and Western—both primitive and civilized—and no one, least of all the Russians, could agree as to which strain predominated. It was difficult therefore to know whether to fear her or to treat her as a friend. In a world where so many things seemed certain, Russia remained a "riddle," a "mystery," an "enigma." One could not talk long about Russia without resorting to a special vocabulary.

The mystery, however, involved not so much her present as

her future. The great question, endlessly debated, was whether she would eventually embrace Western ways or whether she would become the powerful exponent of a way of life alien to that of the West. Of her present backwardness there was no question. In 1900 Russia was what we should today politely call an "underdeveloped country." In 1900 she was simply "backward" and by Western standards uncivilized—a fact which even her friends conceded. Indeed her backwardness was for them her main attraction; it made Western "commercialism" sordid and shabby by comparison. Thus Stephen Graham explained how he had found in the religiosity of Russian peasant life a spiritual serenity which shamed the vulgar hustle and bustle of the Western market place; in the communal life of the *mir* an attractive alternative to the ceaselessly competitive individualism which set men against their neighbors; in the Russian church a truly spiritual Christianity, as opposed to all the religions deriving from Rome.* An article significantly entitled "The Compensations of Illiteracy" summed up Graham's case against civilization. Books, he wrote, cut men off from God, from nature and from one another. The book "has taken us away alone. . . . It has distinguished us; it has individualized us. It has created differences between ourselves and our fellow-men." It was therefore a source of profound comfort to Graham to learn that "in Russia there are no books." In their absence the peasants listened to the voice of God and "read the book of Nature." [1]

Graham was not alone in his devotion to Holy Russia. Dr. Charles Sarolea, a Belgian transplanted to Edinburgh, where

* The popularity of the "germ theory" of history made it possible to see the *mir* and the New England town meeting as having a common origin in the Teutonic forest. Russia, therefore, was despotic in appearance only. See John Fiske, *American Political Ideas Viewed from the Standpoint of Universal History* (New York, 1885), pp. 41–4. Melville Stone, chief of the Associated Press and a frequent visitor to Russia, cited this passage as authority for the statement that the *mir* was in fact the seed of the New England town meeting. Melville E. Stone, "The Russian Revolution," *Russian Review*, III (July, 1917), 37–44.

he became editor of *Everyman*, also looked to Russia for the spiritual salvation of a Germanized Europe. He was convinced that Russia was "the most Christian nation in the world, perhaps the only Christian nation." It was the only country in which one could find "an unadulterated democracy, an absence of class divisions and snobbery, a sense of fellowship and brotherhood, extended to the downtrodden and even to the criminal, which made pity synonymous with piety, and which made all human suffering into a religion." [2] Havelock Ellis, another traveler in Holy Russia, justified Russian backwardness on the grounds that if the Russians were not free, most men were not yet ready for freedom anyway. "I should not myself choose to live in Russia," he admitted. "It is not yet a free country for the man who thinks for himself. But there are not many men who really think for themselves." [3]

The Russophilia of these English intellectuals was an expression of their misgivings about progress and modernity. Nor should it surprise us that such misgivings were more frequently encountered in England than in the United States. The underlying anti-intellectualism of the age, the cult of violence and authority, the taste for the primitive and the exotic—all these evidences of dissatisfaction with modern life, of which the cult of "Holy Russia" was only one, naturally made their first appearance in a society which considered itself highly civilized if not decadent. Yet one finds even in America defenders of Holy Russia, men who were drawn to Russia by what they regarded as the grace and serenity of Russian life. Of these the most unremitting in his efforts to break down what seemed to him an unreasonable American prejudice against Russia was Charles R. Crane. Crane was a progressive in domestic politics, a friend and champion of La Follette, Brandeis and Wilson. Yet he was also an authentic American Russophile. Owing to a conjunction, in youth, of poor health and a considerable fortune (his father had become rich as a manufacturer of elevators),

Crane had travelled all over the world. His travels took him to Russia for the first time in 1898, and that visit proved to be the first of a long series.* The East in general powerfully attracted him, China scarcely less than Russia; and it is significant that he always spoke of Russia as a part of the Orient. The impression is hard to escape that it was just that—the belief that Russia had escaped the road taken by the West, the road soon to become known as "Prussian efficiency"—that appealed to him.

Crane was not a man given to articulating his intellectual premises—not, at any rate, where Russia was concerned—but something of what drew him to Russia comes to the surface in a letter from Europe written in 1900, in which he reported to his wife an interview with no less a figure than the Tsar of All the Russias. "I told him," Crane wrote, "that his people had held to the most charming of the traditions of the Orient [*sic*], the tradition of hospitality and that their manner of exercising it, from the lowest to the highest, was most simple and graceful —that that was one thing they knew better than anyone else in the world and in it they required no instruction."

"Yes," the Tsar complacently replied, "that is one thing we do not want to change—we do not want to change everything."

They went on to deplore "the meagerness of information regarding Russia—the few reliable books and absence of centers of authority." [4] It was Crane's ambition to establish such a center of Russian studies in the United States, to combat the current prejudice. To that end he set up a lectureship at the University of Chicago, to which distinguished Slavs were invited annually. Thomas Masaryk came over in 1902, Paul Miliukov in 1903. Crane also subsidized the career of Samuel N.

* He returned to Russia in 1891, in 1894, in 1896, in 1900, in 1904 and in 1917; see MS autobiography, *passim,* in Charles R. Crane MSS, Archive of Russian and East European History and Culture, Columbia University. He was appointed by Woodrow Wilson as ambassador to Russia in 1913 but declined the position; see Crane to Wilson, Sept. 30, 1913, *ibid.*

Harper, son of the first president of the University of Chicago. If Harper was the first American to make Slavic studies a full-time scholarly career, that was in large part due to the efforts of Crane, who took him with him on several trips to Russia, introduced him to his Russian friends and inculcated in him an abiding devotion to the Russian people. Like Crane, Harper made lasting friendships among the little group of Russian liberals who were seeking to bring Russia up to date (although their efforts, had they been successful, would paradoxically have destroyed much of what attracted men like Crane and Harper in the first place).[5] And in the end it was through the eyes of these Westernizing liberal intellectuals, who constituted the heart of the Constitutional Democratic party (the so-called Kadets), that Crane and Harper saw Russian developments and measured their significance. That was to make it difficult, later on, to view the revolution with detachment, especially for Crane. Harper, on the other hand, though he shared Crane's sympathies, was an inveterate optimist by temperament. He could never have regarded any event as an unmitigated disaster, not even the revolution which swept so many of his friends from the scene. But for Crane the revolution was the end of everything for which he and his friends had been working, the end, possibly, of everything worth working for.

Crane and Harper, when they tried to account for the antagonism of much American opinion toward Russia, were tempted to blame it on the Jews—not all Jews, but those with an ax to grind: "German Jews," Crane once called them, after everything German had become suspect. "A little bunch of them," he complained in 1916, ". . . have for a long time controlled the bridge between Russia and America and so the 98,000,000 Christians here have had no relation with the 170,000,000 Christians over there—although there are the strongest bases for both political and social sympathy." [6] Much later he wrote, with a good deal of bitterness, "We had only warm feelings for the

Russian government and people until the Jews decided that that was an unhealthy mood for us to be in and they set out to cure us—a remarkable example of their malevolent power." *

Yet the man who probably did more to rouse American hostility toward Russia—more, certainly, than any Jew, and probably more than all the Jews combined—was a man whom Crane himself regarded with something like reverence, and the author of one of those "few reliable books" the scarcity of which Crane lamented in his conversation with the Tsar. If there was a single book that accounted for the American prejudice against Russia it was George Kennan's *Siberia and the Exile System,* which depicted for the first time in America the horrors of a police state. Thirty years after the publication of this work in 1891, Colonel E. M. House remembered what a "deep and lasting"

* Crane to House, June 3, 1933, Edward M. House MSS, Yale University Library. He attributed our hostility to Russia in the Russo-Japanese War (an act of ingratitude, since "the Russians . . . for a hundred years, when we were in critical situations, stood boldly for us") to "Teddy's doctrine of giving the Jews at least all they wanted." He also blamed the Jews for blocking his appointment as minister to China in 1909, in revenge for his having spoken up for Russia during the war with Japan. "I seemed to be the only outspoken friend the Russians had and so had to speak out often, and of course had all kinds of abuse from these alien Jews and became well marked, for if you are not 100% for every Jewish thing—both crooked and straight—you are an 'antisimite' [*sic*]—it ought to be a title of honor—and subject to boycott."

Crane's anti-Semitism, if it can be called that, rested on the Midwestern progressive's distrust of the "Jewish" banker. Jacob Schiff was the most frequent object of his suspicion. On the other hand he was on the closest terms with Jews untainted by association with Wall Street: with Brandeis, whose appointment to the Supreme Court Crane strongly commended; with Lillian D. Wald, whom he once referred to as "the finest flower of the Jewish race"; and with Norman Hapgood, who edited *Harper's Weekly* after Crane had acquired control of it in 1913. See Crane to Wilson, May 23, 1913, Jan. 27, 1916; Crane to Josephine Crane Bradley, Jan. 25, 1908, July 11, 1916, Oct. 15, 1916; Crane to Charles William Eliot, June 7, 1914, all in Crane MSS. Nor were his friendly feelings toward the Jews purely personal; he was a firm supporter of the Zionist movement.

Clearly it is too simple to dismiss such opinions as I have quoted above as mere "anti-Semitism." The attitude of Crane and of the progressives as a whole toward the Jews was a complicated thing, which deserves special study in itself.

impression it had made. Kennan "lifted the veil," House said, and "gave us a glimpse of what was happening" in Russia. As a consequence of his disclosures, "every one in the liberty-loving countries of the world welcomed the overthrow of a system that exuded injustice and cruelty in its most objectionable forms." [7]

Kennan himself hated Russia no more than Crane and Harper hated it. But his attitude toward the country was uncomplicated by any feeling for the mystical side of the Russian character. If he loved Russia, that merely made him resent more deeply the political servitude under which the Russians seemed to live: the suppression of free thought; the suppression of the rights of nationalities (as in the case of Poland, Finland and the lesser nations bordering on Russia); the persecution of the Jews. (It was not only the Jews in America who objected to the pogroms; there were no more vivid accounts of them than Kennan's.[8]) He did not of course attribute all these things to qualities innate in the Russian character; it was the Tsar and the bureaucracy, not the people, that he attacked. The "assassinations, expropriations, *pogroms*, and violent crimes of all sorts" which had given the Russians "a reputation for exceptional savagery," were the product of historical conditions which had "abnormally and artificially warped" the character of a people otherwise placid and peace-loving.[9]

From the time of the publication of *Siberia and the Exile System* to his death in 1924 Kennan was acknowledged to be the leading American authority on Russia. He made regular visits and wrote indefatigably in the pages of *Outlook* for a respectable middle-class audience. He founded in the early 1890s the Society of Friends of Russian Freedom, the purpose of which was to aid victims of the Tsarist terror and to cultivate American sympathy for Russia's struggle for freedom. The society drew its membership from among moderate liberals like Kennan himself. William Lloyd Garrison (son of the abolitionist) was one of its founders. Hamilton Holt, publisher of the

Independent, Lyman Abbott of *Outlook*, Jane Addams, Lillian D. Wald, Oswald Garrison Villard, Jacob Schiff and Rabbi Stephen S. Wise at one time or another belonged to it. "The Society," Kennan once observed, "was not the result of Socialist or radical agitation, but was rather an expression of sympathy of freedom-loving Americans with the struggles for political freedom in Russia"—a remark expressive of the impulse which animated the Friends of Russian Freedom and the rather narrow scope of their concern.[10]

If Russia's "backwardness" was a matter of general agreement among her friends and her critics alike, there was nevertheless no agreement as to the direction she would take in the future. Would the differences between Russia and the West become sharper or would they gradually disappear? One school of thought held that "the balance of probability points to a gradual modification of these differences and a closer conformity to Western civilization." [11] Others believed that "the Russian is at heart an Oriental veneered by Western civilization, with a natural leaning toward his origin. It is easier," they thought, "far easier, for the Russian to revert to his original type and become an Oriental than it is for him to be in sympathy with Western nations." [12] The outbreak of the World War and the entrance of Russia into the war on the side of the Allies gave a new urgency to the discussion. Those who took the second view were outraged by the "unholy alliance" with Russia and appalled at the prospect of a Russia still oriental in outlook but greatly strengthened by an Allied victory. The exponents of Russian friendship, seeking to quiet these fears, replied that the mission of "Holy Russia" was to save Europe from German "efficiency." The Russians themselves, according to Graham and his followers in America, saw the conflict as a holy war, the "motto" of which was: "getting rid of the German spirit in life, getting rid of the sheer materialistic point of view, getting rid of brutality and the lack of understanding of others." [13] Charles R. Crane wrote: "I believe we are seeing Russia at her best . . . Russia is fighting to become emancipated from Prussian domination and her whole heart is in this war." [14]

After 1914 it was difficult for Americans, even American liberals, to cling to their suspicions of Britain's ally. *Outlook* made the startling announcement that although Russia was politically "more absolutely autocratic" than Germany, "socially" it was "far more democratic"—a drastic departure from the earlier *Outlook* line.[15] The *Independent* assured itself that "Russia will not, cannot dominate Europe." "The defeat of Germany and Austria will be the defeat of absolutism, even of Russian absolutism. Liberty will rule Russia also, and there will be no more persecution of Jews or Christians." [16] Samuel Harper, a strong Allied partisan, went so far as to deny that Jews were being persecuted at all; the stories of pogroms in Russia, he decided, were invented by German propagandists.[17]

Many liberals found it difficult to deny that conditions in Russia were as bad as ever, if not worse. At the same time they insisted that conditions were bound to improve. Men like Kennan, who had always been inclined to see the darker side of Russian life, now became prophets of Russia's speedy regeneration. Kennan, like many others, declared that the struggle had brought about in Russia a great national revival, a "spiritual uplift," a new unity in which all the old divisions and the old bitterness would be forgotten.[18] The government, he thought, would patriotically reform itself in order more efficiently to prosecute the war. When the Tsar in August, 1914, announced that Jews would shortly be admitted to full civil rights and that Poland, hitherto governed as a conquered province, was to enjoy local autonomy, Kennan hailed the arrival of the millennium. Events soon dispelled the illusion of progress and reform, however. By April, 1915, Kennan was writing that the Tsar and the bureaucracy would "never leave the old road until they are driven from it by force."[19] Now he believed that the war, instead of eliminating divisions, would so aggravate them as to set off the long-awaited revolution. Revolutions in Russia, he pointed out, always followed wars. He did not mention the fact that in the past they had always followed Russian defeats, never victories. He assumed that the present war, unlike any other in Russian history, would end both in victory and in revolution.[20] He also convinced himself that the revolution would be a mild parliamentary affair, not a social upheaval. It would in no way impair Russia's military effectiveness as an ally. A constitution, "a substitution of civil for military law in time of peace," "a change in the franchise," "an enlargement of the legislative power of the Duma," "a removal of the restrictions that now hamper popular education," abrogation of the laws restricting freedom of speech—these would be the fruit of the revolution.[21] And when all these things had come to pass, Kennan predicted, "the Russians . . . will think less of conquest and territorial expansion, and the world will have less reason to regard them with anxiety or fear."[22]

This was good news, no doubt, but a number of liberals remained unconvinced. One's enthusiasm for the Russian alliance diminished in proportion to one's lack of enthusiasm for the war. In England the war was opposed by a little group of Fabian socialists which included Norman Angell and Henry Noel Brailsford. In July and August, 1914, their "Neutrality League" issued a series of tracts arguing for British neutrality on the grounds that a German defeat would merely deliver Europe into the hands of the Russians. Angell and Brailsford were violently attacked for expressing these heretical opinions; a follower of Stephen Graham accused them of "unwittingly sowing the seeds of another war" by encouraging Englishmen to hate Russians.[23] If people were not hostile they were merely indifferent to talk of the Russian menace; "the subject," as Angell later had to admit, "simply did not 'bite.'"[24] This "all but complete disregard of the position of Russia; and what a Russian victory over Germany, a victory made possible by our power, might involve," appeared to him in retrospect "the most astonishing thing about the public discussion, such as it was, which preceded the outbreak of war." "Curiously enough," he recalled, "it was the more intelligent military men who saw the importance of the point. One of them, repeating, I think, a common adage amongst them, said: 'It will take us five years to get the Russians into Germany—and fifteen to get them out.' It will take rather more than fifteen," Angell wrote in 1951.[25]

Liberals in America were at first fully aware of this aspect of the matter. On the day after Germany declared war on Great Britain, Charles R. Crane wrote to Woodrow Wilson: "The most awful aspect of the whole thing to me is . . . this: that Asia is growing rapidly in political power. With that situation facing the Christian world, for it to engage in this fearful war is to run the risk of placing Europe at the mercy of Asia." [26] But for most people these considerations proved to be fleeting. Thus Crane was able shortly to assure himself about Russia that "whatever else Russia at her worst threatens, she does not threaten Europe, and certainly does not begin to be the menace to the peace of Europe that Germany has been these last forty years." The "Russian spirit," he decided, was "not a military one." [27] Only a handful of men remained apprehensive for very long about the consequences of a Russian victory.

One of these men was Colonel House. His diary reveals a constant preoccupation with the subject of Russian expansionism. In June, 1914, he told the Kaiser that "Russia was the greatest menace to England and it was to England's advantage that Germany was in a position to hold Russia in check, and that Germany was the barrier between Europe and the Slavs." (The Kaiser understandably agreed with this opinion.) [28] Shortly after the outbreak of the war House wrote to Wilson in words strikingly similar to those of Crane: "The saddest feature of the situation to me is that there is no good outcome to look forward to. If the Allies win, it means largely the domination of Russia on the Continent of Europe; and if Germany wins, it means the unspeakable tyranny of militarism for generations to come." [29]

These thoughts were set down at a time when other liberals had already accepted the interpretation of the war as a simple conflict of democracy versus autocracy, in which Russia, as well as Britain and France, was presumed to be moved by the noblest and most generous impulses. In March, 1915, House outlined a strategy in essential agreement with that advocated by Angell and Brailsford. "What we need to do is to play for time," he wrote. "Time will make Germany democratic and there will be no more danger in that direction than from the United States, England, or France. Russia is another problem, which may or may not have to be dealt with in the future." [30] Even after the February revolution, which in other quarters swept away what little was left of the old liberal fear of Russia, House remained wary. In April, 1917, he reminded Balfour that the West "had to take into consideration the Russia of fifty years from now rather than the Russia of to-day. While we might hope it would continue democratic and cease to be aggressive, yet if the contrary happened, Russia would be the menace to Europe and not Germany." He asked Balfour "not to look upon Germany as a permanent enemy." [31] So grave were the Colonel's misgivings about Russia that he sometimes wondered whether the best solution of the Russian problem was not to split up the Empire into a number of autonomous units, thereby rendering it impotent.[32]

The most consistent advocate of the anti-Russian point of view in the United States was the *New Republic*, which derived its attitude in large part from Angell and Brailsford, both of whom frequently contributed, in these early days, to the columns of that paper. In the very first issue of the *New Republic*

Brailsford published an analysis of the war as a struggle for "the empire of the East," a contest between Russia and Germany for the domination of eastern Europe, in which the sympathies of Englishmen and Americans should be on the side of Germany.[33] In January 1915 he derided the "Slavic hope," pointing out that there was no reason to think that a Russian military victory would lead to revolution. The revolution of 1905, he noted, had followed a crushing defeat. A Russian victory, which everybody seemed to expect, would be likely to have the opposite result; it would bolster up not only the autocracy but the pan-Slavic ideology which animated it. And the aims of the Russians, as Brailsford reminded the readers of the *New Republic,* were not those of the Western democracies. If the Allies believed that they were fighting Prussian militarism, "the truly Russian orthodox Panslavist is fighting the German enlightenment. What he hates in Germany is not its militarism but its rationalism, its religious tolerance, its socialism, and what he would call its materialism." [34] It was not long before the editors of the *New Republic* adopted this view of things as their own. There was "no real cultural bond" between Russia and the West, they decided, and "except for historical accidents" Russia might have been fighting on the side of Germany—that is, on the side of the militaristic, not the enlightened, Germany—against the Allies. Nor was such a realignment of forces yet out of the question. The possession of Persia and "the right to conquer India" might yet induce Russia to desert the Allies and enter an alliance with Germany and Japan. No doubt this was all a bad dream; but the possibility could not be dismissed. The Western peoples might one day "awake to the fact that the world had changed over night, and that the dream was no longer this new Holy Alliance of reactionary powers, but [their] own pious plans of progress." [35]

There appeared to be some evidence that a grand alliance of reactionary powers was actually contemplated. William C. Bullitt, correspondent of the Philadelphia *Public Ledger,* in the autumn of 1916 published a series of articles in the *Public Ledger* and *New Republic* based on his observations during a trip to Germany the previous summer. He depicted Germany as torn between East and West; while the reactionaries dreamed of an alliance with Russia which would enable them to conquer Britain and France, the liberals, fearing and hating Russia, looked upon the Western nations as their real friends. The reactionaries, the "Von Tirpitz party," according to Bullitt, hope "to form an international league of highwaymen with Russia and Japan. Japan's share of the swag is to be the Philippines, the Dutch Indies and Australia; Russia is to get Asia Minor, Persia and India; while control of the seas and the African possessions of England and France are to fall to Germany!" Militarily this policy demanded "a crushing attack upon France and a defensive on the eastern front." The party led by Bethmann-Hollweg, on the other hand, called for "an offensive on the eastern front and the defensive in the west." It aimed eventually at a negotiated peace with Britain and France. "The Chancellor's supporters believe Russia is Germany's ultimate enemy. Therefore, they look to the east for territorial gains and to the west for peace and alliances. The followers of Von Tirpitz consider England Germany's only implacable enemy; they look to the west for territorial gains and the east for peace and alliances." *

* Bullitt in Philadelphia *Public Ledger,* Oct. 30, Oct. 31, Nov. 1, 1916. The same thesis is presented in his "Worse or Better Germany?" *New Republic,* VIII (Oct. 28, 1916), 321–3.

Six months later the Zimmermann note would be seen as proof of the designs of the reactionary pro-Russian party. "In the background of the Zimmermann note," one paper observed, "may be seen the hope still cherished in Berlin of a separate peace with Russia, and the formation of a great league including Germany, Austria, Turkey, Bulgaria, Russia, Japan and Mexico." Des Moines *Register,* March 4, 1917.

German attitudes toward Russia were in fact far more complicated than Americans supposed. Bethmann-Hollweg did at times hope for peace with the West, but he also attempted (both before and after the February

Bullitt in none of these articles gave a source for his interpretations of German politics, but his views doubtless reenforced the fear of a Russian-German rapprochement.* It was in order to prevent such an alignment that anti-imperialists advocated what the *New Republic* in an editorial of December 23, 1916 for the first time referred to as a "peace without victory." [36] The West, ran the argument, had to win the confidence of Germany, that is, of the liberal element in Germany, and had to maintain Germany as a barrier to Russian expansion. The mere threat of a crushing defeat, by strengthening the hand of the German reactionaries, might throw Germany into the arms of Russia; defeat itself would certainly do so. A negotiated settlement, therefore, resulting in an "inconclusive peace," would

---

revolution) to negotiate a separate peace with Russia. And although the High Command held the views attributed to them by Bullitt, Ludendorff and Hindenburg, who were at least as reactionary as Von Tirpitz or Falkenhayn, insisted on Russia's complete and utter defeat. Far from looking to the East for "peace and alliances," these militarists agitated throughout the early years of the war for the transfer of troops from the western to the eastern front. As always, Americans exaggerated the extent to which foreign policies were determined by ideology alone. See John W. Wheeler-Bennett, *Wooden Titan: Hindenburg in Twenty Years of German History* (New York, 1936), pp. 46–9, 84–6; Klaus Epstein, *Matthias Erzberger and the Dilemma of German Democracy* (Princeton, 1959), pp. 164–81.

* His notes of "a conversation I had with Mr. [Gottlieb] Von Jagow in August [1916]," in the Bullitt MSS, Yale University Library, suggest that he relied heavily, if not exclusively, on that authority. Von Jagow was Foreign Secretary until 1916. Bullitt quotes him as saying: "I should prefer to make peace by way of London and Paris, rather than to make peace by way of St. Petersburg. But the English get wilder every day and I see no chance of liberal England getting the upper hand. People have talked a lot in the past three months about the possibility of peace with England, [but] the possibility has always been very remote. The thing I am afraid of is that President Wilson will allow himself to be drawn into an entente with England and France which would exclude Germany. The English, I know, are doing everything they possibly can to bring about such an entente. The result of it would be that we should have to form an alliance with Russia and Japan. And I do not want to do that. Those dirty little yellow apes of Japanese! I am afraid of them."

Ernesta Drinker Bullitt, *An Uncensored Diary from the Central Empires* (Garden City, 1917), pp. 27–8, 41–2, records similar conversations with private individuals.

in the long run better safeguard the security of the West than an illusory military success, which would in fact leave matters worse than they were to begin with. For in the absence of the German barrier, what price would the Allies have to pay for Russian friendship? The price, as the *New Republic* soon learned (long before the publication of the secret treaties by which the Allies in advance had divided among themselves the prospective spoils of victory), had already been paid. "Russia," the editors announced in December, 1916, "has received a definite promise of Constantinople in the event of a victory by the Allies." The implications of this bargain, they thought, were tremendous. First, the war would have to be indefinitely prolonged, "for assuming Germany can be beaten, she would have to be rendered helpless before she would succumb to the Russian ambition." [37] Second, the Allies, if they consented to the "partial or the complete emasculation of Germany and the corresponding aggrandizement of Russia," would be making themselves "dangerously dependent on Russian forbearance. They cannot afford to weaken Germany," the *New Republic* warned, "unless they are prepared to trust their own future security and that of continental Europe to Russian good will." [38] Given the unlikelihood of reform in Russia, let alone revolution, Russian good will appeared to be a most uncertain foundation on which to build the new and better world which the war was supposed to bring into being.

The strategy advocated by the anti-imperialist minority in England and America, in opposition to the official strategy of "crushing German militarism," rested on the premise that Germany was going to be easier to live with in years to come than her neighbor to the east. The demand for an "inconclusive peace" sprang not from sentimental considerations but from a fear of the consequences of disrupting the present European balance of power. "Any misgivings we may have entertained about the cause of the Allies," the *New Republic* said in explanation of its policy, "have always turned upon the contribution that Russia has made to the Allies. . . . The New Republic has argued in favor of an inconclusive peace, largely because it apprehends the consequences on the eastern frontier of a decisive victory for the Allies. . . . We believe that Englishmen and Frenchmen would eventually regret acquiescence in a course which would tend to weaken Germany as compared to Russia." [39] As for "democratizing Germany," in the early years of the war that was the slogan of patriotic orators and pamphleteers. Anti-imperialists argued that the Allies could not democratize Germany if they wanted to, any more than they could make over Russia in the image of the West. Only the Germans, they insisted, could democratize Germany. But if it came to that, an indigenous democracy seemed far more likely to take root in Germany than in Russia, where the obstacles to change of any sort appeared to be overwhelming.*

No sooner had the anti-imperialists arrived at this view of the world, however, than they began to abandon it. Germany's posture became increasingly menacing; perhaps anti-imperialists found it even more menacing than it actually was just because they had expected so much of Germany. Her refusal to abandon submarine warfare was interpreted in the United States as the triumph of the military party, of those who aimed "to make Germany the leader of the East against the West, the leader ultimately of a German-Russian-Japanese coalition against the Atlantic World." The *New Republic* now decided that it was the duty of the United States to join the fight against Germany —not to destroy her, "but to force her and lure her back to the

* At the same time it cannot be too strongly insisted upon that anti-imperialists did not yet regard a German revolution as a condition of peace. They did not even regard it as a likely event. Thus Ernesta Drinker Bullitt, after reading H. G. Wells' *What Is Coming: A European Forecast* (New York, 1916)—much of which, as she noted, was "based on the idea that there will be a revolution in Germany"—dismissed the idea as absurd. Germany, she declared, was "the last country in which such a thing is likely to-day." *Diary from the Central Empires*, pp. 196–7 (Sept. 15, 1916).

civilization in which she belongs. She is a rebel nation as long as she wages offensive war against the western world." [40] Not all readers were able to follow the editors in this reasoning, however. "Where now is your logic?" demanded a reader who still held fast to the original *New Republic* line. Germany, he pointed out, was the only one of the belligerents who could not be called a "rebel nation" in the sense of making war against the West. "It was Great Britain and France," he insisted, "which became traitors to the western world when they allied themselves with the great eastern Powers [*i.e.*, Russia and Japan] and it is primarily for the interests of those Powers that this war is now being fought." [41] Such voices as these, however, were hard to hear in the uproar following Germany's resumption of unrestricted submarine warfare in February, 1917.

Meanwhile the prospects for revolution in Russia had brightened. As early as September, 1915, the *New Republic* thought it detected "straws" in the "wind of discontent." [42] Even Brailsford, whose opinions carried so much weight in the offices of the *New Republic,* was beginning to think that Russia was ripe for revolt. Like George Kennan, he envisioned the revolution as strictly a parliamentary coup d'etat. The revolution of 1905, he explained, had not taken place until the end of the Russo-Japanese War. Then, the danger from outside having passed, all varieties of revolutionaries were free to put forward their own far-reaching and conflicting programs, with the result that the forces of progress dissipated their strength in conflicts among themselves. In 1915, however, with a foreign war still raging, the Left would have to unite around a common program. Circumstances thus guaranteed that the revolution would "involve neither social upheaval nor economic reconstruction" but would take the form of "a Whig revolution, a 1688 rather than 1789." [43] Like everyone else, Brailsford now assumed that Russia could have her revolution and still go on fighting.

By the beginning of 1917 the *New Republic* was publishing

letters which indicated a widespread acceptance of these assumptions. One lady demanded, "Why . . . are we not focussing our attention on [Russia's] internal affairs?" "If out of the sacrifice of this war the next generation sees an educated, self-governing Russia, Europe may be brought nearer peace than by any league to enforce it." [44] A Swarthmore professor complained that no one was pointing out "the possible bearing on the question of peace of the progressive awakening in Russia of which we hear so much." Was it not now possible to hope that Russia would join the Allies in offering liberal peace terms to Germany, on condition that the German people throw off their "masters"? And was it not "just possible that democratic articles of peace might help to call the bluff of the bureaucracy and tip the scales definitely to the side of progress in Russia?" [45] All of this foretold with remarkable accuracy the strategy followed by Woodrow Wilson in 1918.

If American anti-imperialists believed that German reactionaries contemplated an alliance with Russia and Japan, they were equally convinced that the reactionaries of Russia were fully in accord with this sinister design and waited only for an opportunity to desert the Allies and sign a separate peace with the Kaiser. By the time of the February revolution the fear of a separate peace had become an obsession.

It was the Russian liberals themselves who first leaped to the conclusion that the Tsarist government was not simply inept but was deliberately plotting to deliver the country into the hands of the enemy. Paul Miliukov, leader of the Kadets, in a powerful and emotional oration before the Duma on November 14, 1916, charged the government with having instituted negotiations for a separate peace. Since the speech was suppressed in Russia, the exact scope of Miliukov's charges was never very clear. It was not clear whether he actually accused Boris Stürmer, premier and minister of foreign affairs, by name. But it was widely believed that he had. One version which was circulated in the United States quoted Miliukov as having displayed a document which he said showed "every mark which [Stürmer] received from Germany from July 1901 to July 1916." * Western liberals needed no further proof to convict Stürmer—or for that matter the Tsar himself—of treason. The word of Miliukov was enough.

Other stories from Russia were repeated and believed. It was reported in American papers that Stürmer had accepted a bribe of nine million dollars to negotiate a treaty with Germany; that he had actually negotiated the treaty "and that the refusal of his country to accept it caused his downfall"; that "the conspiracy . . . was on the verge of success" and was foiled only by the army, which issued "an ultimatum . . . demanding that the Duma be recognized forthwith as the spokesman of the Russian people." [46] Not only Stürmer but other ministers of the Tsar were accused of complicity with the Germans, notably Protopopov, minister of the interior in the cabinets of Stürmer and his successors, and Sukhomlinov, sometime minister of war.[47]

* Typescript translation, unidentified, in Harper MSS. Another version of the speech was published in *Current History*, V (March, 1917), 1068–70. The speech attracted a good deal of attention in the United States; see, *e.g.*, Arthur J. Brown, "The Struggle to Save Russia," *Asia*, XVII (June, 1917), 250. Harper circulated his version among friends; see Frederic M. Corse to Harper, Dec. 22, 1916, Harper MSS.

Just what Miliukov said, however, remains something of a mystery. The French ambassador, who did not hear the speech himself, wrote in his diary on Nov. 14, 1916: "Miliukov formally accused Stürmer of treason and double-dealing. In support of his charge of treason he referred to the provocative role of the police in the strikes in munitions factories, the secret communications with Germany, Protopopov's talk with the German agent, Warburg, at Stockholm, and so on. . . . He wound up as follows: 'If I am asked why I open such a discussion during the war, I reply that it is because M. Stürmer's ministry is itself a peril during the war.'" Maurice Paléologue, *An Ambassador's Memoirs*, tr. F. A. Holt (London, n.d.), III, 92. Most secondary accounts follow Paléologue. See C. Jay Smith, *The Russian Struggle for Power* (New York, 1956), p. 441; Bernard Pares, *The Fall of the Russian Monarchy* (London, 1939), pp. 391–2; Michael T. Florinsky, *The End of the Russian Empire* (New Haven, 1931), pp. 108–10.

In neither of these cases was there any more evidence of treason than in the case of Stürmer, although there was plenty of evidence of stupidity and incompetence.[48]

All these rumors could be traced to the liberals in Petrograd, often by way of the press of western Europe, sometimes through their spokesmen or friends in the United States. No doubt the Kadets believed their own propaganda, as successful propagandists must; but the charge of subversion was totally without basis in fact. The government could perhaps be accused of a want of energy in carrying on the war. Yet even this want of energy was at bottom the fault not of the government's inefficiency and corruption, much less of treason, but of Russia's primitive economy. What the Kadets mistook for subversion was economic disintegration. It was difficult, as the opposition was soon to discover for itself, to conduct a war without ammunition or guns or to transport what supplies could be produced by Russia's inefficient industries to the front when transportation was in a state of total collapse. Not even liberal ideas would make the trains run. Under these circumstances the government might better have been blamed for helping to start a war which the country was in no condition to fight, than for seeking to quit it; but in fact the government had no intention of quitting the war. It was as blind to Russia's real condition as the liberal opposition or as the liberals' Allied friends, who confidently expected Russia to roll back the well-equipped, well-disciplined German troops on the eastern front. Only the Bolsheviks (and a few of the Mensheviks) seemed to grasp the fact that Russia was unequipped to carry on a modern war, or even to survive as a modern state. If the rest of the world had understood at the outset this simple truth, it would not necessarily have been able to prevent the rise of the Bolsheviks, but it would have been far better prepared to deal with them once they had seized power. Their understanding of the fact of Russia's primitive condition, about which there had once been so much speculation in the West, conferred on the Bolsheviks an inestimable advantage.

Western liberals—anti-imperialists and war liberals alike,—although they were aware of Russia's weakness, tended more and more to attribute her weakness to evil rulers.[49] Nor did they fail to see the uses to which this theory might be put, in persuading those who still opposed the war of the war's justice and necessity. If the Tsar was against the war, who could refuse to be for it? * In all countries it was only the reactionaries, obviously, who opposed the war—and with good reason, it seemed to liberals. It was clear to the latter, and therefore, they assumed, to their opponents as well, that the war would lead to revolution not only in Russia but in Germany and to a great upsurge of democracy throughout the world. It would sweep away at one blow what remained of the old order. In the process it would eliminate inequality, oppression, and war itself. It seemed reasonable to suppose, therefore, that the crowned heads of Europe were conspiring to end the struggle before it swept them away in the wreckage of the old regime.

By the time the United States entered the war liberals everywhere had come to believe that the war was only superficially a war among nations, that it was at bottom a struggle, conducted simultaneously within all the countries concerned, between the masses and their oppressors; a struggle which would end inevitably in the triumph of "the people." This interpretation of the war was not at once adopted. As we have seen, liberals, and anti-imperialists in particular, at first tended unconditionally to oppose participation in the war, and to scoff at the notion that it would advance the cause of democracy. They ridiculed the no-

* Thus Emmaline Pankhurst, the English suffragette and a great champion of the war, thanked Samuel Harper for sending her an article of his on the Russian situation, adding: "I am making use of the information, that an agitation for peace in Russia was promoted by reactionaries, as I think that this is an illuminating fact which will have a good effect upon the minds of our 'suffragette' [and pacifist] readers." Emmaline Pankhurst to Harper, May 12, 1915, Harper MSS.

tion that Germany could be democratized by force or that Russia could enjoy both revolution and victory at the same time. Not until Germany, by provoking the United States to the verge of war, made it difficult any longer to trust her good intentions, and not until events in Russia seemed to justify the expectation of imminent political upheaval, did anti-imperialists finally accept the view that the war would set loose elemental popular forces before which autocracy and oppression would have to give way. Thus while the war quieted, but did not finally put an end to, the old fear of Russia, the prospect of the collapse of Tsarism in turn persuaded many liberals of the desirability of prosecuting the war to a finish.

These developments led the original exponents of "peace without victory," against their original judgment, at last to acquiesce in the proposition that the democratization of Germany had become the *sina qua non* of Western security—a proposition which enabled those who wished to see Germany crushed to prolong the war indefinitely, on the grounds that Germany was not sufficiently democratized to be trusted to make peace.* The shifting emphasis of the anti-imperialist interpretation of the war also raised expectations with regard to Russia which in retrospect one can see were almost bound to be disappointed. It was unreasonable to expect that Russia could leap overnight

* This profound but subtle shift in the liberal interpretation of the war has gone almost entirely unnoticed by historians of the subject. Such standard works as Charles Seymour's *American Diplomacy during the World War* (Baltimore, 1934) do not mention it; neither do more recent studies, not even Arno J. Mayer's *Political Origins of the New Diplomacy* (New Haven, 1959). Laurence W. Martin, *Peace without Victory: Woodrow Wilson and the British Liberals* (New Haven, 1958) assumes, as the title of his book indicates, that "peace without victory" remained the liberal program throughout the war. He does not take into account the possibility that the demand for a change of government in Germany completely undermined it. See, on the other hand, the article by George F. Kennan, "Walter Lippmann, the *New Republic*, and the Russian Revolution," in Marquis Childs and James Reston, eds., *Walter Lippmann and His Times* (New York, 1959), pp. 41–4. My own interpretation is greatly indebted to this essay.

into the twentieth century. It was unreasonable to expect that a mere change of regime could immediately alter the social and economic conditions which had produced the Russian autocracy in the first place. The first instinct of American anti-imperialists was closer to the truth than were their second thoughts about Russia. The real question was not when the revolution would occur but whether Russia would ever undergo such a revolution as the Western liberals had in mind.

What was it about the war that swept away the old fear of Russia and replaced it with the belief that Russia, like the rest of the world, would inevitably be democratized as a consequence of the war? All this could not have been accomplished in a few months' time. The war must simply have brought to the surface a deeper fear—the fear of Germany and what she stood for. And if the fear of Germany was able so easily to displace the fear of Russia, the fear of Russia must not have gone very deep in the first place.

We have already seen that Russia's attraction for Western liberals (for those liberals, at least, who admitted to such an attraction) was precisely her "backwardness." Russophilia in the West was a form of rejection of the gospel of progress, to which the West was irrevocably committed but about which it had reservations deeper and more widespread, one suspects, than this brief survey of opinion has been able to indicate. Even as they gave lip-service to progress, Western liberals must have wondered at times whether progress did not destroy more than it created. One could see in Russia, where the older ways survived, just how much had elsewhere been lost. Thus Russia came to have for American liberals something of the significance of the American South: it became a museum of preindustrial antiquities, in which were preserved all the things that liberalism itself had wiped out wherever it had had power to do so.

What did Germany stand for? In the minds of American

liberals, she stood for nothing if not for progress, at the altar of which liberals everywhere (even in Russia) were presumed to worship. German "efficiency" was a byword long before the war. But whereas in the period from 1865 to 1914 efficiency was something to be admired and emulated, after 1914 it was something hateful; it came to be known as "Prussian efficiency," and it became the duty of civilized people to destroy it. But again, is it likely that such a revolution in opinion could have taken place overnight? To be sure, one's first impression is that it did. Before 1914 American progressives had had only the friendliest feelings toward Germany. A generation of progressives had quite literally gone to school to Germany, and one could probably discover that progressivism owed as much to German as to native influences. "Efficiency" was the motto of the progressive movement and Germany was its model.

Yet in view of what happened after 1914 one is justified once again in wondering how profound were the misgivings about progress and "efficiency" which the progressive movement may have concealed. One wonders finally whether American liberals in turning on Germany after 1914 were not in some sense turning upon themselves. Such a train of speculation leads to some remarkable though not very heartening conclusions about American progressivism, superficially so optimistic a faith. It also makes it possible to understand the transformation of the liberal war program from "peace without victory" to "making the world safe for democracy." That in turn, as we shall see, explains why liberals found it so difficult to understand the Russian revolution.

II

The February Revolution: The Peril of Peace

THE February revolution in Petrograd (March 9–14, 1917, by the Western calendar) appeared to justify all the optimism which Americans had invested in the Russian future. The old regime collapsed; a government of moderate liberals was triumphantly installed; Russia took her place at last among the great democracies. Yet the prophets of Russia's regeneration almost at once displayed a curious uneasiness about the fulfillment of their own prophecies. Enthusiasm for the revolution was not lacking, but most of it derived from the belief that the revolution would in one way or another contribute to the defeat of Germany. The tributes paid by most Americans to Russia's adoption of democratic institutions seemed formal and perfunctory. That the revolution had made Russia more democratic evidently mattered less than that it had made her more belligerent; and even that, it shortly appeared, was open to question. Morris Hillquit justly complained that most of his countrymen regarded the revolution as "merely an incident of the world war" and measured its significance according to "its possible bearing on the outcome of the war." [1]

The belief that the revolution was directed against the treasonable influences around the Tsar captivated liberals and conservatives alike. One paper declared flatly that the "immediate object" of the revolution was not "the radical change of the form of government" but the elimination of the "pro-German, anti-Russian influences surrounding the Czar and controlling the Government." [2] The revolution therefore put to an end the possibility of a separate peace, as other papers were quick to note. It sounded "the knell of the Russo-Jap-German alliance which was back of the Zimmermann note to Mexico." [3] It dissipated the "haunting nightmare" of a "menacing coalition . . . between the two eastern empires [Russia and Germany] for the domination of the world." [4] In a word, it did away with the "Russian menace."

So pervasive was the anti-German, pro-war theory of the revolution that some people concluded that the whole thing had been made to order by the Allies themselves.[5] Even those who should have known better, like Samuel Harper, did nothing to discourage such delusions. When asked by Lansing for his opinion of the revolution, Harper replied that it was provoked by the Tsar's attacks on the *zemstvos* and the municipalities and by his pro-German proclivities. The aim of the revolutionists, he said, was "to create conditions that would make it possible for Russia to bring into force all her strength. [It] means therefore more effective prosecution of [the] war until victory." [6] In July, 1917, Harper still held to the view that "had there not been a change of government, a revolution of some kind, Russia would have been out of the war and perhaps even on the side of Germany, through the treasonable [actions] of the men kicked out last March." [7]

By removing the Tsarist government from the scene, by sweeping away the "Eastern peril," the February revolution removed what for most liberals was the chief stumbling-block to participation in the war on the side of the Allies. The New York *World* was probably correct when it claimed that any lingering opposition to the Allies in America (aside from outright pro-German sentiment) could be set down to "anti-Russian sentiment which honestly dreads Russian aggrandizement as a threat against civilization." [8] Whether one feared the fact of Russian aggrandizement or simply the moral blot on the character of a country entering into an alliance with "a decadent and besotted Caesarism" (and most liberals tended to look at the matter in the latter light), the revolution removed the fear.[9] It purified the Allied cause. "The war can now be visualized, without embarrassing reservations, as a conflict between the principle of democracy and the principle of autocracy," the Springfield *Republican* declared.[10] It was probably not too much to say, as the New York *Evening Post* later observed, that the revolution

> decisively swung the uneasy balance between our desire to serve the cause of right in Europe and our doubt whether such service could not best be rendered by keeping this country out of the bitter conflict. With the cause of Russian freedom thrown into the scale there was an instant change of view. . . . Socialist rhetoric and German vituperation may speak of America as forced into war by her capitalists or by the need of safeguarding her loans to the Allies. Men of reason know that with the uprising of the Russian people the moral issue for ourselves was clarified.[11]

The revolution put to rout those who still protested that the war would not necessarily make Russia or any other place safe for democracy. Nor were pacifists long in learning how the revolution would be used against them. "[N]ow the Russian Revolution is put down to the credit of war," one of them said, "and by war we are to 'democratize the world'! What folly and blindness." [12] Foolish and blind as this view may have been, it nevertheless swept everything before it. The revolution, exclaimed the *Evening Post*, "is the first visible sign of that democratization of all the world which must come if civilization is to profit by the unparalleled bloodshed of this unspeakable world-war." [13] Especially compelling was the prospect that the revolution would spread to Germany, to lighten the work of the Allied armies. "If Russia, the perfect example of absolutism, turns to democracy," asked Stoughton Cooley in the *Public*, "what possible hope of survival can there be for the reactionaries in other lands?" [14]

It was not long before people had occasion to reconsider some of these opinions. The revolution, it appeared, far from hastening the downfall of the German empire, might undermine the Russian war effort instead. Alarming reports began to filter in—reports of opposition to the war, of agitation for "peace, land and bread." Some pessimists already began to despair of Russia's continuation in the war.[15]

What especially gave Americans pause was the war-aims program of the Petrograd soviet, which the soviet in May, 1917, forced on the Provisional Government itself. The authority of the liberal regime headed by Prince Lvov, in which Paul Miliukov held the position of minister of foreign affairs, was challenged from the outset by the soviet, or "council," of the workers and soldiers of Petrograd, a body dominated throughout the spring and summer of 1917 by the Social Revolutionaries and the Menshevik faction of the Social Democrats (not yet by the Bolsheviks). The fact that the conflict between the Provisional Government and the soviet turned on questions of foreign policy, while the land issue, which was more important but less immediate, was relegated temporarily to the background, served to confirm the erroneous impression in the United States that the revolution was essentially a dispute among Russians as to what part Russia should play in the war.

The soviet feared, with good reason, that the Provisional Government would allow itself to be bullied by the Allies into promising to go on with a war which was now almost unanimously condemned by the Russian Left, and which the Left was convinced could end only in disaster. On March 27, the soviet therefore advised the workers of all countries to take matters into their own hands and put a stop to the slaughter.[16] A thrill of terror ran through the Western world. Miliukov, an avid expansionist himself, promptly sought to put the fear to rest. Russia, he said, would never quit the war until she was in possession of Constantinople and the Straits (and by implication, until the Allies had achieved comparable gains). His statement had the desired effect. What those who took it at face value did not know, however, was that not even a majority of the Provisional Government shared Miliukov's extreme views. The Provisional Government, however, did not hasten to enlighten them. Instead it attempted to preserve an appearance of unanimity. Even Kerensky, the single socialist in the cabinet, repeatedly denied that Russia had any intention of making peace, although nobody was in a better position to know just how intense was the popular desire to end the war. Americans did not discover until Miliukov had been forced out of office that his policy commanded no appreciable support.

Notwithstanding its desire to give off an outward impression of calm, the government could not indefinitely resist the pressure of the soviet. On April 10 it issued a declaration of war aims, in which it renounced its own claim to "annexations and indemnities" at the expense of Germany and her allies. This was a drastic step, for Russia had earlier signed treaties with Britain, France and Italy, in which each had promised not to make peace until the others had achieved certain minimal territorial objectives: Constantinople in the case of Russia; Alsace-Lorraine, the Saar, the Rhineland and parts of Asia Minor in the case of France; control of the Adriatic in the case of Italy; most of Asia Minor in the case of Britain.[17] In renouncing her claim to Constantinople, Russia was not necessarily threatening to leave the war. Not only the Provisional Government but the Petrograd soviet affirmed again and again their abhorrence of a separate peace. Even the Bolsheviks at first opposed a separate peace with Germany, and although by the end of April they had reversed themselves and voted for it, the Bolsheviks themselves remained for a long time a minority in the soviet.[18] But when they disavowed any desire for territorial gains the Russians were clearly inviting the Allies to follow their example and to make an immediate general peace with Germany. From this time forward a general peace was to be the cardinal aim, although unfortunately not often the avowed aim, of Russian diplomacy.

Owing to the opposition of Miliukov, even the revision of war aims could not at once be announced as a diplomatic objective. Miliukov as an expansionist wanted Constantinople for Russia; but beyond this he was desperately afraid, as a Western-oriented liberal, of doing anything that would force a break between Russia and her Western allies. He therefore attempted to avoid communicating to the Allies the government's provocative note of April 10, calling for an end to "annexations and indemnities." When at length, on May 1, he reluctantly sent out the text, he attached to it a note of his own in which he promised once more to "fulfill Russia's obligations to her Allies." Rumors of discord within the government, he said, were "absurd," invented by the enemy in order to weaken the Entente.[19]

In the West the effect of Miliukov's note was reassuring. In Russia, however, its publication on May 3 led to the first great crisis of the revolution. Demonstrators paraded in the streets, calling for the resignation of Miliukov and even for the overthrow of the government. For two days matters hung in the balance. In the end the government sacrificed Miliukov to the mob. It qualified his statements on war aims in such a way as to leave him no choice, since he still clung to Constantinople, except to resign. Guchkov, another liberal expansionist, also resigned as minister of war. The government was reorganized so as to give the moderate socialists a stronger voice in it and, presumably, thereby to restore harmony between the soviet and the Provisional Government.

Confronted with these startling events, the war liberals in America first attempted to make light of the attack on Miliukov and then, when the attack succeeded in driving him from power, to extract from the result some crumb of hope. At the very least, they pointed out, the admission of socialists to the cabinet had resolved the issue between the government and the soviet. No doubt the socialists would be less dangerous in office than in opposition; faced with the responsibilities of power, they would abandon their utopian dreams.[20] Of Russia's real condition—of the economic breakdown, the longing for peace, the appalling demoralization of the army—there was as yet little inkling among most Americans, although once again evidence on the subject was not lacking. It was known, for example, that Guchkov had publicly implored the troops not to desert from the army or fraternize with the enemy—surely an indication of desertion and fraternization on a large scale. A few papers did cite Guchkov's appeal as a reason for doubting whether Russia would be very effective in the summer campaigns.[21] But whatever misgivings Americans may have had were constantly soothed by the statements of the Provisional Government itself, which sought desperately to keep Russia's wounds hidden from view. In the absence of any appreciation of the country's inability to carry on the war, the question invariably presented itself, in the United States, as turning on her desire to do so, and it was easy for Americans to convince themselves that if only the Russians could be fired up with enthusiasm for the war, if only they could be made to understand their stake in the defeat of Germany, they would gladly take up arms again. From the first, Americans exaggerated the extent to which they could influence the course of events in Russia.

What little influence Americans could wield, in fact, was chiefly negative. By tact and patience it was perhaps possible to avoid making matters any worse than they were. On the other hand whatever positive effect American policy exerted on the revolution always turned out to be a bad effect. Thus although a restatement of war aims would not necessarily have strengthened the Provisional Government and kept Russia in the war, the truculent refusal to discuss the subject at all undoubtedly hastened the government's demise. Truculence, however, was the course urged by those who were supposed to know Russia best. George Kennan, for instance, advised Lansing to "give no encouragement whatever to the Council of Workmens & Soldiers Delegates, or to the coalition ministry if it stands for 'peace without annexations or indemnities.'" That formula, he said, "might mean the leaving of Alsace & Lorraine to Germany; the turning over of Turkish Armenia to Turkey; and the freeing of the Central Powers from any pecuniary responsibility for the destruction of Belgium, Servia, & Montenegro. Great Britain & France," he predicted, "never will consent to that programme, and I hope we never shall. I doubt very much whether the Russian people & the Russian army ever consent to it." [22] William English Walling, a former left-wing socialist who had become a vehement supporter of the war, a vehement advocate of "victory" over Germany, sternly declared, "The time to begin to combat this 'no annexation, no indemnity' propaganda is now." [23]

Whatever one may think of their opinions as to what should have been done about the Russian crisis, the mere fact that Kennan and Walling admitted the existence of a crisis set them apart from most of their countrymen. Kennan in particular was alert to the gravity of the situation, Miliukov's resignation having shaken whatever hopes he may have entertained at the outset. "I continue to regard the situation in Russia with great anxiety," he wrote to Jacob Schiff in the middle of May. He doubted, he said, "the permanency of the modus vivendi" brought about by the reorganization of the cabinet.[24] A month later he wrote to Lansing, "I can't see much that is encouraging in Russia yet." [25] The wording of his letters to Schiff and to Lansing suggests that he had never had much hope for the revolution to begin with. Evidently, therefore, the rather guarded optimism which he had expressed in some of his early articles on the revolution did not reflect his real opinions. Late in March, for instance, he predicted that as a result of the revolution, the war would "ultimately . . . be carried on with greatly increased vigor and effectiveness." [26]

But it was characteristic of commentators on Russia that they were invariably more optimistic in public than in private. It was characteristic also that the pessimists, although they understood better than most Americans the dangers with which the revolution threatened the orderly progress of democracy, were unusually unimaginative about what should be done to meet these dangers. Faced with a threat to democracy, they could suggest nothing better than the removal of the threat by force, a policy of "blood and iron." It was people like Kennan who continued throughout the revolution to call for a "strong man" who would forcibly suppress every trace of radicalism in Russia, and who early lost patience with Kerensky because he would not undertake such a purge of the opposition. Realism again and again, in the course of the controversy over the revolution, identified itself with repression.

Anti-imperialists, on the other hand, "accepted" the revolution, as they liked to put it. But they did so only when they had convinced themselves that the dangers of which the opponents of the revolution spoke did not exist at all; only when they had decided that the revolution was nothing more than a radical extension of Western democracy. Their attitude toward the Petrograd formula was a case in point. The *New Republic* at first found the formula "negative and sterile." "A settlement based exclusively on the status quo ante," it declared, "would constitute a confession of bankruptcy on the part of European statesmanship." [27] The Philadelphia *Public Ledger* and the Springfield *Republican* objected to the formula on the same grounds.[28] Upton Sinclair, a pro-war socialist of anti-imperialist inclinations, found it inadequate because it said nothing about the democratization of Germany, which he considered a "fundamental and inevitable demand in this war." [29] Colonel House went so far as to put down the Petrograd proposals to German influence; he suspected that "some sort of an agreement [was] growing up between the socialist forces in Russia and Germany." [30] Their opposition to a peace without annexations and indemnities, that is, to a "peace without victory," was an indication of the degree to which American anti-imperialists had already abandoned their original view of the war.

Yet although they were at first horrified by the Petrograd formula, anti-imperialists were not unaware of the need for a redefinition of the aims of the war. Although they demanded not only the indemnification of Belgium and the democratization of Germany itself, both of which the Petrograd formula seemed to preclude, they were not eager to fight for the secret treaties. Quite apart from the intrinsic undesirability of a division of spoils, the war aims of the Allied governments were inconsistent with the anti-imperialist strategy for the democratization of Germany, which was to make an offer of reasonable, nonannexationist terms that would induce the German people to throw off the Kaiser and make peace. If the German people were threatened with the destruction of their empire, they would be afraid to lay down their arms.

To these considerations, which predisposed anti-imperialists, even after they had left "peace without victory" behind them, to favor a moderate and reasonable peace, there was now added another: the need to keep the Russians in the war. As early as May 19, 1917, the *New Republic* advised Wilson to press the Allies for a redefinition of war aims as the only means of appealing to Russian idealism.[31] The Russians, obviously, were restive; they wanted peace. Or did they simply want to be assured that the Allies were fighting for democracy, and not for national aggrandizement? Without much effort anti-imperialists convinced themselves that the latter was in fact the case. They came to see the redefinition of war aims less as a means of clearing away the obstacles to peace than as a grand and noble gesture which would appeal to Russian idealism and renew the Russian ardor for a "holy war." The Russians, they began to think, would continue to fight once the Allies had purged their cause of all taint of sin.

Experts in textual exigesis set to work on the problem of reconciling the war aims of the *New Republic* with those of the Petrograd soviet. H. N. Brailsford discovered that "no annexations, no indemnities," did not necessarily imply a return to the *status quo ante,* as liberals had feared. What the Russian socialists wanted, Brailsford decided, was simply to be assured that in continuing the war they would not be fighting for the narrow ambitions of Allied imperialists.[32] Charles A. Beard, prompted by the *New Republic's* editorials on war aims, hit upon the same idea. "We must convince the Russian revolutionists that the things they hold dear are really at stake in the eastern trenches. . . . We must convince them that this is not at bottom, or even potentially, a capitalist war for colonies, markets, and concessions." [33] Lincoln Steffens upon his return from Russia in June 1917, with the authority that the fact of visiting Russia was henceforth to confer on even the most casual of tourists, urged the same views on Colonel House.

> The Russians can be made to fight, but only by an act of the Allies. In a highly exalted state of mind, the effect of the revolution, they think that if all the Allies would reduce their purposes (or raise them) to a demand only for permanent peace (no punishments; no compensation; no extension of territory; and a promise to let the questions of the sovereignty of the lesser nations be answered by the lesser nations) [*i.e.*, "self-determination"], then we could have peace. And if we couldn't, if Germany refused to hear on this basis, then,—then the Russians would fight.
>
> It may be an illusion, but the Russians think they are asked now to fight, not to achieve idealistic ends, but to carry out certain secret treaties among certain of the Allies. Whatever it is, illusion or

fact, this belief and the psychological condition of the Russian mind are facts which should be and can be dealt with, if understood.[34]

What is especially interesting in this passage is the unequivocal assertion that if Germany refused an offer of fair terms, the Russians would resume the war.[35] Nor was there any doubt in Steffens' mind that the German government would never accept such terms, since it was presumably fighting for objectives even more imperialistic than those of the Allies. Thus the offer of reasonable terms became a means of embarrassing the German High Command and of hastening its downfall. At the same time the refusal of the German government to negotiate would make the Russians see the necessity of continuing the war until Germany was democratized.

Once they had succeeded in defining the phrase, "no annexations, no indemnities," to their own satisfaction, once they decided that, far from implying a return to the *status quo ante* it merely expressed "the profound truth," as Lincoln Colcord put it, "that no real democracy can harbor predatory thoughts . . . and that no governments truly representative of their peoples could subscribe to reactionary foreign policies," American anti-imperialists became enthusiastic exponents of the Petrograd formula.[36] The war liberals, however, continued to oppose it on the grounds that any discussion of peace terms was premature. This attitude became official when the Committee on Public Information announced in a bulletin circulated among newspaper editors: "Speculation about possible peace is another topic which may possess elements of danger, as peace reports may be of enemy origin, put out to weaken the combination against Germany." [37]

So far as Russia was concerned, men who took this position felt that any appearance of disagreement among Americans themselves over the question of peace terms would encourage dissidence in Russia, whereas if Americans stood unanimously for war and against all talk of peace, the Russians would take heart from their example. Thus Charles Edward Russell, a war socialist, and like all war socialists more energetic in his support of the war than even the conservatives, advised Lansing to take a strong position against the Russian peace initiative. Peace without annexations and indemnities, he said, was a "sentimental and impossible delusion," and a clear statement to that effect by the American government would "greatly help stabilize things in Russia and elsewhere." [38] His visit to Russia in the summer of 1917 as a member of the Root mission confirmed Russell in this opinion. What the Russians needed to be convinced of, he declared, was "that this Nation stands solidly behind its allies in this war." [39] Thereafter he devoted himself to discouraging peace talk in the United States, while at the same time urging the government to organize a gigantic campaign of propaganda in Russia designed to impress upon the Russian mind the rectitude of the war and the blessings of democracy.[40]

With Samuel Gompers, William English Walling, and Frank Walsh, and with the active encouragement of the administration, Russell helped to found the American Alliance for Labor and Democracy, an organization designed to prevent the infiltration of anti-imperialist ideas among the ranks of labor.[41] Before the founding conference of the Alliance at St. Paul in September, 1917, Russell declared that talk of peace was "interpreted by the Russian people as meaning that the United States does not want to fight," and therefore weakened the "faith of the Russian people," undermining their will to resist the German armies. "Riga," he exclaimed, "was captured by United States Senators La Follette, Gronna and Stone." [42] It was this message which Russell and his cohorts broadcast throughout the land, with results highly gratifying to the CPI.[43]

Nothing caused the war liberals greater anxiety than the proposed "peace conference" at Stockholm, announced by the Petrograd soviet in May. The soviet's decision to call an international conference of socialists to discuss peace terms reflected its growing impatience with regular diplomatic procedures. The Allied governments, it appeared, were united in their opposition to any revision of the secret treaties. It was to bring pressure on them by a dramatic display of world opinion in favor of the Petrograd formula, and even to threaten them with destruction from within, that the soviet revived an idea with which pacifists had played since the beginning of the war. Unfortunately even the Stockholm conference depended on the willingness of Allied governments to allow their nationals to attend. The British government after heated debate decided to allow representatives of British labor to make the trip. In America, however, the State Department refused to issue passports to Morris Hillquit, Victor Berger, and Algernon Lee, who had been appointed by the Socialist party as delegates to the conference. The war liberals were delighted. George Kennan, in reply to those who argued that it was wise to conciliate the soviet in its search for peace, insisted that the refusal to issue passports to Hillquit, Berger, and Lee would "have a *good* effect in Russia by discouraging the pacifists & pro-German schemers, & by strengthening the hands of Milyukov and Guchkoff." [44]

Berger, however, protested that the administration was "riding rough shod over the constitution." [45] A convention of pacifists met in Madison Square Garden on May 30–31, 1917, to endorse the Russian peace formula and the Stockholm conference. The People's Council of America, its very name a translation of "soviet," was the most immediate and tangible manifestation in America of the impact of the Russian revolution. From its founding until it was finally hounded out of existence by the authorities in the autumn of 1917, it remained the rallying point for pacifist opinion, although in this capacity it was sometimes challenged by the American Union against Militarism. The Union tended to accept America's decision to enter the war as irreversible and to concentrate on the defense of civil liberties at home. Both organizations, however, accepted the Petrograd formula as part of their program.

But even the pacifists did not always make it clear how the formula was to be defined. Frank Harris, who as editor of *Pearson's* at this time professed radically pacifistic views, took it as implying a return to the *status quo ante,* and supported it as such. Harris, for all his eccentricities, was one of the few people to understand that what the Russians wanted was peace, not a holy war for democracy; he predicted that they would settle for a separate peace if they failed to get a general one.[46] Alexander Trachtenberg, a Russian emigré and anti-war socialist, also saw that the Russian revolution was "really an anti-war revolution." [47] But a number of pacifists—probably most of them—fell into the anti-imperialists' error of thinking that the Russians wanted only to purify the war, not to end it. Thus Judah Magnes, addressing the rally in Madison Square Garden, declared that the Russian armies would "have the spirit to continue the war on one condition—that their own idealistic war aims be made the war aims of their Allies." [48]

Anti-imperialists, together with such pacifists as Rabbi Magnes, continued throughout the summer of 1917 to clamor for a restatement of war aims. The Allied cause, they insisted, was tarnished with imperialism. Unqualified supporters of the war, on the other hand, maintained that the cause was already pure and the Allies' aims in no need of redefinition. It was perfectly obvious, they argued, that the United States was fighting for democracy. Surely it was equally obvious to the Germans and the Russians; it was necessary only to tell them so. It was for this purpose, as well as to make a rather general gesture of American sympathy for the revolution, that a mission headed by Elihu Root was dispatched to Russia in May, 1917. Among the members of the mission were Charles Edward Russell and Charles R. Crane.[49]

Just what led Wilson to appoint Root for the position will

probably always remain a mystery. But the kind of considerations that must have prompted the sending of a mission to Russia in the first place can be inferred from notes by George Kennan of conversations with Oscar Straus, who was perhaps the first to suggest that a mission be sent. On April 9, 1917, only a week after the United States entered the war, Straus proposed sending a "Commission to Russia," as Kennan put it, "to help [the] Provisional Gov't in any way possible & particularly in its struggle with Socialists & radicals. His idea," Kennan said, "was to save American lives in the war by preventing collapse of Russ. Govt through internal dissension. He had submitted plan he said to Andrew D. White [former ambassador to Russia], Col. House & Secy Lansing & all approved provided Provisional Govt gave its consent." [50] In the minds of Straus and Kennan at least, the mission was thus deliberately designed to throw cold water on the soviet's campaign for a revision of war aims; and if the choice of members was any clue to Wilson's motives, this was the purpose of the administration as well. The Root mission was America's answer to Stockholm.

Inasmuch as all the members of the Root mission were out of sympathy with the aims of the revolution, the failure of the expedition either to persuade the Russians to stay in the war or to warn Americans at home of the gravity of the situation might have been predicted in advance. Sailing from Seattle on May 20, the party arrived in Petrograd on June 13, by way of Vladivostok and the Siberian railway. On June 21–25, they made an excursion to Moscow, returning immediately to the capitol, where they remained until the second week in July. Everywhere their path was strewn with oratory, both Russian and American. Samples of the latter have been preserved in the papers of Charles Edward Russell. "We make war that we may have peace," Russell told the Russians.[51] The war was a war for democracy, and democracy was a precondition of socialism.[52] Indeed it was, in the West; but in Russia the precondition of socialism, or of any other kind of reform, appeared to be peace. How was society to be reconstructed in the midst of a devastating world war? And if reconstruction were postponed, who was to say whether anything would be left of Russia, after the war, to reconstruct?

Russell had no answer to these questions. But at least he was aware, as most of the other members of the mission were not, of the widening chasm between the soviet and the Provisional Government. It was clear to him that these organs were rival governments locked in a deadly struggle for mastery. Indeed Ambassador Francis complained that Russell spoke "disrespectfully and openly" of the Provisional Government, "maintaining that they [the soviet] have the power." [53] He was, in truth, "too much of a Socialist," as Algernon Lee wrote to Morris Hillquit, "to be welcomed by the folk with whom Root hobnobbed." [54] The other members of the mission "pooh-poohed the idea" that the soviet was of more importance than the government itself. Arno Dosch-Fleurot of the New York *World*, after talking with members of the mission, was convinced that "they had not grasped that the real Government of Russia was the Soviet." Russell, according to Dosch-Fleurot, was "the only member of the . . . mission who seemed to understand the mass-movement of the Russian population," and he "was regarded in the mission as a well-meaning crank." [55] But neither was he welcomed by the Russian socialists. On the morning of his first visit to the soviet he sought out Bessie Beatty, the radical young correspondent of the San Francisco *Bulletin*, and begged her, she told Algernon Lee, "to dig up a piece of red ribbon, a red silk neck-cloth, anything good and red . . . As luck would have it," Lee wrote to Hillquit, "she couldn't find a scrap of anything red. An hour later, though, she sees him on the street, with a flaming scarlet necktie and a red rosette in his coat lapel—and then, alas! ignoring these manifestations of his revolutionary soul, the heartless Bolsheviki snubbed him as cruelly as had the rich bourgeois[ie]." [56] The ambassador, meanwhile, made it clear that Russell's usefulness in Russia, in his opinion, had reached its end. He warned the State Department that Russell would "make trouble" if he stayed in Petrograd.[57]

The Root mission, having been "wined and dined by all sorts of eminently respectable elements," as Lee observed, and having assured the Russian people of the undying esteem in which they would always be held by Americans (provided, of course, that they carried on the war), took its departure from Petrograd on July 9, 1917, late enough to witness the beginning of the great advance of the Russian army into Galicia but too early to see at first hand the moral effects of its total collapse twelve days later. By July 19, when the Russian troops began their headlong retreat, the Root mission was within two days' journey of Vladivostok. By the 21st, they were at sea. By August 8, its members (all except Charles R. Crane, who had prolonged his stay in Russia) were back in Washington, assuring everyone that the Russians would never make peace until the German army was beaten to pieces.[58] They admitted in their report that there was a question whether the Provisional Government would "have the power to continue the war." [59] But they did not emphasize the point, either in public appearances or in conversations with officials. Lansing was "astounded at their optimism. I cannot see upon what it is founded," he confessed. But Root and his colleagues stood firm in their optimism. "When I expressed doubts," Lansing wrote, "as to Kerensky's personal force and ability to carry through his plans in view of the strong opposition developing against him, they assured me that everything would come out all right and that Russia would continue the war against the Central Powers with even greater vigor than under the Czar." [60]

Naturally this view of things was reflected in the press, which relied on the Root mission and on the statements of Ambassador Francis for firsthand reports on Russia's condition. The ambassador was a particularly fruitful source of optimism. He found comfort even in the rout of the Russian armies. Defeat had "strengthened the hands of the government," according to one of his reports, by creating a "universal demand for stronger discipline."[61] Even Samuel Harper continued to send home words of encouragement and reassurance.[62] Repeatedly he complained that reporters in Russia, because of their antirevolutionary bias, were sending out only the most discouraging news, when in fact the reporters were sending out the most optimistic news they could find.[63]

Harper, returning to the United States in September, 1917, predicted that the Kerensky regime would survive until the meeting of the Constituent Assembly in December, which would then unify the country.[64] Even those who, like S. R. Bertron, admitted that the Russians were "tired of war," doubted that Russia would make a separate peace.[65] Of all the members of the Root mission, only Charles R. Crane seems really to have understood the direction in which matters were drifting. On his way home in September, he told a correspondent in Stockholm that Russia was beyond redemption. "Things have been growing steadily worse right along," he said. "They are still getting worse and the end is not in sight yet." Russia was "the sick man of Europe" and needed "the rest cure."[66] Where the other Americans in Russia still hoped to see the emergence of a vigorous coalition of socialists at the head of a reunited Russia, Crane had lost whatever confidence he may have had in the socialists. Miliukov, his friend of long standing, now supported the counter-revolution, and it is possible that Crane too had thrown in his lot with the forces gathering around the Cossack general A. M. Kaledin. Some of the Americans in Russia suspected that Crane was giving money to Kaledin.* Whether or

* George F. Kennan, *Soviet-American Relations, 1917–1920* (Princeton, 1956), I, 176–7. It should be noted that because Crane remained in Russia after the other members of the Root mission had returned to the United States, he was not among those who delivered the optimistic report to Lansing in August. Not until December 11 did Crane call on the Secretary of State. At that time he may have urged support of Kaledin.

not that was the case, there can be no doubt that he was, even at this early date, completely disillusioned with the revolution.

The Provisional Government, as noted, attempted to oblige the Allies by launching an offensive into Galicia in July. This decision touched off a series of violent demonstrations in Petrograd. Soldiers rose up in revolt rather than be sent back to the front. On July 17, huge crowds gathered in the streets demanding "All power to the soviets!" At this point the soviet did not want power badly enough to seize it, however. Even the Bolsheviks were frightened. Without leadership the revolt quickly collapsed. Trotsky was arrested; Lenin escaped to Finland. The forces of the Right urged Kerensky to make a clean sweep of the opposition. War liberals in the United States joined them in demanding bold, dictatorial action. But Kerensky would neither satisfy the extremists of the Right nor meet the demands of the Left for peace, land, bread. The Provisional Government under his direction continued to drift aimlessly. From time to time it issued optimistic statements for foreign consumption, which served to hide from the world the real condition of the country.

Not all Americans were oblivious, however, to the plight of the Provisional Government. Colonel House, for one, was at least intermittently aware of the imminence of disaster and of Russia's desperate need for peace. At times House spoke as if the disintegration of Russia made an immediate peace absolutely imperative—even, it seemed, a peace on the basis of the *status quo ante*. Thus in August, 1917, he advised Wilson to reply to the peace appeal of Pope Benedict XV in such a way "as to leave the door open" for negotiations. "It is more important, I think, that Russia should weld herself into a virile republic than it is that Germany should be beaten to her knees. . . . With Russia firmly established in democracy, German autocracy would be compelled to yield to a representative government within a very few years." [67]

At other times, however, as in the closing passages of this same letter, House spoke as if he wanted the President not to attempt to bring about an early peace but merely to discredit the German government, by exposing the contrast between German and Allied war aims. "[A]nswer the Pope's proposal in some such way as . . . to throw the onus [*i.e.*, for continuing the war] on Prussia," House advised. "[S]ay . . . that it is hardly fair to ask the people of the Allied countries to discuss terms with a military autocracy—an autocracy that does not represent the opinion of the people for whom they speak." [68] At first House seemed to have been implying that a political upheaval in Germany was no longer to be considered a prerequisite of peace. The German revolution, he seemed to say, could wait; the important thing for the moment was to give Russia time to consolidate her own revolution. The existence of democracy in Russia would then exert an inexorable pressure on Germany to change her ways—a pressure more powerful than that of Allied arms. But in the concluding parts of his letter to Wilson, House appeared to fall back on the democratization of Germany as an essential condition of peace. The reply to the Pope became a tactical maneuver. The United States, by refusing to negotiate with an unregenerate Germany, was to bring about "almost revolution" in Germany, as House put it in a subsequent letter.* But what if the revolution misfired? Then the war, presumably, would go on. The Russians' need for peace receded once again into the background. Like all Americans, Colonel House fell

* House to Wilson, Aug. 17, 1917, Wilson MSS, 2d series. "You can make a statement," he added, "that will not only be the undoing of autocratic Germany, but one that will strengthen the hands of the Russian liberals in their purpose to mould their country into a mighty republic." This line of reasoning may reflect the advice of Lincoln Steffens; see above, page 37.

easily into the habit of thinking that the Russians would fight once the aims of the war were made perfectly clear, once the purity of the Allied cause, in contrast to German "frightfulness," was exposed for all to see.

No episode of the war illustrates more clearly the ambiguity of the campaign for a revision of war aims, or the part played by the Russians themselves in confusing the issue, than the discussion revolving around the papal note. On August 1, 1917 the Pope issued an appeal to all the belligerents urging them to consider means of ending the war. Immediately he was denounced by Allied imperialists as an accomplice of the Kaiser. Lansing advised Wilson flatly to refuse to discuss peace. "I would only say that the Pope, probably unwittingly or out of compassion for Austria-Hungary, probably has become in this matter the agent of Germany." [69] Wilson appeared to be swayed by this advice, for he considered, for a time, making no reply at all.[70] House feared that the President was on the verge of a "colossal blunder." [71]

House had not yet abandoned hope, however. If the Provisional Government, through its ambassador in the United States, Boris Bakhmetev, urged the Allies to make a conciliatory reply to the Pope as a means of reviving the flagging spirits of the Russian people, it would be difficult for the Allies to refuse. Bakhmetev's approval of a policy of "leaving the door open," House thought, would be "an additional lever with the President." [72] The Colonel was therefore gratified to find, after conferring with Bakhmetev on August 19, that he and the ambassador were evidently in agreement. Bakhmetev "suggested," according to House, "that the President should call an Allied conference in order to formulate peace terms and announce them to Germany as the common Allied terms." They discussed how such a conference might be brought about. They "could not see how it was possible unless some terms were stated." House thought that if Wilson "could state it as being the position of all the Allies, that this country was willing to treat with the people of Germany but not with an autocracy which did not represent the people, that would be the first move." Territorial questions could be put off until later. Bakhmetev appeared to agree.[73]

In the course of their conversation House let it be known that Wilson was receiving different advice from others. He "did not mention names." But after a moment Bakhmetev said, "I find no sympathy in Lansing. When I talk of these matters to him, he does not appear sympathetic or to have any real understanding of Russian liberal opinion." [74] Yet two days later Bakhmetev told Lansing, according to the latter's account, "that his Government indicated that [the] Pope's appeal could not be accepted as it did not end military autocracy," a position with which Lansing himself was in full accord. The same day the Russian Embassy released a formal statement to that effect.[75]

This development threw House and his friends into consternation. Lincoln Colcord, the correspondent of the Philadelphia *Public Ledger*, who saw House regularly and knew his opinions as thoroughly as it was possible to know them, in a dispatch to his paper tried frantically to correct the impression that the Russian government intended to turn a cold shoulder to the Pope. "The correct interpretation to be placed upon this sentence, according to the friends of the Russian Embassy [House?], is . . . that she recognizes the fundamental fact that democracies cannot treat with autocracies." [76] But from his colleague in Washington, William C. Bullitt, Colcord heard that Bakhmetev opposed making any reply to the Pope.[77] When House heard of this, he wrote to Bakhmetev calling attention to the fact that his published statement did "not seem to harmonize with our conversation." [78] Bakhmetev was off reviewing a parade in Boston; House sent Colcord to give him the letter in person. On the afternoon of August 21, Colcord caught up with the ambassador on the reviewing stand.

"Have you seen the papers to-day?" he asked. "Your statement is being interpreted contrary to the talk you made to the Colonel on Sunday." He showed the ambassador a copy of the New York *Times*, which printed the statement of the Russian Embassy under the headline, "RUSSIA WILL SAY 'NO' TO THE POPE."

"That is all wrong," said Bakhmetev. "The statement was given out by the Embassy on advices from Petrograd, but it was not intended to convey that impression at all. It was done very stupidly."

"How do you interpret the sentence: 'It is considered in Russia that the very bases of the Vatican's proposals are inconsistent with the democratic aims of the Russian people in this war, and are not acceptable from that point of view?' "

"I interpret that as referring to the fact that Germany is not a democracy, and that democracies cannot in the nature of the case treat with autocracies. That is just what we talked on Sunday."

"But a totally different construction is being placed upon the sentence," Colcord persisted. "And Secretary Lansing got a totally different impression of your position from your talk with him yesterday afternoon."

"I am so sorry," the ambassador said. "Tell Colonel House that I made exactly the same talk to Mr. Lansing that I made to him on Sunday."

"He construed it in the diametrically opposite sense," Colcord said. Then he asked whether Bakhmetev intended to make a public denial of the interpretation placed on his statement by Lansing and the press.

"Perhaps I will," Bakhmetev said. "I must be careful of my words." [79]

That evening, however, when he telephoned House and asked whether he should issue a denial, House advised against it. "He has done enough now to be recalled," House wrote in his diary, "and the sooner he gets out of the papers, the better it will be for him and everyone." [80]

Bakhmetev assured House that he had acted on his own initiative throughout, having had no advice from his government on the subject but only "the views which came to him from unofficial sources." [81] But in public, as well as in his interview with Lansing, Bakhmetev had given the impression that he spoke for the Provisional Government. It is hard to believe that he was unaware of the importance that attached to his words.

But the point of this curious episode is not that Bakhmetev was indiscreet (which he probably was) but that the issues and ideas involved in the discussion of the papal note were so obscure that it was possible simply by saying the same thing to different people to set off a heated controversy. Bakhmetev, after all, had told Lansing nothing that he had not told House. What he said, on both occasions, was that the Allies should make it clear to the Pope that they would treat only with a representative government in Germany, a government which could be trusted to keep its word. But whereas this assertion seemed to House to "leave the door open" for negotiations, to Lansing it seemed to close it firmly in the Kaiser's face.

When finally incorporated by Wilson into his reply to the Pope (August 29, 1917), the idea met with the same reception: it pleased everybody for totally different reasons.[82] Wilson's note, in which he declared that it was impossible for the Allies to "take the word of the present rulers of Germany as a guarantee of anything that is to endure," led anti-imperialists to expect, as Herbert Croly wrote, "that a really vital peace discussion . . . will be taking place during the coming Fall." [83] Walter Lippmann, who had opposed making the democratization of Germany a condition of peace, was "more than happy" with the President's note, although it seemed clearly to demand that Germany change her government if she wanted peace. [84] Lincoln Colcord, like Lippmann, regarded the demand for a representative form of government in Germany as "essentially a meddling of the first rank in German internal affairs"; yet he too claimed Wilson's reply to the Pope as a victory for the anti-imperialist interpretation of the war.* Even pacifists approved of the note as a step in the direction of peace.[85] Conservatives, on the other hand, as well as most war liberals, acclaimed it because they thought that it would put an end to all talk of a negotiated peace. The United States and the Allies, as the Emporia *Gazette* put it, had "bound themselves to a fight to the finish, a decisive end which can be accomplished only through a crushing defeat of Germany." [86] It was in this light that Wilson's note was accepted by the American people, whose ardor for "victory" knew no limits.

What confused the war-aims question, as we have noted before, was the demand for the democratization of Germany, which tended to prolong the war instead of bringing it to an end and which therefore discouraged the Russians instead of giving them new strength with which to carry on the fight—a fight in which they no longer had much interest. It was of no concern to them what form of government Germany chose to

* The whole episode made him appreciate, he said, "the nature of the Colonel's political genius." He was convinced "that there will not be a diplomat or statesman in Europe who can match him when the peace conference comes. He will dominate the conference, and have things measurably his own way." Colcord MS Diary, Aug. 25 [1917].

Yet Colcord sensed the ambiguity of Wilson's reply to the Pope. It seemed to him that the newspapers "over-emphasized the German-autocracy phase of the note . . . But of course the President gave them the cue to do this; he over-emphasized that phase himself." House seemed to agree. "Yes," he said, "and that is what I would have liked to change in the note. That is, I would not have emphasized that phase myself; the President's emotions led him to do it. But when I thought it all over, and took into account the necessity for appealing to the support of the Allies, I decided to make no objection." *Ibid.* Aug. 29, 1917.

For Colcord's views on the democratization of Germany, see Colcord to House, Oct. 19, 1917, House MSS. Much later Colcord, like most anti-imperialists, came around to the view that Germany's democratization had to be a primary condition of peace. See Colcord to House, Aug. 11, 1918, House MSS. For a similar metamorphosis *cf.* Paul M. Warburg to House, July 15, 1917 and Oct. 17, 1918, *ibid.*

adopt. They wanted peace. American anti-imperialists, however, still labored under the delusion that some such statement as Wilson's reply to the Pope was just what the Russians had been clamoring for. "Russian radicals are now assured that the sympathies of the United States are with them," the *New Republic* declared, "and that their aspirations for a just peace are our aspirations. The President in effect subscribes to the Russian peace formula." [87]

The Russian "radicals" could hardly have found much encouragement in these words. But they bravely—and foolishly—hid their disappointment and sought to preserve the fiction of Allied unity. The Kerensky government encouraged Americans to think that in replying to the Pope, Wilson had replied to the Petrograd soviet as well. But the Kerensky government in truth no longer reflected the mood or the wishes of the country. Patriotic speeches, the government's stock in trade, were no longer good politics or even good taste. "The soldiers in the trenches . . . want only one thing now—the end of the war. Whatever you may say here, the soldiers are not going to fight any more." Thus a soldier, fresh from the front, addressed the soviet. Even there, Sukhanov recalled, his words caused a "sensation." "Exclamations were heard: 'Even the Bolsheviks don't say that!' " [88]

The Kerensky government was falling to pieces. Having survived attacks from the Left, it was menaced late in August by an uprising of the Right, led by the dashing General Kornilov. To protect himself against Kornilov, Kerensky had to arm his enemies on the Left, who gained the credit for saving the day. Thus as a result of the affair the Bolsheviks found their position greatly strengthened. For the first time they commanded a majority in the soviet, where, turning a deaf ear to all appeals for a "united front," they waited the opportunity to seize power for themselves. The opportunity, they began to think, lay not far ahead.

America, like Russia, was tired of Kerensky. Several papers, including the New York *Times* and the New York *Tribune*, hailed Kornilov as the "strong man" who would deliver Russia from her tribulations.[89] Most of the war liberals, together with the anti-imperialists, deplored the Kornilov uprising. That was not so much, however, because they disapproved of Kornilov himself as because they feared that civil war in Russia would render the country impotent in the face of a German advance.[90] The St. Louis *Post-Dispatch* waited until Kornilov had retired from the field before deciding that he was an "arch-traitor." [91] Even then the *Post-Dispatch*, like all papers of its strong pro-war inclinations, continued to hope for the emergence of a "strong man." It attributed Kerensky's failure to his "willingness to compromise," to his refusal to see "the value of force in unsettled, revolutionary times." [92] The *New Republic* and the *Nation* (and the *Nation's* alter ego, the New York *Evening Post*) were almost alone among liberal journals in arguing that the Allies themselves were partly to blame for the troubles of the Provisional Government.[93]

The precise nature of these troubles was still only dimly understood in the United States; in some places, their existence was not even suspected. Americans were therefore surprised to read in the papers for November 3, 1917, an interview with Kerensky by a correspondent of the Associated Press, in which the harassed premier for the first time admitted that his government found itself in a difficult and dangerous predicament. Russia, he confessed, was "worn out" and could not carry on without help from the Allies. In the first years of the war she had "saved France and England from disaster" by engaging the Germans in the East. Now she claimed "as her right that the Allies . . . shoulder the burden." [94] The State Department attempted to minimize this cry of distress, while privately deliberating whether it would be wise to inform the Russians "that they might not get assistance unless they intended to do their share of fighting." [95] The public was outraged. What right had Russia to be worn out? the New York *World* demanded. Serbia was not worn out, France was not worn out.[96] "[W]e were not prepared for so great a disappointment in Kerensky," said the St. Louis *Post-Dispatch*.[97] At the same time Americans still did not seem to understand the extent of the Russian collapse. They still talked of a dictator who would restore discipline and order.

Kerensky's interview was directed not at the American public but at the inter-Allied conference which was then about to meet in Paris. This conference represented the last hope of the Provisional Government, the last opportunity for the Allies to abandon the secret treaties and prepare for peace. Kerensky's friends in the West sensed the gravity of the occasion. Colonel House was fully aware that the Russians were "eager for peace." [98] Ambassador Bakhmetev, abandoning his reticence on the subject of war aims, urged him that "it was essential for the War Council to recognize Russia's political as well as her war needs." [99] House left for Paris on October 29, determined to force the issue with the Allied governments. Behind his back, however, Lansing was assuring Ambassador Francis in Russia, who was afraid the Allies might do something to encourage the extremist element, that the forthcoming conference could under no circumstances consider terms of peace.[100] In the House of Commons Bonar Law assured his colleagues that the Allies did not intend to "discuss the aims of the war at all, but only methods of conducting it." [101] Colonel House had lost his fight before he set foot in Europe. By the time the conference finally convened, after a series of postponements, the Bolsheviks were in power in Russia. It was ironic but also fitting that the Provisional Government itself, fearing an open conflict with the soviet over the representation of Russia at the conference, had asked for the postponement.[102]

To the end, anti-imperialists believed that a revision of war aims would have saved Kerensky and prevented the triumph of the Bolsheviks. But as the Springfield *Republican* wisely observed, "[N]othing would [have satisfied] the forces behind the bolsheviki but an early peace. A revision of war aims, however radical in eliminating every selfish imperialist ambition, or nationalist desire for new annexations of territory on the side of the entente, would have utterly failed to satisfy the maximalist socialists," or, it might be added, the great majority of the Russian people, "unless the restatement of war aims had carried with it the immediate end of the war." But whether the "American conscience" was therefore "clear, so far as Russia [was] concerned," was by no means as obvious a conclusion as the *Republican* permitted itself to think.[103] If the United States could not, in 1917, have saved the Russians for the war and for the West, it could at least have avoided repeatedly and unnecessarily antagonizing them. It might even have explored the possibility of bringing the war to an end, as the Russians hoped it would. With so much at stake, nothing could have been lost by such a step—nothing, that is, except the prospect of total victory over the horrible Hun.

III

The Judas of the Nations

THE optimism of the press, of the officials in Washington and, until the last moment, of the Provisional Government itself, had left Americans unprepared for the sudden collapse of the Kerensky regime. In fact, as we have seen, Kerensky's support had been ebbing away ever since the Kornilov affair, after which he had tried to placate Kornilov's supporters by appointing them to cabinet posts. On October 25, the Bolsheviks, sensing that the moment was ripe, voted to prepare to overthrow the government. On November 5, they captured the Fortress of Peter and Paul without bloodshed; on November 7, after a short siege, they took possession of the Winter Palace. Five days later Kerensky fled to England. By November 15, Moscow as well as Petrograd was in Bolshevik hands. The Provisional Government had ceased to exist.

Although the Bolsheviks had figured in the news from Russia since May, and especially since the July uprising, there was still a great deal of doubt in the United States as to who they were and what they stood for. One paper explained that the term "bolsheviki" meant "most demandful," and continued for weeks to refer to the Bolsheviks as the "most demandfuls," sternly rebuking a reader who suggested that "bolsheviki" meant "majority" (that is, a majority of the London convention of the Social Democratic party in 1903): "If the Bolsheviki and their American sympathizers look upon that party as the Russian majority, events will undeceive them." [1] The widespread belief, reinforced by Trotsky's leading role in the events of the next few months, that Trotsky rather than Lenin was the leader of the party, explained much of the confusion surrounding the objectives of the Bolsheviks.[2] As for what the party believed in, where it stood in the spectrum of Leftist opinion, Americans commonly made the mistake of identifying the Bolsheviks as anarchists of some kind; a mistake the implications of which can best be explored at a later time.[3] More loosely Russia's new rulers were thought of as agitators, fanatics, pacifists, doctrinaire idealists.

Their uncompromising idealism was the subject of much complaint. The St. Louis *Post-Dispatch* conceded that "the Bolshevik platform has many appealing doctrines" but declared that "their leaders have been so intemperate and visionary, have shown themselves so susceptible to reptile German intrigue, have revealed such an inadequate conception of the only means by which the revolutionary gains are to be preserved, that they have forfeited claims to confidence." [4] In the same vein but with greater emphasis the *Public* called them "ideologists who flourish on decomposition and chaos; . . . the Russian examples of doctrinaire impossibility, [dependent] for following upon the hysterical, criminal and impatient socialist fanatics of the country. Among them," the *Public* was confident, "are few really enlightened men." [5] The New York *Evening Post* was more optimistic; it hoped that "the calm hand of fact" would fall "with sobering touch" even "upon the heaving shoulders of the Bolsheviki." [6] The Emporia *Gazette* also hoped that the Allies would discover some means—perhaps the withholding of further exports to Russia—of "sobering a freedom-drunk people." [7] The Bolsheviks' power for evil, it appeared, lay in their ignorance, their ineptitude, their unreasoning impatience in rejecting half a loaf as worse than none at all. Of the two standard caricatures of the Bolshevik to which cartoonists invariably resorted, the East Side agitator (always bearing a strong resemblance to Trotsky) and the brutish, uncomprehending peasant, the second seemed more expressive of prevailing opinion. But the outstanding characteristic even of the bomb-throwing anarchist was not so much his contempt for respectability and virtue as his incredible naïveté. If he was depicted as a German agent, he was the unwitting tool, not the accomplice, of the Kaiser.

In the ensuing controversy over whether the Bolsheviks intended to make a separate peace with Germany and whether the Allies should break with the new regime or attempt to conciliate it, the "idealism" of the Bolsheviks was taken for granted. The question was whether or not their idealism was hopelessly misguided, whether ideas were irrelevant to the conduct of a war or whether ideas were weapons which at times were more effective than artillery. Those opposed to cooperation with or recognition of the Bolsheviks based their objections not, as one paper claimed, on the "socialistic plans" of the new regime, but on "the apparent attitude of the governing group toward a continuation of the war"; more precisely, on the naïve belief, which the Bolsheviks appeared to share with their American supporters, that the Germans would listen to reason.[8] The hope that in the long run anything except the force of arms would impress either the German government or the German people appeared to men of this mind as the wildest lunacy; it struck them as no less absurd when expressed by the Bolsheviks than when expressed by American pacifists. Their indictment of Bolshevism scarcely differed, indeed, from their indictment of all those who, since the outbreak of the war, had insisted that a redefinition of war aims was the clue to peace.

When Trotsky broke off negotiations early in February, 1918, and declared that the Bolsheviks would neither fight nor sign a German peace, the war liberals threw up their hands in despair at such innocence; "he lives in a world of phantoms," one paper sighed.[9] Another more charitably conceded that "the Trotsky attitude of passive resistance was one of historical interest. . . . But against such an enemy as Prussianism," it went on, Trotsky's pacifism "seemed hardly to have done more than to preserve Bolsheviki consistency." [10] The Springfield *Republican* could hardly believe that the Bolsheviks were as "credulous and ignorant" as they seemed, and wondered whether their "unsophistication" was not a "mask." [11] The Milwaukee *Journal*, however, had no doubts on this score; it dismissed the Bolsheviks' "dream of peace" as "impractical, as their other idealistic dreams may yet prove to be," and hoped that the German armies would teach them some lessons in politics.[12] Charles Edward Russell agreed that only a sound thrashing would bring them to their senses. The Bolsheviks, he wrote, were "dreamers," "amiable obsessionist[s]." The typical Bolshevik, according to Russell, reasoned as follows: "At twelve o'clock he would beat upon his bell in Petrograd. At one o'clock the proletariat in all countries would stand forth and declare the new order, and by sundown in all the world the old social structure would have been pulled down and a new one erected." A Western realist could only shake his head at such innocence. "It was a sad disillusion that awaited these moon-struck dreamers. The world was in a state of war." [13] Another writer reflected, a little later:

> Where the fanatical Russians made their mistake was in believing that revolutionary propaganda alone would suffice to bring imperialism to ruins, without armies to support it. All the honest bolsheviki were as interested in ruining Hohenzollernism as we were, but they failed to distinguish between the admittedly imperfect democracies of the western powers and the wholly vicious autocracy of German militarists. With a faith in the power of extremist propaganda that can be described as either sublime or fatuous, they threw away their weapons, laid their heads on Germany's block, and remained calmly confident that the German proletariat could not resist their wistful look.[14]

Nor did the anti-imperialists challenge this interpretation of Bolshevik motives. They objected only to their opponents' tendency to dismiss the appeal to men's minds as of less importance than bombs and bullets. Those who were already committed to the theory that a "diplomatic offensive" had to accompany a purely military attack on the Central Powers found it easy enough—found it, indeed, a matter of necessity—to defend Bolshevik diplomacy. From Petrograd Arno Dosch-Fleurot wrote that "the Russians, by their peace move, are doing the Germans more damage now than at any time by their fighting." [15] If Lenin and Trotsky failed in their experiment at Brest Litovsk, their failure would reflect on the whole strategy of weakening the German government by exposing its iniquity before world opinion. Pacifists especially were inclined to believe that Brest Litovsk was a critical test of "democratic diplomacy." As David Lawrence reminded Oswald Garrison Villard at the height of the negotiations:

> It seems to me that you non-resistants ought to be crowing over what is happening in Russia. It is the first experiment in national non-resistance that I have ever heard about, and probably the first that anybody else in this generation has either. . . . Trotzky not only will not make peace with Germany, but will not make war. Fear of the moral effect of an attack on the Russian people which might cause uprisings at home dissuades Germany from walking on over the Russians.[16]

Some Americans, impatient in wartime of any policies except those resting on armed force, took the Bolshevik revolution as conclusive proof of what they had been saying all along, that Kerensky's fatal weakness lay in his temporizing with the radical opposition. The man whom conservatives and even some war liberals had welcomed as a "democratic dictator" had failed them; he had been too much the democrat and too little the dictator; he had not, after all, proved to be a Napoleon, only another La Fayette. Henceforth their search for a man who would not shrink from forceful measures took on greater urgency, and they insisted less and less on the democratic qualifications which a dictator should ideally possess.

Such a solution of Russia's difficulties naturally did not commend itself to those who looked upon force as a poor substitute for imaginative foreign policies; it did not even commend itself to all of those who regarded the revision of war aims as of distinctly secondary importance to a decisive military victory over the Germans, and who scoffed at the Russian peace program as the most blatant nonsense. The Des Moines *Register* is an example of a pro-war, anti-Bolshevik paper which at this stage of the revolution was nevertheless quick to condemn anything which smacked of counter-revolution. The *Register* was inclined to see in the Bolsheviks the secret agents of the Kaiser; it predicted that Russia's withdrawal from the war would soon follow as a result of their rise to power.[17] Nevertheless it denied and continued for a long time to deny that Russia's salvation lay in a return to "order." It refused to believe that Kerensky's fall could be attributed to his failure to exercise dictatorial powers, insisting instead that he had lost his grip on the country only when he fell out with the non-Bolshevik socialists. In the opinion of the *Register,* no Russian government, however forceful, could regain power without the support of the parties of the Left.[18] Russia, as such papers never tired of pointing out, could not go backward, even if that were desirable; her future lay in the direction of more liberty, not less. On that proposition it was still possible for most war liberals to find common ground with the anti-imperialists.

The war liberals did not, however, go so far as to blame Allied mistakes for the fall of Kerensky. Anti-imperialists, on the other hand, insisted that the Allies were chiefly to blame for that event, because they had not only held aloof from the repeated pleas of the Provisional Government but on the very eve of the Bolshevik uprising, at the height of Kerensky's distress, had allowed their most reactionary spokesmen to deride and condemn the Russian position. The indifference of the Allies to the Russian demand for a restatement of war aims was "monstrously disastrous," in Amos Pinchot's opinion; after the refusal of the inter-Allied conference to discuss war aims, "it became a question of months how long Kerensky could hold Russia together." [19] "It is no exaggeration," said the New York *Evening Post*, "to say that Bonar Law gave the signal for the disappearance of Kerensky and the emergence of Lenine." [20] Walter Weyl accused the Allies of "evading, delaying and talking [until] they killed or at least helped to kill the Kerensky government. They did what Germany alone could never have accomplished." [21] In his biography of Wilson, William Allen White stated categorically that Wilson "could have stopped [the Russian] debacle." [22] Arthur Bullard of the Committee on Public Information remembered how the Americans in Russia had

> waited in desperate impatience for the answer of our governments to [the] appeal of revolutionary Russia. There was not a ghost of a chance that Russia would stay effectively in the war if her allies refused to co-operate in her hope for a general peace. . . . [But] there was a fighting chance of stabilizing Russia . . . a chance of kindling renewed ardor in the army. If the Central Empires had refused—as I believe they would—to accept a democratic peace, then it would have been possible to make the Kaiser appear the one great counter-revolutionist.
>
> We will not know until men still young write memoirs in their old age why the Allies refused to define their war aims. If Mr. Wilson could have formulated his fourteen terms in July instead of January there would have been some hope. But the refusal of the Allies to even discuss the Russian proposals was fatal as far as Russia was concerned; it dampened the ardor of all our friends and it gave a new and tremendous weapon to our enemies.
>
> It was not till this refusal had become clear that the Bolsheviki dared to advocate a separate peace with Germany.[23] *

* This was the prevailing view among anti-imperialists. For a rare dissenting opinion see Moissaye J. Olgin, "Mass Rule in Russia," *Asia*, XVIII (March, 1918), 191–2. Olgin thought it "doubtful . . . whether any statement of war aims, however definite and democratic, would have stopped the decay of the Russian army." "The masses," he wrote, "did not want to fight. The demoralization of the army had begun even under the

Wilson himself, in his address to Congress of December 4, 1917, seemed to endorse the theory that the Allies were themselves to blame for the collapse of Kerensky. Reminding Congress that "the wrongs, the very deep wrongs committed in this war . . . cannot and must not be righted by the commission of similar wrongs against Germany and her allies," he went on to say:

> All these things have been true from the very beginning of this stupendous war; and I cannot help thinking that if they had been made plain at the very outset the sympathy and enthusiasm of the Russian people might have been once for all enlisted on the side of the allies, suspicion and distrust swept away, and a real and lasting union of purpose effected.*

Their obsession with war aims led the anti-imperialists to view the purposes of the Bolsheviks primarily in the light of the previous history of the war-aims controversy. They observed, for instance, that the shrill cries of alarm, of "separate peace," of "German intrigue," which had so far greeted every Russian effort to raise the question of war aims had proved utterly baseless. Not one of the Russian parties, not even the Bolsheviks, avowed a separate peace as one of its objectives. As for alleged German intrigue, the same charge had been so recklessly flung about by patriotic orators in attacking everything from Senator

old regime. Centrifugal forces had developed long before the Revolution. The new order, necessarily shaking the very foundations of military discipline, only increased the confusion." Added to that were "lack of food, lack of munitions, lack of management, lack of transportation facilities." "Under such conditions," Olgin concluded, "no government favoring a war policy could meet with success." It would be difficult to argue with him.

* Ray Stannard Baker and William E. Dodd, *The Public Papers of Woodrow Wilson* (New York, 1927), III, 133–34. It is interesting to note, however, that this paragraph was added almost as an afterthought. Earlier drafts of the passage, on Wilson's typewriter, in the Woodrow Wilson MSS, 2d series, Library of Congress, contain no references to Russia. No doubt it was at the insistence of House, who in turn was influenced by Bullard and Ambassador Bakhmetev, that the paragraph in question was inserted in the final draft of the message; and it may be questioned, therefore, whether Wilson was very deeply committed to the interpretation of events which it contained.

La Follette to the music of Brahms to the right of labor to bargain collectively, that anti-imperialists could no longer take it seriously. They began to suspect, and with good reason, that what the opponents of a discussion of war aims really feared was not so much a separate peace as any peace at all. All the more reason then, in their estimation, why the question should be raised, as well by the Bolsheviks as by anyone else. From an anti-imperialist perspective the party of Lenin and Trotsky appeared radical only in its evident determination to force a discussion of a subject which had so far eluded every attempt to discuss it, and to do so even at the risk of offending the Allies, a risk which Kerensky had been unwilling to take. But Kerensky's failure seemed to show that nothing less than extreme measures, subject to just such risks, would shock the Allied governments out of their intransigence. That the Bolsheviks in bringing up the war-aims question again were moved by a purpose radically different from that of previous regimes was a possibility which anti-imperialists overlooked.*

* Arno J. Mayer in his admirable book, *Political Origins of the New Diplomacy* (New Haven 1959), seems to me to err in treating the war-aims question as if it eventually boiled down to a choice of "Wilson or Lenin." In the United States at least the question was not raised in this fashion, not even by Wilson himself, until late in the revolution, if then. At first, those who believed in a revision of war aims, in "open diplomacy," in the technique of defeating Germany and/or shortening the war by political rather than military means, never saw any antagonism between what Wilson and Lenin were doing—that is, as long as they believed that Wilson was on their side. As indicated above, they regarded Lenin's diplomacy as complementing Wilson's. Those who opposed the Bolsheviks were precisely those who never had any faith in the "new diplomacy" to begin with; who opposed a restatement of war aims as unnecessary, and who held that Germany could be defeated only by armed force. They opposed Lenin for much the same reasons as they opposed Wilson, except when they thought Wilson was on their side. Wilson himself, at those moments when he was most confident in the political, as opposed to the military method of defeating Germany, was inclined to view the Bolsheviks with a certain tolerance, if not with sympathy, as in his address of Dec. 4, 1917.

If liberals had seen that Lenin's anti-imperialism was not the same as their own, the whole history of these years would have been quite different.

Such a step as the publication of the secret treaties, which the Bolsheviks found in the archives of the foreign office—an act denounced by the war liberals as "perfidious," etc.—from this point of view appeared justifiable if not desirable.[24] Amos Pinchot was applauded at a mass meeting in New York when he declared, "The Russians have been the only people that have dared to tell the truth about the war." [25] The *Nation* thought that "whatever the motive, the act scarcely goes, in impropriety, beyond the giving out by the Provisional Government last summer of the correspondence between the Czar and the Kaiser [the "Willy-Nicky" letters, referring to the period of the Russo-Japanese War!]. The intent, in either case, was to discredit a previous regime." [26] Far from regarding the act as reprehensible, Villard's *Evening Post* republished the treaties in English, and anti-imperialists congratulated him on having performed a valuable public service.[27] "You deserve a public testimonial of some kind," wrote Albert Jay Nock. A philosophical anarchist, Nock tended to read his predilections into the conduct of the Bolsheviks. He hoped that Villard would write an editorial making it clear that "the treaties are not published by the Russians as a text for distrust of this or that government, form of government or set of men, but as a text for distrust of *all* government, of government per se. That is really what the Continental democrat has mostly on his mind at the present time." [28]

Even the Bolsheviks' long-awaited opening of negotiations for an armistice, December 2, appeared to anti-imperialists as merely the most imaginative in a series of maneuvers designed, as the *Evening Post* put it, "less to frame a peace than to force a discussion of peace." Indeed it was, except that its object was to revolutionize not only the Central Empires, but the Allied nations as well.[29] "Unless Lenine is willing to do business with William II," Simeon Strunsky wrote, "the Russian people will have to wait for their immediate peace." [30] It was hard for such people to see how the Allies could lose, no matter what was the outcome of the Bolsheviks' strategy: if the Kaiser were overthrown, fighting could cease on all fronts; if he remained in power, the Russians would resume the war rather than sign the sort of peace he would be likely to dictate.

The *New Republic*, which in spite of its vigorous support of the war remained the rallying point for anti-imperialist opinion, was for the moment far more pessimistic than the people for whom, in a loose sense, it spoke; it was more skeptical both as to the likelihood of Russia's remaining in the war and as to the beneficent designs of the Bolsheviks. On December 1, it wrote: "There is no longer reason for doubting that the factions which insist upon an immediate peace are far more powerful than the western peoples had believed. Nor is there any longer doubt that those factions are permeated with resentment toward Russia's western allies." [31] The *New Republic* saw what other anti-imperialists ignored, that the publication of the secret treaties was designed to discredit the Allies as much as to revolutionize Germany; and not merely to discredit them, that is, to force them into renouncing "annexations and indemnities," but to incite their peoples to rebellion. Nor did the editors see anything hopeful in the Bolsheviks' decision to sue for an armistice. But even the *New Republic*, while conceding that "the Russian army will not count again as an important factor in the balance of military force during the present war," continued to believe that "in the long run, the Russian revolution will not be the accomplice of the German autocracy, but its deadliest enemy." In spite of the fact that "the salvation of the republic may depend upon an early peace," the *New Republic* ventured to predict that "no Russian revolutionary party, whether maximalist or minimalist, will make a separate peace with the existing German government." Only the triumph of reaction in Russia would lead to a separate peace, for "a reactionary dictatorship could not survive except in alliance with the German autocracy in hostility to the democracies of the west." The *New Republic* for months to come continued to urge these precepts upon its readers as the only safe guide to policy. As long as they remained the starting point for an understanding of the revolution, the conclusion was inescapable that "while the present Bolshevik government lasts it is the business of Allied diplomacy to avoid an open break with it." [32]

Colonel House sent the same advice from Paris. On November 28, he notified Wilson that there had been "cabled over and published here statements made by American papers to the effect that Russia should be treated as an enemy. It is exceedingly important," he warned, that "such criticisms should be suppressed." They would "throw Russia into the lap of Germany." [33] House was informed by Lincoln Colcord that Bakhmetev, although he would not agree with Colcord that the Bolsheviks had "in a sense reaffirmed the original policies of the Russian revolution" ("reaffirmed," the ambassador thought, was "too positive a word," whereas in his opinion the policies of the Bolsheviks had been "largely negative"), nevertheless shared the anti-imperialist belief that the Bolsheviks had "presented the same issue [as raised by the Provisional Government] in a debased form."

> Bakhmetev will never recognize the Bolsheviki government [Colcord wrote] . . . But in his opinion Kerensky will not regain power too easily or too soon. He recognizes that Kerensky's real failure has been not to push home the original demand for a revision of the war aims of the Allies. This is the program which the Russian people want, the program which is the basis of the whole revolution.[34]

In Russia, meanwhile, everyone except Ambassador Francis, according to Arthur Bullard, had come to favor attempting to reach a *modus vivendi* with the Bolsheviks. Bullard himself was critical, at first, of the new regime; he wrote to George Creel in November that the Bolsheviks were "only one small faction of the socialist movement" and that having overthrown the

Provisional Government by force, and lacking the support of the majority, they could hold power only "by sheer terror." He thought that the United States should refuse to recognize them, basing its action "not on repugnance to their fantastic social experiments, but on sound democratic grounds." [35] Within two weeks, however, he had decided that Bolshevism, whatever else it might be, was "a sincere effort to fight German Imperialism (all imperialism) in a more effective manner," that is, with propaganda rather than with guns.[36] About the same time he wrote to Creel in praise of Raymond Robins of the American Red Cross, the leading advocate of cooperation with the Bolsheviks: "Of all the officials of our Government, whose trail I have encountered here, he has been the most important, the most intelligent . . . almost unique." Most of the President's representatives, he complained, were by contrast "out of accord with that fine patience towards the mistakes of a struggling Democracy, which has marked Mr. Wilson's policies." Evidently Americans were less democratic abroad than at home. "Crane, for instance, whom I like and respect, is one of our best democrats at home. Here, he quit the minute his little group of friends got lost in the appalling shuffle." [37] By January Bullard had reached the conclusion that there was

> a very real similarity between Trotsky's theory of how to overthrow German imperialism and that of Mr. Wilson. Both believe that to really make an end of the Imperialistic domination of Germany, we must have for allies the Anti-Imperialists of Germany. Both believe that to gain these ends the Entente must renounce all schemes of conquest which will stir a defensive patriotic sentiment in Germany.

The renunciation by the Allies of the secret treaties therefore seemed in Bullard's estimation more imperative than ever. He suggested that Wilson could force the Allies to act by getting congressional approval of his own liberal war aims.[38]

Other Americans in Russia agreed with Bullard's appraisal

of the situation. General Judson, chief of the American military mission (whom Robins earlier described as "the biggest American I have met in Russia"), early concluded that Russia would stay in the war "but without fighting much." [39] He thought that there was "one chance in a thousand that if armistice or peace terms fail a reasonably united Russia will stay in a state of war for a time longer." [40] Only the Bolsheviks, he believed, had support enough to perform such a feat as this implied; no other party had even one chance in a thousand of holding out against the popular clamor for peace. Judson, Robins, and Colonel William Boyce Thompson of the Red Cross, Robins' foremost ally, not only demanded a revision of war aims as the best means of keeping Russia in the war, but stressed the need for communication with the Bolsheviks through some individual whom the Bolsheviks trusted. Since the ambassador opposed their efforts to get in touch with the Bolsheviks, they began to agitate for his removal. The State Department on December 15, upheld Francis and recalled Judson, but this mishap served only to convince them that the full facts were not known in Washington and to make them all the more eager to lay their version before the country.[41]

Like Bullard, like all proponents of cooperation with the Bolsheviks, Robins and his friends started from the premise that the aims of Bolshevik and Wilsonian diplomacy were essentially the same. Robins, with his evangelistic temperament, advanced this view with the same fervor with which, in 1912, he had thrown himself into the Progressive party's crusade for social justice. He admitted that Russia was out of the war, so far as any further military efforts were concerned. "But," he added, "if support is given by the Allies to the present Bolshevik [*sic*] government . . . it is entirely possible to use existing Russian opinion and governmental activity to undermine the morale of the German army." Bolshevik propaganda, in other words, might prove as effective an ally in the war against German militarism as Russian arms. "Already," Robins said, "this insidious poison is being distributed to the German soldiers along the Russian front." [42]

To impress these opinions on the authorities in Washington, Colonel Thompson sailed for America on November 28, 1917. He stopped briefly in London, where his friend Thomas W. Lamont arranged an interview with Lloyd George. Thompson told his story to the Prime Minister: "Let's make these Bolsheviks our Bolsheviks; don't let the Germans make them their Bolsheviks." "The Prime Minister," according to Lamont, "was very much taken with that phrase. Said he emphatically, 'I will pick out the best man in England, and will send him to Russia with the best man in America whom President Wilson will pick out. Together they will go to those people and see if they cannot work out a better destiny.' " [43] Americans had not yet learned that Lloyd George could say one thing and do quite another; Thompson and Lamont thought they had scored a signal success.

Fresh from this triumph and armed with memoranda from Robins, Judson, and other authorities, they landed in New York on Christmas Day, 1917, and began a strenuous campaign of proselytization. They saw Colonel House, who seemed sympathetic.[44] Thompson found eager listeners in Washington. George Creel hardly needed to be converted; he had been listening to Bullard. He reported to the President that Thompson had "more first-hand information than any one yet reporting," and urged Wilson to see him.[45] Thompson called on McAdoo, on Lansing, on Frank Polk, on Theodore Roosevelt; he gave out a long interview to the New York *World;* he published a series of articles in the New York *Evening Post.*[46] His message seemed to meet with great approval not only among anti-imperialists, but among members of the war party who had until now showed little interest in the possibility of holding Russia to the Allies by gestures of conciliation. Theodore Roosevelt wrote rather apologetically after reading Robins' "Considerations of the Present Conditions in Russia":

> I regard the letter as far and away the most illuminating and instructive statement of the situation that I have seen. I shall, of course, govern my conduct and my utterances hereafter absolutely by it. I am particularly glad to get it because in my not unnatural indignation at much of the conduct of the Bolsheviki I have used expressions which I shall hereafter avoid. There is no danger whatever of my ever getting to sympathize in any way with the reactionaries in Russia; but I had supposed that the Bolsheviki were necessarily purely ephemeral, possessing some unpleasant analogies with the men of the red terror in the French Revolution—and of course it has been a very bitter thing to all of us who have sons on the western front to feel that they might be overwhelmed by a huge German offensive which was set free by the defection of Russia under the lead of the Bolsheviki.
>
> I very seriously question whether any other individual, except perhaps (and only perhaps) some General, has rendered anything like the service that you have rendered to civilization and to the allied cause during the last five months.[47]

George Foster Peabody, certainly no Bolshevik, effusively praised Thompson's articles, and Senator Calder of New York had them inserted into the *Congressional Record*.[48]

The President himself, it is true, refused to see Thompson, but the sixth of his Fourteen Points, as Thompson confided to Frank Polk, "accomplished nine tenths of what he had in mind." [49] His refusal to see Thompson was attributed by the Colonel and his friends merely to personal pique; the President, they thought, was still annoyed because Thompson, the previous summer, had suggested spending several million dollars of the government's money on propaganda designed to strengthen Kerensky. A friend wrote to Thompson that Lamont, after having talked to Creel,

> said that the trouble with Wilson was that he had imbibed Lansing's prejudice which was based on the idea that you were a man of bad judgment because you talked of such an enormous sum as three

million dollars a month for propaganda! To this has been added the prejudice of Francis with his petty jealousy. While T. W. [Lamont] did not say it, of course a great difficulty has been the personality of Crane who was one of Wilson's earlier supporters and has Wilson's ear every time Russia is mentioned.[50]

But Wilson's silence did not dispel the illusion of success in Thompson's camp.

Other travelers returning from Russia argued in favor of the Robins-Thompson thesis. Samuel Harper, who was still enthusiastic about the revolution and kindly disposed toward Robins, spread the glad tidings among his large circle of friends. He advised Richard Crane in the State Department (son of Charles R. Crane) that although Trotsky was "not working for the same kind of democracy for which we are fighting," "up to a certain point he takes a line that fits in with ours." "[H]e will use us," Harper predicted, "just as we are using him, and it is a question of wits." [51] Harper fell in with the demand for a restatement of war aims and the dismissal of Ambassador Francis. "To play this rather dangerous game, it would seem that a more active man than the present Ambassador might be advisable." [52]

Lincoln Steffens continued his efforts to promote an understanding of the revolution. Russia could still be saved, he insisted, if the Allies purged their cause of evil and selfish ambitions. He too was looking for a man to replace Ambassador Francis, someone whom the Bolsheviks trusted and who could explain America to the Russians. He enlisted his former protégé Walter Lippmann in the search, and Lippmann in turn approached Colonel House:

[Steffens] says that Trotzky's reasoning is as follows: "The United States is not a democracy. Mr. Wilson is the President of the United States, and he talks the language of democracy. According to the doctrine of Marx it is impossible for a plutocracy to bring forth true democracy. Therefore the President must be insincere!" Steffens believes, quite shrewdly I think, that the only way to reach

Trotzky is to give him the assurance needed on the authority of somebody in whom he has complete confidence. That is to say, if somebody who is a friend of Trotzky could say to him that the President means what he says, it would make a great difference in Trotzky's behavior.[53]

Still another traveler who helped to spread the Robins gospel was the sociologist Edward A. Ross, who left Russia in November "in full possession," as Robins assured his wife, "of all the facts of this most interesting hour." [54] Ross seems to have been carefully rehearsed by Robins; shortly before his departure he wrote to Robins suggesting that if he were "to make any impression at Washington," he would have to have from Robins, "in order to memorize it, a list of indications (utterances and actions) of Lenin and Trotzky which do not jibe with the theory that they are German agents." He also asked to meet Lenin and to "see the 'red guard' drill, see their armament and get an idea of the number of soldiers and armed workmen the Maximalists here can count on." [55] Presumably he returned to America with a lively sense of Soviet power. But although he expected momentarily to be called to Washington, he does not seem to have been asked for his opinions until the following July.[56] His influence for the moment was confined to writing and lecturing on behalf of cooperation with the Bolsheviks.

The newspaper correspondents in Russia probably had as much to do with shaping liberal attitudes at this point as these travelers—perhaps even as much as Robins and Thompson. Arno Dosch-Fleurot of the New York *World*, Louis Edgar Browne and Isaac Don Levine of the Chicago *Daily News*, M. Phillipps Price of the Manchester *Guardian*, and Arthur Ransome of the London *Daily News* all believed that the purposes of the Bolsheviks were fundamentally akin to those of the Allies. Because their opinions were repeated almost daily and because they were presented as facts, which gave them an appearance of great authority, they had tremendous influence in propagating this view. They did not, of course, wilfully distort the facts upon which they based their judgments. Most of their information was of unimpeachable authenticity. It was in the inferences which they drew from this information that the Allied correspondents, like all Western observers in Russia, allowed themselves to be guided by their own hopes and fears. Thus Dosch-Fleurot, throughout the period of the Brest Litovsk crisis, sent one dispatch after another predicting that the Bolsheviks would never sign a separate peace with Germany, a prediction that turned out to be highly inaccurate. But Dosch-Fleurot's confidence in this proposition derived from interviews with Trotsky himself. On October 28, two weeks before the Bolshevik seizure of power, Trotsky told Dosch-Fleurot that what the Bolsheviks wanted was not a separate peace, but an immediate general peace on the basis of "no annexations, no indemnities." They did not expect the German militarists to accept these terms, he said. But when they refused to accept them, they would be overthrown by the German masses. If for some reason the German revolution failed to materialize, "then every soldier in the Russian Army," as Dosch-Fleurot put it, "will know he is fighting to save the revolution . . . If Germany refuses they will fight like lions." [57]

This was an accurate enough presentation of Trotsky's own thoughts, and events for a time fell out as he had predicted. Negotiations between the Bolsheviks and the imperial German government opened at Brest Litovsk on December 22, 1917. The Bolsheviks presented as a basis for discussion a set of terms highly favorable to themselves, to which Von Kühlmann, the head of the German delegation, replied on December 25, in language so conciliatory that it was construed by the Bolsheviks as an acceptance of the very liberal terms they had proposed. The next day, however, General Hoffmann informed the Russians that "forcible annexation," which the Germans had agreed to eschew, was not to be construed as precluding the "voluntary" secession from Russia of Poland, Lithuania, and Courland, and their union with Germany. The Bolsheviks, who seem genuinely to have believed that Germany intended to return to Russia territories occupied by German troops, returned in some confusion to Petrograd, December 27, for advice. But all this was no more than what Trotsky had predicted; and since the German people still showed no sign of throwing off their government, Western liberals naturally assumed that the Bolsheviks, having exposed for the benefit of the Russian people the kind of treatment which the revolution could expect at the hands of the German imperialists, would now resume the war. "Russia has turned again to war," announced Dosch-Fleurot on January 2, and there appeared to be abundant evidence to bear him out.[58] Feverish preparations for defense were being taken in Petrograd; Trotsky made warlike speeches; *Izvestia* warned Germany that Russia would never consent to the loss of Poland and Lithuania.[59] In fact, however, the Petrograd soviet and the central executive committee of the Bolshevik party had already decided on January 1 that resistance was out of the question. Negotiations were therefore resumed on January 8, Trotsky replacing Joffe as head of the Russian delegation, in the hope that his oratory would inspire revolutionary movements within the Central Empires.[60]

Trotsky, who now emerged as the central figure in the drama, received increasingly favorable attention in the United States. His book, *The Bolsheviki and World Peace*, written earlier in the war, was resurrected and published by Albert Boni as proof

> that TROTZKY wants WORLD PEACE, not a separate peace—that the BOLSHEVIKI are ANTI-PRUSSIAN—ANTI-HOHENZOLLERN—ANTI-HAPSBURG. Trotzky tells in this book how he would make the world SAFE FOR DEMOCRACY. He says, "Russian freedom must not be had at the expense of the freedom of Belgium or France." [61]

The book was serialized in the major American newspapers and caused editors to marvel "that his Marxian and doctrinaire fallacies do not prevent him . . . from thinking straight on the immediate problems confronting the Russian people and the democratic forces of the central powers." [62] It is hard to understand the success of Trotsky's book in the United States unless one remembers that it was read by people who had previously written him off as an impractical idealist. Americans were surprised and pleased to find that "he has no illusions as to Prussianism." [63]

Throughout most of December and January, especially during the period in which negotiations at Brest Litovsk were suspended (December 27—January 18), large numbers of liberals—more than at any other time—were disposed to look with patience, if not with sympathy, upon the Bolsheviks and to accept the theory that a restatement of war aims might help them to keep Russia in the war. Not only the *New Republic, Nation,* and New York *Evening Post,* but the Springfield *Republican,* Philadelphia *Public Ledger,* Des Moines *Register,* Chicago *Daily News,* and St. Louis *Post-Dispatch* now advocated a more conciliatory policy. Even the New York *World,* which earlier had characterized Soviet Russia as "the Judas of the nations," relented somewhat in its scorn of the Bolsheviks.[64] The St. Louis *Post-Dispatch* spoke for many moderate liberals when it came to the conclusion, early in January 1918, that "adverse opinion concerning the sincerity of Russian Bolshevik leaders may have to be revised. Their action on the German peace negotiations indicates a sincere effort to accomplish peace in accord with their avowed purposes." [65] The *Public Ledger* was the scene of intense conflict between its liberal editors and its conservative readers, but for a time the editors seemed to have succeeded in their campaign, encouraged throughout by Colonel House, to make the *Public Ledger* a liberal paper.[66] In ringing tones they deplored American hostility to Russia and begged their readers to remember that "in the long run German imperialism and militarism could be met by no more deadly menace than the permanent establishment of democracy in Russia." [67] The paper gave a great deal of space to Colcord's dispatches from Washington, and allowed him in addition to submit a number of signed editorials. Colcord in turn maintained his friendship with Colonel House, who had recommended him to the *Ledger* in 1916.[68] Conversations with House naturally encouraged Colcord's delusion that the policy of the anti-imperialists was now the policy of the administration, and this understanding no doubt helped to strengthen the editors, John J. Spurgeon and H. B. Brougham, in their wavering allegiance to anti-imperialist principles.* Faithful readers cried out in alarm at the paper's apostasy, but to liberals the startling renaissance of the *Public Ledger* was a sign of the changing temper of the times.[69] The collapse of the *Ledger's* anti-imperialism a few months later, it may be added, ought to have been an equally significant portent.

Throughout the period of the negotiations at Brest Litovsk the distortion of news, which can be taken as a reliable index of what Americans wanted to believe, consistently favored the advocates of conciliation instead of discriminating against them, as it did in every other period of the revolution. Thus the New York *World's* headlines announced on January 3: "Peace Parleys Are Interrupted; Russia Likely to Resume Fighting"; on January 24: "Bolsheviki Likely to Yield if Allies Refuse to Give Aid"; on February 28: "Workmen Prepare to Die Defending Russian Capitol"; on March 16: "Russian Soviets Ratify German Terms, but No Lasting Peace Is Seen"—all of which created a highly misleading image of the likelihood of Russia's return to the war

* Spurgeon especially was inclined to drag his feet. At one point he came to Colonel House to apologize for the paper's slow progress. "He was afraid I was not satisfied," House noted, "with the progress the Ledger was making toward liberalism, and he wished to tell of the difficulties. The Ledger, as I already knew, had a most conservative clientele and if he went as fast as Brougham and Colcord desired, it would disrupt the finances of the paper." There follows a revealing sentence: "He seemed relieved to know that I agreed with him, and that I had placed a restraining hand on them both." House MS Diary, Aug. 23, 1917.

and hence strengthened the position of those who argued that American policy should be based on that assumption. Nor was the *World* alone in its misrepresentation of Russia's desire to fight.[70] The record of American papers during the Brest Litovsk crisis suggests that the shortcomings of the press in its coverage of the Russian revolution were to be attributed not to a "capitalistic" bias, as anti-imperialists came to believe, but to the inveterate optimism of American editors. It happened that from December, 1917, to February, 1918, the Bolsheviks and their friends were the ones to benefit from their reluctance to disturb their readers with unpleasant information. What Americans most wanted to believe at that moment was what anti-imperialists had been telling them for months: that the Russian revolutionists would continue to fight if the Allies publicly cleansed their cause. In no other period of the war could the New York *World* have given such conspicuous coverage, as well as its editorial endorsement, to the long dispatch from Dosch-Fleurot, February 22, 1918, in which he blamed Allied diplomacy for the whole Russian debacle. The *World* not only endorsed this interpretation, which it had long derided, but printed it as news on the front page under an eight-column headline: "ALLIES THEMSELVES ARE TO BLAME FOR RUSSIA'S DEFECTION." [71]

The advocates of conciliation benefited also from the widespread impression that the administration favored their position. They themselves did all they could to foster this impression. David Lawrence wrote from Washington to the *Evening Post* on February 1, that the government was on the verge of recognizing the Bolsheviks.[72] Before submitting his story Lawrence had taken it to Colonel House for inspection. "I gave him the right steer," House noted afterward, "and he wrote the article as it appeared." [73] That House thought he had given Lawrence the "right steer" suggests the degree to which he himself was ignorant of Wilson's real opinions in regard to Russia. Lawrence, however, naturally assumed that House spoke with some authority for the President. House was also in almost daily contact with Lincoln Colcord; no doubt he misled that writer in the same fashion. But some of Colcord's stories could probably be traced to Colonel Thompson. On January 15, for instance, Colcord reported that "State Department officials" regarded "with undisguised satisfaction the political turmoil which has arisen in Germany as a result of the abortive first peace conference with Russia at Brest-Litovsk." They felt, Colcord said, "that the view of the situation taken by President Wilson in his last address [the Fourteen Points speech] was "intrinsically the true view, and hence one on which to base a definite policy," a policy which could not "well fail to be other than one of support to the brave efforts which the Soviet is making . . . to sustain its direct and unselfish principles." [74] Ten days later Colcord, like Lawrence, predicted that the United States would "shortly . . . recognize the Government of the Soviet in Russia." [75]

It is doubtful that anyone in the State Department, even someone who sympathized with the policy in question, would have taken the responsibility for giving out information so completely misleading. But Frank Polk left a brief account of a conversation with Thompson which suggests that he made no effort to correct Thompson's mistaken view of presidential policy, probably because he himself did not know what that policy was.[76] Under the circumstances Thompson could easily have concluded that the State Department agreed with all he said, and once he had got such an impression, it is not hard to imagine him zealously spreading it.

Thompson was undoubtedly the source of Herbert Bayard Swope's story in the New York *World*, January 11, 1918, in which Swope with a great show of authority declared that Wilson's speech was a move toward some working agreement with the soviets, and in which he predicted the dismissal of Francis. The ambassador had misled the State Department, according to Swope, into thinking that the Bolsheviks contemplated a separate peace, when everyone knew that their object was a general peace without annexations or indemnities. Swope attributed the change in policy, reflected in Wilson's speech of January 8, to the influence of certain devoted but unsung public servants, whose names he did not reveal, although he threw out some strong hints. "The representatives of the Committee on Public Information sent to Russia . . . helped to remove the misunderstanding. And there were others . . . Red Cross officials and those with no public connection—who saw the truth and told what they saw when they returned to Washington." Their reports, according to Swope, enabled the President to "see wherein the Russian scheme of things had spiritual kinship with those ideals he had phrased as the aspirations of America." [77]

In this instance, the anti-imperialist interpretation of Wilson's policy did not go unchallenged. William English Walling a few days later issued a testy rejoinder in the New York *Times*.[78] Dismissing Swope as ignorant and uninformed, and Swope's fellow prophets Dosch-Fleurot and Arthur Ransome as hopelessly biased, Walling stated that Wilson and Ambassador Francis, far from regarding Bolshevik war aims as consonant with those of the United States, took the position that the Bolsheviks "were moving toward a separate peace which would have been a German peace." That this was the object of the Bolsheviks, he added, was "an absolutely established fact." In attempting to trace the source of the "pro-Bolshevist and anti-Francis agitation," Walling for some reason overlooked Thompson and attributed the gossip to "some emissaries of the Committee on Public Information," an allegation which, as might have been expected, provoked a furious counter-attack by George

Creel.[79] * Whether or not Walling's statement was a reference to Arthur Bullard—it could presumably have applied as well to Ernest Poole or even to Edgar Sisson—is not clear, but Bullard certainly took it as such.†

If ever a policy of cooperation with the Bolsheviks could have been adopted by the United States, it was during the period of the negotiations at Brest Litovsk. Yet such a policy was never seriously considered even then. The impending dismissal of Francis, as the State Department reassured the ambassador's son, was a myth. Polk told Perry Francis on February 4, as the latter wrote to his father, "that there was absolutely nothing

* Walling, himself a socialist, then complained to the State Department that "Creel was surrounded by a number of Socialists who were poisoned with the Socialist viewpoint"! See Polk MS Diary, Jan. 15, 1918.

† He kept a clipping of Walling's article, which is now in the Bullard MSS. On March 24, 1919 he wrote to Sisson (in *ibid.*): "I want to get my position on Bolshevism in print. I find some people—probably due to Walling's denunciations—believe I'm pro-Bolshevik."

Both Sisson and Poole were known at this time to favor the Robins-Thompson policy, although both of them, like Bullard, shortly changed their minds. For Sisson, see below, pp. 88, 113 ff. Poole hovered uncertainly between the anti-imperialism of many of his friends (including his brother-in-law, Walter Weyl) and a romantic fondness for Old Russia. He was the author of a number of books on Russian peasant life. He served with the CPI in Russia throughout the period of the revolution.

House's relation to the Swope story is not clear. Swope sent him the story after it appeared and invited him to comment on it. See A. L. Schlosser of the New York *World* to House, Jan. 14, 1918, House MSS. Whether or not House did so is unknown. Shortly thereafter, however (probably at lunch on Feb. 4; see House MS Diary, Feb. 4, 1918), he suggested to Swope, as the latter put it, that "we might meet at stated times for the purpose, generally, of exchanging ideas, but, more particularly, of having you suggest those thoughts in that line of effort which you think would be most conducive to a helpful cooperation in the winning of the war." Swope to House, Feb. 9, 1918, *ibid.* Whether House made this suggestion because he was disturbed by Swope's article and wanted to keep an eye on him or because he liked the article and saw in Swope a suitable vehicle for his ideas is hard to say; but the latter supposition seems the more likely. It is important to note in this connection that House was in the process of dropping Lincoln Colcord. "I find that when he stays in Washington he loses his perspective hopelessly," House complained about this time. MS Diary, Jan. 27, 1918.

to be worried about, and that Thompson had not seen the President, and later in the conversation that Mr. Crane had seen the President,—which I construed to mean that Thompson had been endeavoring to get an interview, but that the President had no time for him." Later Crane also assured the ambassador's son that "Thompson had no standing with the powers that be." * The rumor that the United States intended to recognize the Bolsheviks was likewise unfounded. When Bakhmetev came in alarm to Lansing, the Secretary told him there was "nothing to it," and Polk reassured him in precisely the same words.[80] Gradually it began to dawn on Thompson and his friends that the President had no intention of seeing him; that Judson's recall was a far more reliable indication of administration policy than anything Wilson might have seemed to say in his Fourteen Points speech; that Walling and Crane remained the President's favorite advisers on Russian affairs.

Nor were Wilson and Lansing as far apart in their views as the Thompson faction believed. Both the President and the Secretary of State were greatly impressed by Walling's memorandum on "The . . . Danger of . . . Revolutionary Movements in . . . Europe," which, if read carefully, furnishes a revealing glimpse of the considerations which at this point guided administration policy. Walling began by pointing out that the only reason for cooperation with the Bolsheviks was

* Perry Francis to his father, Feb. 14, 1918, David R. Francis MSS, Missouri Historical Society, St. Louis. See also Polk MS Diary, Feb. 4, 1918.

What was true of Thompson was true in even greater measure of Robins. The fact is that Wilson had a violent antipathy to Robins. House told Lincoln Colcord in August, 1918, "that from the first the President absolutely refused to rely on Colonel Robins' judgment in the Russian matter. 'I could have told you at the beginning of the year,' said Colonel House, 'that everything which Colonel Robins said and did in Russia, and that his very presence in the heart of that scene, was daily doing injury to the cause of the Soviets in the eyes of the Administration.' " Colcord, unpublished article, "Woodrow Wilson and Russian Policy," n.d. [1919–1920], Lincoln Colcord MSS.

"to encourage their efforts to revolutionize the peoples of Central Europe." But this was a dangerous game:

> We forget that the continuing success of Bolshevism in Russia and the growing strength of pacifist strikes in Germany and Austria immensely aid the already dangerous pacifist movements among the working-men of France, England and Italy—movements united in the demand for a Stockholm conference to bring about "an immediate democratic peace."

Therefore, Walling concluded, "To aid the German Socialists (positively) and the Bolsheviki (negatively) is not only playing with fire, it is almost certain to end the war before German defeat or American victory." [81] Wilson said of Walling's paper: "It seems to me to speak an unusual amount of truth and to furnish a very proper basis of the utmost caution in the conduct of . . . affairs . . ." [82] Lansing thought it "remarkable." [83] It was indeed. Not only did it clearly point out the implications of cooperating with the Bolsheviks, but it called into question the whole strategy of ending the war by a political assault on German morale, the strategy outlined by Wilson himself in his "Peace without Victory" speech, the strategy to which anti-imperialists believed he was still committed. Walling was saying that the Allies, in appealing to the German socialists to throw down their arms, ran the risk not only of bringing about a premature end of the war, but of Bolshevizing (not democratizing) Germany itself. Thus the former left-wing socialist urged the administration to abandon the rhetoric of internationalism, to regard the war not as a class struggle but as a conflict of national states, and henceforth to subordinate all other considerations to the single objective of inflicting a decisive military defeat upon the German Empire.

Wilson's Fourteen Points address, as we have seen, was incorrectly taken by anti-imperialists (and also by many conservatives) as an indication that the President had "implicitly recognized the government of the Soviets," as Lincoln Colcord wrote.[84] One of Amos Pinchot's friends conjectured that "somebody [Wilson] trusts evidently has let him in on the fact . . . that the Bolsheviki are good people, that they are in to stay, and that they are doing more to win the war for the Allies and to further the cause of human freedom than all the other armies in the field." [85] The conservative Baltimore *Sun* shared the belief that the speech implied "that the representatives of the Bolsheviki at Brest-Litovsk—and, therefore, by implication the Bolshevik Government itself—are sincere and in earnest." [86] Yet it may be doubted that this is exactly what Wilson meant to say. It is true that in making the speech at all he yielded to the view, formerly his own but recently championed mainly by Colonel House, that a statement of war aims would not only persuade the Russians to stay in the war, but would create a "chasm," as House said, between the people of the Central Empires and their rulers.[87] Wilson had not yet read Walling's memorandum on the dangers inherent in this policy. At the same time it should be noted that his words of sympathy for the Russians were hardly more than a gesture. Wilson did not "recognize" the Bolsheviks; he did not even recognize the formula of "no annexations, no indemnities." As one paper pointed out, the speech required Germany to evacuate Alsace-Lorraine, Belgium, Serbia, Montenegro, Roumania, Poland and western Russia—"terms such that only a militarily defeated Germany can accept." [88] Indeed the speech, like most of Wilson's wartime speeches, could be read as a fighting document, closing the door to negotiations with Germany and serving notice on the Bolsheviks that they could expect no sympathy from the Germans or, if they accepted a German peace, from the United States. It could even be interpreted as an appeal to the Russian people over the heads of the Bolsheviks, inciting them to throw off a government which had "shamefully tricked" them, as the New

York *World* put it.[89] Such a variety of interpretations shows that the speech by no means clearly recognized the validity of Bolshevik diplomacy, as anti-imperialists assumed.[90]

If the war liberals looked with favor upon the new regime in Russia when it showed intentions of carrying on the war, most of them quickly changed their minds when it became clear that the Bolsheviks would not, after all, resume hostilities against Germany. Many people up to the last minute expected the Bolsheviks to reject the treaty, and its ratification came therefore as an acute shock, which heightened their resentment. But the optimism of Americans was understandable, for the Bolsheviks kept the world in doubt as to their intentions until the very end. They were themselves badly divided on the question of accepting the German terms. The Germans, on January 18, had presented to the Russian delegation at Brest Litovsk an ultimatum according to which Germany was to remain in possession of all Russian territories then occupied by her troops. A majority of the Bolshevik party leaders now favored a "revolutionary war." It required all Lenin's powers of persuasion to move a majority of the central committee on January 24 to approve Trotsky's compromise policy of "no war, no peace," for which Lenin himself reluctantly voted because his own policy—acceptance of the German terms, no matter how harsh—commanded so little support. In short there was a great deal of sentiment in the Bolshevik party for resistance of some sort, and very little for peace. But when Trotsky, on February 10, announced to the world that the Bolsheviks would neither sign the treaty nor take up arms, and when the German armies, in complete disregard of the opinion of mankind (which Trotsky had counted on to deter them) resumed their advance into Russia, the central committee, on the evening of February 18, with Trotsky's approval, hastily voted to reopen negotiations. Even then a militant minority, led by Bukharin, held out for war to the death. Over their impassioned objections, the new terms, which were somewhat stiffer than the ones Trotsky had turned down, were signed at Brest Litovsk on March 3, and ratified by the Fourth Congress of Soviets at Moscow on March 15.[91]

In the face of these disappointing events liberals in America tended to become more and more righteous. "Russia," declared the *Public*, "is paying dearly for the uncritical idealism that has tolerated these doctrinaire impossibilists." [92] A month earlier the same magazine had seen "no conclusive reason why Russia should not be on the battlefront next summer." [93] The New York *World* rebuked the Russians for their unwillingness "to fight and die for their liberties." [94] Even the New York *Evening Post* now dismissed the "prattle of a holy war for the defence of the Revolution" as "not sincere" and suggested that the Allies could save Russia only by encouraging the opponents of Bolshevism.[95] George Foster Peabody spoke for a large number of war liberals who had momentarily looked with some favor upon the Bolsheviks when he wrote in disappointment to Amos Pinchot late in February:

> I wonder how you are feeling about the Russian debacle? I confess that my early suspicions of Lenine and Trotzky as acting under pro-German provocation were very much modified by the particularly fine manner in which the conference at Brest-Litovsk was carried on by the Russians—especially Trotzky's brave words. . . . [More recent events, however,] seem to me to indicate a far planned German program to recover the grip which they lost when Lvoff and Miliukoff and the others proved loyal to the Allies' program. I could never forgive the imprisonment of Baboushka, and, of course, the willingness to kill Russians when they would not kill Germans was inexplicable. Lenine's safe conduct thru Germany must also be taken into the account.[96]

But the manner of Lenin's passage through Germany had not disturbed Peabody when he wrote to Newton D. Baker a month and a half earlier, "I am overjoyed at the situation and Russia's influence in disintegrating Prussian autocracy is working as I suggested to you I thought it would."[97] It was the conclusion of peace, not the manner in which Lenin returned to Russia or the imprisonment of Katherine Breshkovskaya (which was in any case a myth), which finally convinced Peabody, as it convinced most of the war liberals, that the Bolsheviks were German agents.

The war correspondents continued to predict that Russia would remain in the war, but their words no longer guided the policies of the papers for which they wrote. Arthur Ransome's stories were now printed in American papers with the explanation that his views were those of an out-and-out Bolshevik sympathizer.[98] Lincoln Colcord fell out with the management of the *Public Ledger* and left the paper in August, 1918; the editors reverted to a cautious conservatism.[99] Browne and Dosch-Fleurot kept their jobs but lost their illusions about the Bolsheviks. Both of them left Russia in the general exodus of foreign correspondents following ratification of the treaty. Dosch-Fleurot pronounced the revolution "a corpse."[100]

In Russia Robins continued to hope for the best, but Bullard and Sisson parted company with him. The latter, having discovered, as he thought, documents which conclusively proved that the Bolsheviks were in the pay of the German government, was preparing to publish to the world this evidence of their iniquity. "Sisson has become my bitter enemy," Robins was soon writing to his wife.[101] Bullard had no faith in Sisson's documents but even less faith, now, in Robins, whose untiring efforts to believe the best of the Bolsheviks had undermined Bullard's confidence in his intelligence, and whose conspiracies against the ambassador, against Sisson, and finally against himself, raised doubts about his character as well. By March 14, Bullard regretted that he had once spoken so highly of Robins. "He has been one of the worst personal disappointments of my life," he wrote to Creel.[102]

Robins persuaded himself that the Congress of Soviets might

refuse to ratify the treaty if an offer of Allied assistance were forthcoming. He did not see that although Trotsky may still have had hopes of forestalling ratification of the treaty, which was as distasteful to him as it was to Robins, he was by now more interested in getting the Allies to call off the Japanese, who were clamoring to be allowed to intervene in Siberia.[103] It was primarily with the ominous developments in the Far East in mind that Trotsky encouraged Robins and Bruce Lockhart, Robins' British counterpart, to hope that Russia might renew the war.[104] The central committee, with Lenin's approval, on February 22, authorized Trotsky to approach the Allies in order to ascertain what aid Russia might expect from them. But as George F. Kennan has pointed out, Lenin at no time conceived of the acceptance of Allied aid as an alternative to ratification, which he continued to urge even after he had cast his vote for the "acceptance of potatoes and arms from the bandits of Anglo-French imperialism." [105] In his conversation with Robins on March 5, which was to become the center of so much controversy, Trotsky made no promise that the treaty would be rejected. What Robins construed as a promise was no more than a series of questions. If the soviets refused to ratify the treaty, Trotsky wanted to know, what kind of support could they expect from the Allies? What did the Allies intend to do if Japan attempted to seize Vladivostok and the Siberian railway? [106] Robins, however, afterwards referred to Trotsky's statement as if it had bound the Bolsheviks to a definite course of action.[107] His version of the events of March, 1918, became an article of faith among American anti-imperialists. They now added to their indictment of American and Allied policy the blame for having left Russia with no choice except to sign a separate peace. The conduct of these governments since the outbreak of the revolution in March, 1917, began to reveal, it seemed to them, a consistent pattern of cynicism, deceit, and fraud.

How widely Robins circulated his version of events is not immediately evident, for when he returned to the United States in June, 1918, the State Department forbade him to make his story public.[108] For nine months Robins observed a strict official silence. But there was no way for the State Department to prevent Robins from talking to his friends. In Washington Robins saw, among others, Lansing, Newton D. Baker, Herbert Hoover, Hiram Johnson, La Follette, Felix Frankfurter, Louis D. Brandeis, Charles R. Crane, and William C. Bullitt. "The word goes over," he reported.[109] On July 12 in New York he talked to William Hard—Bull Mooser, free-lance journalist and frequent contributor to the *New Republic*—and to Herbert Croly. The latter wrote to him a few days later to thank him

> for taking the trouble and the time to give me such a complete account of your experiences in Russia, and your reasons for wishing our government at the present time to cooperate in certain practical ways with the Soviet government. It was really an extraordinary experience for me to listen to such a sustained and brilliant piece of narrative, exposition and argument.[110]

Croly arranged a luncheon on July 22, in the rooms of the *New Republic*, attended by Francis Hackett, Alvin Johnson, Phillip Littell, himself and Robins, at which Robins once again launched into his narrative.[111] Robins also brought with him from Russia a long article by Arthur Ransome, which the *New Republic* published.[112] On July 23, Robins lunched again with Hard, who was later to do so much to popularize Robins' experiences in Russia.[113] On August 1, after a brief trip to Chicago, he and his wife spent the night at Walter Weyl's country house in Woodstock, leaving Weyl "worn out" but "anxious to write down enough about the Russian situation to enable me to remember the main points." [114]

Just how much of his story Robins allowed to become known is not clear. His long letter to Theodore Roosevelt of August 24, 1918, if that can be taken as a sample of what he was circulating, makes no mention of his dealings with Trotsky, the heart of his narrative.[115] Neither did he mention them to Raymond Clapper of the United Press, who saw Robins in Washington in July and whose account of the conversation, together with Robins' letter to Roosevelt, constitutes about all the available direct evidence as to the nature of what Robins was telling people.[116] Clapper noted merely that Robins had pleaded for American cooperation with the soviets as "the natural indiginous [*sic*] form of local government" in Russia.[117] It is possible that Robins in his various wanderings told people no more than he told Roosevelt and Clapper, no more than people could have discovered for themselves. At the same time it is difficult to believe that a man of his fervor and volubility could have repeated his story as often as he apparently did and each time could have left out the most striking part of it.

In any case Americans were not dependent only on Robins for an account of his dealings with Trotsky. Presumably any number of people in the State Department would have known of them, although not everyone would have wanted to publish them to the world. William C. Bullitt, however, who at this time was doing intelligence work for the State Department, was an anti-imperialist by conviction and an exponent of Soviet-American friendship; nor was he noted for reticence.[118] Raymond Clapper mentions his name, though rather ambiguously, in connection with the circulation of Robins' story.[119] In Russia Robins' activities must have been known to the whole American community in Petrograd; both Albert Rhys Williams and John Reed brought the news with them back to the United States. Reed, not at all handicapped in this respect by the State Department's confiscation of all his papers and documents, published the story in full in the *Liberator* for November, 1918.[120] Williams was cited by Upton Sinclair in the January, 1919, issue of his magazine as the source for the same story, which Sinclair also gave in detail.[121] The fact that an account of the episode also appeared in the Manchester *Guardian* suggests that still others, Bruce Lockhart, for instance, knew the tale and helped to spread it.[122]

Whatever their source, the rumors of American perfidy in dealing with the Bolsheviks during the Brest Litovsk crisis were remarkably plentiful. Samuel Harper was appalled at the number of "loose or carelessly quoted statements about Russia" that he was obliged to listen to in the course of his active social life. "I have just about decided to become a hermit," he confided to a friend.[123] Theodore Roosevelt told Robins in September, 1918, that he had "been informed that before they [the Bolsheviks] made the Brest-Litovsk Treaty they sought economic help at Washington and were turned down," and asked Robins whether the story was true.[124] Max Eastman's *Liberator* stated the rumor as fact in its October issue.[125] The *Nation* on November 16, demanded to know whether it was true

> that the Administration knew, at the time of the Brest-Litovsk negotiations, that the Soviet government, represented by Lenine and Trotzky, was opposed to the projected treaty, and looked forward to signing it only because of the physical impossibility of resisting the German demands unless the Allies, or some of them, came to its aid? [126]

Lincoln Colcord knew the story, for he wrote to Colonel House that all of the charges recently made by Hiram Johnson in the Senate could be proved by "documentary evidence of the most conclusive and unimpeachable sort [and that this material] exists in America." [127] Johnson himself must have been equally certain of the truth of the charges before rising in the Senate on December 12, 1918, to denounce the administration's Russian policy, although it was not until after he had delivered the speech that he asked Robins for the documents in support of it.[128] His attack took the form of a series of rhetorical questions. Was it true that American aloofness was "largely" responsible for the fall of Kerensky? that the Bolsheviks had repeatedly offered to cooperate with the American government in matters of trade, and had repeatedly been rebuffed? that the Creel committee had deliberately distorted and misrepresented news from Russia? Was it true that Trotsky, through Robins, had offered to reject the treaty of Brest Litovsk in return for a promise of material aid? [129]

The administration declined to answer Johnson's questions, as it had persistently sought to stifle any discussion of its Russian policy. Naturally this reticence made the government's case look weaker than it was. A flat statement of what had actually transpired in Petrograd would have shown at once that the government had never had any real assurance that the Bolsheviks would carry on the war if aided by the Allies. When the text of Trotsky's famous proposal was finally revealed to the public by Senator Johnson, Samuel Harper demanded, "Why the dickens didn't the State Department give this out months ago? The text of the proposal itself, if one can call it that, is enough, if one reads it carefully." [130] The whole episode strikingly illustrated the futility of the State Department's policy of secrecy, which succeeded only in arousing apprehensions about American diplomacy where the facts of the matter would have put them to rest. Because Lansing refused to let Robins talk, it was naturally assumed that Lansing had something to hide.

When Robins finally spoke out in public, therefore, before the Overman committee of the United States Senate on March 6, 1919, anti-imperialists were only too ready to believe rumors which the government was evidently anxious to suppress. They found it unnecessary to look closely at Robins' enthralling story, when the presumption in favor of its validity was so great. "Mr. Robins's testimony is decisive," the *New Republic* declared,[131] and Lincoln Colcord, somewhat later, wrote confidently, "His facts have all been proved, and his advice justified." [132] Robins was, moreover, a powerful speaker, as obviously honest as he was eloquent. "Robins is a spell-binder," Harper admitted, "and puts it over in great shape. His speech here at the City Club was most plausible." [133] John Franklin Jameson thought his speech before the Overman committee was "the most interesting I had ever heard in Washington." [134]

Not only the force of Robins' character accounted for the enthusiasm with which anti-imperialists received his words. His story, after all, conformed to certain known facts. Trotsky was anxious to prevent ratification of the treaty (as well as to forestall Japanese intervention); so deep indeed was his hatred of the treaty that he never brought himself to vote for ratification, but merely abstained from voting against it.[135] He had approached Robins, with the approval of the central committee, with a proposal which showed that the Bolsheviks at least considered making an appeal for help. Robins' theory was therefore, as Samuel Harper said, plausible; nor was it in a deeper sense altogether unsound. It is true that Trotsky's request for help was not as binding as Robins thought it was. It is also true that Robins' telegram containing the text of Trotsky's statement did not reach Washington until ten days after the ratification of the treaty, a fact which he never seems to have known.[136] But a message from Ambassador Francis containing the substance of Robins' conversation with Trotsky was received by the State Department on March 15, while the debate in Moscow was still in progress.[137] The officials in Washington knew, therefore, that an offer of aid to the soviets was their last chance to prevent ratification of the treaty. Moreover, it must have occurred to them at some point in their deliberations that the soviets, whatever their intentions, could not in any case fight without guns. The government did not, after all, act in complete ignorance of how matters stood in Russia. When Francis asked whether the government considered Wilson's message to the Congress of Soviets (with its austere notice that "the government of the United States is, unhappily, not now in a position to render the direct and effective aid it would wish to render" [138]) an adequate reply to Trotsky's questions, the State Department answered in the affirmative.[139] In passing up the chance, such as it was, to prevent ratification, the government could defend itself only on the grounds that the chance was too slender to offer any hope. More imaginative statesmen, however, might at least have been willing to get the credit for having made an offer which was refused. It is hard to see what was gained, under the circumstances, by intransigence.

The anti-imperialist indictment of American policy was to that extent justified by the facts of the case. At the same time one can hardly help thinking that anti-imperialists would have blamed America and the Allies for Russia's withdrawal from the war even if the facts had been less persuasive than they were. It was no coincidence that those who most eagerly took up the Robins thesis were the same people who from the moment of the Bolshevik coup had predicted again and again that the new government would never consent to sign a separate peace. They had staked their hopes and their reputations as political prophets on this proposition; they had a vested interest in it; only with the greatest difficulty could they have admitted that they had been mistaken. Hence their attempt to show that the Bolsheviks had signed the peace only because the Allies gave them no encouragement to reject it.

There was another reason for their reluctance to admit that they had not known the Bolsheviks as well as they had thought. If the Bolsheviks could not be trusted, which of the Russian factions could? Men who did not object to delivering Russia into the hands of a "strong man" were only too eager to get rid of the Bolsheviks. But for anti-imperialists—indeed, for most liberals—the rule of a strong man implied military government, a secret police, the censorship of thought: the very "Prussianism" which the Allies claimed to be fighting. They preferred even the reign of the Bolsheviks to what they could only regard as a return to tyranny. It was too early to see that Bolshevism itself was a form of tyranny; its outlines could only dimly be made out; its implications were not yet seen. Much of what the Bolsheviks attacked in Western society—imperialism, exploitation, "annexations and indemnities"—American liberals also objected to. Their experiments with "open diplomacy" naturally commended themselves to pacifists and anti-imperialists. The disaster which befell them at Brest Litovsk earned them the sympathy of all who were convinced that they had done everything possible to avert it. Thus while anti-imperialists in the United States could not shut their eyes to the menacing attitude of the Bolsheviks, they continued to believe that time and sympathy would dull the edge of their anger.

IV

Standing By Russia

THE unhappy outcome of the negotiations at Brest Litovsk silenced the advocates of the "new diplomacy." The case for a political appeal to the German Left in conjunction with a military attack on the Right rested on the imminence of a democratic upheaval in Germany. Brest Litovsk appeared to invalidate this assumption; the German people acquiesced in what Americans regarded as the outrageous terms imposed by the German High Command upon prostrate, defenseless Russia. "[T]he German people seem to be more completely under the dominance of their cynical Junker class than I had thought," wrote Norman Thomas to Lillian D. Wald.[1] Overnight the hope that Germany was on the verge of revolution evaporated. Nothing but a military victory, it appeared, would bring Germany to terms. "For the present," William C. Bullitt advised Colonel House, "we had better fight and say nothing." [2] "Political expedients have failed," wrote Herbert Bayard Swope. "So, for the time being, words must be laid aside in favor of the arguments of the bullets." [3] Even radical socialists now agreed that the war must be fought through to "victory." Max Eastman declared: "The hypothesis of international working-class revolution against war was tried out by Lenine and Trotsky, and it failed. Whether it failed entirely because of the attitude of the Allied governments, has become an historic question. It failed." [4] Nations seemed still to command more allegiance than classes. John R. Commons saw in the failure of the German socialists to heed the call of the Bolsheviks the final refutation of Marxism, which failed to anticipate the growth of "patriotism," that is, of nationalism.[5]

The collapse of the Bolshevik "peace offensive" seemed for a time to have silenced opposition to the war altogether, although some pacifists contended that opposition had merely been driven underground by the government's relentless persecution.[6] Morris Hillquit offered his services to the government as a propagandist. "It is now clearer than ever," he told an audience of socialists, "that Prussian and Austrian junkerdom is the foe of liberty and peace." [7] During his campaign for mayor of New York, in the autumn of 1917, Hillquit had publicly refused to buy a Liberty bond; in April the New York board of aldermen, which included seven socialists elected during the Hillquit campaign, endorsed the third Liberty Loan.[8] A mass meeting of socialists in New York cheered Wilson and called upon all socialists to support the war.[9] A strong movement sprang up for repeal of the St. Louis platform, supported, among others, by such publications as *Pearson's Magazine* and the *Liberator*, whose editors had previously opposed the war.[10] Allan Benson, socialist candidate for President in 1916, resigned from the party in protest against its continued opposition to the war.[11] Floyd Dell allowed himself to be drafted into a "war against the chief enemy of Soviet Russia." [12] Everywhere pacifists painfully reexamined their position. Norman Thomas wrote in great agony of spirit:

> Frankly, my own feeling with regard to the war is undergoing something of a change. On religious grounds I am still obliged to think that war is a hideously unsatisfactory method of righteousness but the Russian situation and the progressive abandonment of imperialistic aims by the Allies under pressure from the President and British Labor remove the reproach of hypocrisy from us. . . . Things change so fast that one is at a loss what to think.[13]

The essence of the pacifist position had been the assumption that the Allies and the Central Powers were equally in the wrong.

After what Americans, almost without exception, took to be the revelation of German iniquity at Brest Litovsk, it was difficult any longer to refuse to distinguish between the two sides. The Germans, so it seemed, had acted like the Huns George Creel made them out to be. On the other hand the Allies seemed to many pacifists and anti-imperialists to have repented of their sins. Lloyd George's speech of January 4, and Wilson's more sweeping Fourteen Points were hailed everywhere as signs of a change of heart. In their eagerness to be convinced of the Allies' good intentions anti-imperialists chose to forget that nothing Wilson or Lloyd George had said altered the fact that the secret treaties remained in force. The *Public*, for instance, declared that "the Grand Alliance has accomplished the difficult and dangerous task of changing its basis. We may consider the whole groundwork of 1914 as definitely repudiated."[14] Yet in fact nothing had been repudiated at all—neither the treaties themselves nor the unwritten understanding among the European Allies that Germany had to be so decisively defeated that she would never again be able to threaten the safety of her neighbors. That anti-imperialists were able so easily to ignore the obstacles that still lay in the way of what they considered a just peace suggests that they were more interested in the ritualistic aspect of the war-aims question than in its substance; that what they demanded of America and the Allies was not so much an act as an attitude of renunciation. One has the feeling that they were more concerned about America's soul than the map of Europe. They demanded nothing more than that the President of the United States go on record as opposing the more extreme territorial ambitions of the Allied powers, as if this gesture were enough to purge all suspicion of sin.

There was another, more immediate reason for the rush of pacifists, socialists, and anti-imperialists to the colors; another reason why peace with Germany had suddenly become unthinkable. That was simply the fear that peace in the West would leave Germany free in the East to exploit the advantages of the Treaty of Brest Litovsk, "to quench remorselessly," as one paper put it, "the burning flax of democracy in Russia." [15] In theory a negotiated peace, if it had ever been possible, ought still to have been possible after March, 1917; what kind of peace Germany made with Russia was not necessarily any indication of what kind of peace she might be willing to make with the West. But to have made peace with Germany at that point would have meant not merely leaving the Brest Litovsk settlement intact, but implicitly approving it. For those who still believed that the Russian revolution was "the greatest net gain of this war so far," as William Allen White wrote to a friend, a peace achieved at Russia's expense was the worst calamity that could befall the cause of democracy.[16] It was the liberals—anti-imperialists and war enthusiasts alike—who now clamored for war to the bitter end, while a few conservatives (in England, if not in the United States), were beginning to glimpse the profound social consequences of an indefinite continuation of the war. Lord Lansdowne, a Tory and an imperialist, predicted in his celebrated letter to the London *Daily Telegraph*, November 29, 1917, that to prolong the war would "spell ruin for the civilised world." [17]

Anti-imperialists, instead of leaping to Lansdowne's defense, derided him. "Lord Lansdowne's letter," cried H. G. Wells in the *New Republic*, "was the letter of a peer who fears revolution more than national dishonor." The Tories had led the world into war, he said, and now were the first to want to back out when they perceived that the masses had turned the war against them. "Far rather would they make the most abject surrender to the Kaiser than deal with a renascent republican Germany." [18] American anti-imperialists joined in the attack on Lansdowne as the spokesman of "caste and privilege." * Raymond Clapper,

* Nothing more clearly illustrates the significance which the demand for revised war aims had come to have, in the minds of American liberals,

citing Wells' article, decided that "conservatives here . . . fear Russian Bolshevikism more than German militarism—and they prefer peace with German autocracy rather than see German[y] really liberalized." [19] Lincoln Colcord wrote in alarm to Wilson that "men everywhere . . . are saying that it would be better for Germany to be in Petrograd than for the Bolsheviki to remain longer in control. That," he added grimly, "is going to be the next platitude on which the hopes of mankind are to be wrecked." [20]

What is surprising, however, is not that a few of the enemies of the revolution should have come at last to the conclusion that the war, from a conservative point of view, had gone further than they had intended, but that so many of them continued to resist the logic of their own anti-Bolshevism. It was true, as anti-imperialists suspected, that they were beginning to fear Bolshevism more than German "militarism," but it was not true that they wanted to compromise with Germany in order to save the world from Bolshevism. That was the policy clearly dictated by their reflections on the unexpected turn the war had taken—by William English Walling's "Memorandum on Revolutions," for example.[21] Yet Walling, Lansing, and, indeed, every anti-Bolshevik in America, resisted to the end the conclusion to which their observations logically led. If Bolshevism was indeed

than the comment of the *Public*, XX (Dec. 7, 1917), 1165–6. "The strength of Lord Lansdowne's letter," according to the *Public*, was "his demand for a definition of war aims"; the "weakness" of the letter was his "bid for premature peace."

Some liberals at first mistook Lansdowne's views for those of an anti-imperialist, instead of a Tory pacifist; that is, they assumed that he was interested not in an immediate peace but simply in a "political offensive," as the *New Republic* put it, XIII (Dec. 8, 1917), 138–9. See also Springfield *Republican*, Dec. 1, 1917. Colonel House, after talking to Lansdowne, found that they "scarcely disagreed at all." House MS Diary, Nov. 14, 1917. House could hardly have understood Lansdowne's position. The essential difference between the anti-imperialists and Lansdowne was that they demanded the democratization of Germany as a condition of peace while he did not. That was all the difference in the world, as those who understood Lansdowne's position quickly realized.

a greater menace than Kaiserism, why not make peace with the Kaiser? But peace was the last thing the anti-Bolsheviks demanded. Like the anti-imperialists they continued to insist that not only Germany but Russia as well must be "saved" for the West, and that to that end the war must be prolonged indefinitely. Like the anti-imperialists they rallied around Wilson's ringing affirmation, on May 18, 1918, of America's determination to "stand by" Russia.[22]

It was over the question of what "standing by" Russia meant in practice that agreement broke down. The phrase was characteristically Wilsonian; it could be interpreted by everyone to his own satisfaction. As Ray Stannard Baker wrote to Frank Polk from Europe:

> Mr. Wilson's remark in his Red Cross speech to the effect that he intended to "stand by Russia" . . . has curiously been accepted and heralded in both camps. It has been seized upon by the imperialistic party as a new war cry: a new argument for crushing Germany. After the Russian collapse the first reaction of this group was to "let Russia stew in her own grease," withdraw the British ambassador, and have nothing to do with the Russian radicals. As they began to see the danger in the unexpected penetration of Germany into the heart of Russia with its sword pointed at the vitals of the British empire in Asia, the cry for Japanese intervention from the East was raised, and there was much veiled hostility toward President Wilson's position in this matter. . . . President Wilson's message of sympathy to the Russian soviets received scant courtesy from the imperialistic and tory press here . . . though it was welcomed by the liberal and labor elements. Since then . . . the German penetration into Russia has become . . . threatening. Mr. Wilson's watchword, "stand by Russia," becomes suddenly, therefore—not at all for idealistic or democratic reasons, but for imperialistic and military reasons—a new policy to be eagerly seized upon.

At the same time, according to Baker, European liberals naturally welcomed the assurance that the Allies would never leave Russia to the Germans.[23]

In America the Red Cross speech was equally ambiguous. To William Howard Taft and Theodore Roosevelt (who never managed to heed for very long the advice which he so profusely thanked Robins for giving him) and to most of the American press, "standing by Russia" meant sending in an army to save the country from German domination and to assist the "loyal Russians" in restoring "order." Most liberals, on the other hand —even those who deplored the Bolshevik revolution—in the summer of 1918 believed that the Allies could rehabilitate Russia only by a program of economic aid. That idea, perhaps because it was so vague in detail, commanded a great variety of support; almost everyone with any liberal pretensions at all, from Robins to Walling, preferred it to military intervention. The American League to Aid and Cooperate with Russia, the chief source of organized support for a policy of aid and relief, counted among its members not only Mrs. Robins, Colonel Thompson, Senators Borah and Owen, Frederic C. Howe, Lincoln Steffens, Norman Hapgood, Thomas W. Lamont, and Lillian D. Wald, all of whom adhered more or less consistently to the Robins-Thompson point of view, but also Samuel Gompers and James Duncan of the AFL, president Frank Goodnow of Johns Hopkins University, E. Chappell Porter of the Russian-American Chamber of Commerce, Melville Stone of the AP, Mark Sullivan, Senator John Sharp Williams, Erving Winslow, Rabbi Stephen S. Wise, and William English Walling, who were all strongly pro-war and anti-Bolshevik.

Herbert L. Carpenter, the official head of the League, and Samuel Harper, its guiding genius, sought without success to maintain an appearance of harmony between the two factions, which agreed on only two points: the importance of economic aid, and the desirability of creating a special governmental agency, independent of the State Department, to oversee and coordinate all phases of Russian policy.[24] This last feature of the League's program, which was never publicly disclosed, reflected not only the central importance which liberals attached to the Russian problem—to the point where they wished to appoint officials who would devote themselves to nothing else—but also the widespread dissatisfaction with what was regarded as the State Department's unimaginative handling of Russian affairs. Naturally this kind of speculation did not commend itself to the State Department, and no doubt it was partly because the campaign for economic aid was so closely associated with the persistent efforts to remove Russian affairs from the department's control that Lansing, who at first favored economic aid, as the summer wore on increasingly inclined to a military solution of the problem.

The proponents of economic aid advocated, as the first step toward implementation of their program, sending to Russia a commission of experts under some distinguished public figure. Gordon Auchincloss, son-in-law of Colonel House, hit upon the happy idea of getting Herbert Hoover to head the commission; perhaps Hoover could duplicate his success in Belgium. Hoover was approached and agreed to serve.[25] Lansing gave his consent to the plan, which at the same time appealed to liberals like Norman Hapgood, who told House that it was "a stroke of genius," and William Allen White, who asked to be appointed to the commission.[26] Wilson, however, refused to commit himself on the subject of Hoover's appointment. Somewhat later Justice Louis D. Brandeis was proposed in the same connection. This suggestion greatly alarmed the anti-Bolsheviks, who feared that Brandeis had been "much influenced by Robbins [*sic*] and was more or less sympathetic with the point of view taken by the New Republic." [27] Harper objected to the choice of Brandeis, as he explained to Frederic Dixon of the *Christian Science Monitor,* because as a Jew he was "the intellectual center of the 'clique' which is composed of men who are not genuine liberals, but who have Brandeis' support because they contribute to his

Zionism. If B. is appointed," he complained, "I just bet that men like Jacob Schiff . . . would get on the job, and into Russia." [28] Harper's friend E. Chappell Porter also feared "the Jewish group in Washington." Some of his Russian acquaintances, he reported, were "very much depressed over their activities." [29] But when Harper and Butler Wright of the State Department paid a visit to Brandeis they were relieved to find "that he was interested . . . only as a citizen, and that he was not taking part in the 'official' discussion of the policy toward Russia." [30] Presumably that meant that the rumors of his impending appointment to the Russian commission were unfounded.

The membership of the proposed commission was not the only subject of dispute among those who agreed in principle that a commission should be sent. All attempts at relief sooner or later foundered on the question of whether relief was to be undertaken in conjunction with or in spite of the soviets. Robins and Thompson and their friends still believed that it was not only possible, but absolutely essential to cooperate with the Bolsheviks. In their opinion the Bolsheviks were "in to stay." [31] It followed from this proposition that "the only possible salvation of Russia," as Thomas Lamont put it, "is to cultivate in some manner the cooperation of the present ruling powers." [32] Others thought they saw a distinction between the Bolsheviks as a political party, and the soviets, which they regarded as institutions indigenous to Russia which would presumably survive a change of regime. They reasoned that the "constructive forces" in Russia, whose good will it was necessary for the Allies to cultivate, disapproved of the Bolsheviks but were deeply attached to the soviet form of government, which in their minds symbolized all the gains of the revolution. They conceded that the Bolsheviks controlled the soviets at the moment but insisted that their control was only temporary. "[T]he Bolsheviki cannot police the country for ever," Harper reminded Richard Crane.* By encouraging the soviets, therefore, while ignoring the Bolsheviks—to the extent to which that was possible—the Allies might bring to the surface the latent democracy of the Russian masses.

For a time it was possible for men like Harper, who retained their faith in the soviets even when they had lost confidence in the Bolsheviks, to defend the views of Robins and Thompson as essentially similar to their own. As late as May, 1918, Harper still spoke with praise of Robins' work in Russia, recommended Thacher's article on economic aid to his friends, and defended Thompson's membership in the American-Russian League against those who objected that Thompson was a wild-eyed radical.[33] "[W]e cannot desert Russia," he wrote to Corse. "I have fought reconciliation [recognition?] hard but have urged some kind of contact, so as to stay in. That is Thompson's idea, so far as I can make out from my conversations with him." [34] But everyone advocated "contact"; the question was, contact with whom? Eventually Harper was forced to recognize the divergence between his own position and that of Thompson and Robins. By the beginning of July he confessed that he was "a bit disappointed" with Robins.[35]

At about the same time he abandoned the distinction between the Bolsheviks and the soviets. After conversations with friends in Washington he decided that although the distinction existed in theory, it was "quite possible that . . . the two *ideas* have become synonomous in the minds of the non-Bolshevik educated classes and also in the minds of the workmen and peasants. . . . If this is the case, then the word soviet, if used by

* Harper to Richard Crane, June 11, 1918, Harper MSS. Richard Crane, it will be remembered, was the son of Charles R. Crane and thus a more important figure in the administration, owing to his father's intimacy with the President, than his rather lowly position in the State Department would otherwise have warranted. But William Appleman Williams, *American-Russian Relations* (New York, 1952), pp. 107–8, greatly exaggerates his importance, it seems to me, as he exaggerates that of Basil Miles, William Phillips and Frank Polk.

us, would not serve as a rallying call to constructive forces." [36] To John R. Mott he wrote, "Russians in whom I have the greatest confidence assure me that the word has been discredited." [37] Once he had lost faith in the power of the soviets to speak for the regenerative forces in Russia, Harper was no longer able to argue effectively against the drift toward forcible intervention in Russia's affairs. He never went as far as his friend Corse, who after sixteen years in Russia as representative of the National City Bank returned to the United States convinced that "for one or two generations Russia will progress much faster under limited monarchy than . . . under a republican form of government." [38] But he was increasingly able to countenance Allied support of Russian factions which were democratic in name only, and although he still held out for economic aid, he was willing to see it accompanied, if necessary, by an army. In the end Harper acquiesced in Wilson's long-awaited decision, August 3, 1918, to join the Allies in sending troops to Siberia.[39]

Not that such men as Harper became friends of the counterrevolution. Liberals who eventually accepted the necessity of "intervention," like Wilson himself, did so only when they had convinced themselves that Russia was in danger of being overrun by German troops, and that in sending an army to Siberia, therefore, the Allies were fighting not the Bolsheviks but the Germans. If they had supposed that they were taking sides in a Russian civil war, most liberals would have been shocked and outraged. Their support of intervention, far from expressing a desire to overthrow the Bolshevik regime, was based on the premise, startling as it may seem to us, that the Bolsheviks did not really exist—except, of course, as agents of the German government. Only in this way could men who still believed in "self-determination" both fight a war and continue to talk like liberals.

The United States would have intervened in Siberia in March, 1918, if the Allies had had their way. Wilson was under intense pressure to act. The Allies still dreamed of restoring an Eastern front. Japanese expansionists looked covetously toward Siberia. The Russian liberals and monarchists hoped for support in the counter-revolution. The pressure on Wilson was as great in March as it was in July. It was so great that Wilson momentarily yielded to it, until recalled by House to his earlier view of the matter.[40] By the middle of the summer, however, House himself had come to favor some form of intervention. In July the decision could be explained in terms acceptable to the liberal conscience; in March that was impossible.

What made the difference was the uprising of the Czecho-Slovak Legion in Siberia in May, 1918.[41] From a liberal point of view that event removed both the practical and the ideological obstacles to intervention. The seizure by the Czechs of the Siberian railway solved the practical problem of how the Western saviors of Russia were to enter the country with their food and blankets, and with whom they were to cooperate once they were there. Nor were American observers slow to see their opportunity. Why not "use" the Czechs? Harper suggested on July 13.[42] But Wilson was already groping toward a solution, as he told House on July 8, "along the double line of economic assistance and aid to the Czecho-Slovaks." [43] The uprising of the Czechs relieved Americans from the embarrassing ideological difficulty of sending "aid" to revolutionary Russia through one of the counter-revolutionary factions. The Czechs were thought to be above participation in local Russian quarrels. That they had in fact already aligned themselves, wherever the opportunity arose, with the parties opposing the Bolsheviks was easily ignored by men anxiously searching for a solution to the Russian problem which would not involve taking the Bolsheviks into account. In American eyes the Czechs were fighting the Germans, not the Bolsheviks. Throughout the long debate over intervention there was no indication that the advocates of aid to the Czechs realized that they were taking sides in a Russian civil war.

Many Americans were at this time under the illusion—an illusion nourished by the wartime habit of exaggerating the prowess of the enemy—that the Bolsheviks, at Germany's bidding, had provided arms to the German prisoners of war, captured by the armies of the Tsar and the Provisional Government, who were scattered all over Russia and Siberia. That explained how the Czechs could be fighting the Germans. In fact most of the prisoners were not German at all but Austrian, and although they numbered about a million they were in no sense an army, as Americans believed. At most only a few thousand of them were armed.[44] Nor did the German government have anything to do with the arming of prisoners of war. In fact it protested against the practice. The armed prisoners were men who had been converted to communism by Bolshevik propagandists and recruited into the army of the international proletariat. As internationalists they were no more friendly to Germany than to the United States. But to people who considered themselves at war only with Germany, the recognition of these facts would have complicated matters by injecting a third force—international communism—into a tidy dualism: the bad Germans versus the good Americans. The facts therefore had to be ignored by everyone except those who had accepted the war in the first place only with reservations, and who were therefore more easily able to give thought to other matters besides the struggle with Germany.

The official rationale of American participation in the Allied expedition to Siberia, as set forth in a statement by the State Department of August 3, 1918, based on Wilson's *aide-memoire* of July 17, made sense only if one assumed that the Czechs were heroically engaged in combat with the German prisoners of war. The State Department's statement did not attempt to conceal the fact that the Czechs no longer seemed interested in leaving Russia, according to their original plan, but were in fact moving westward from Vladivostok toward European Russia, in an effort to reunite their force. At the same time it asserted that the only justification for American intervention was to assist the Czechs.

To assist them in doing what? What objectives were they pursuing that required them to move westward? Anti-imperialists, who knew that the Czechs were by this time cooperating with the Russian whites in overturning Bolshevik authority wherever they found it and in setting up new governments of their own (they took part, for example, in the establishment of an anti-Bolshevik regime at Omsk in June, 1918, which claimed to speak for all Siberia), immediately found in the curious reference to the "westward-moving Czecho-Slovaks" evidence that the government of the United States had openly thrown its influence on the side of the counter-revolution. They assumed that since the Czechs were fighting the Bolsheviks and that since Allied troops were being sent to aid the Czechs, the purpose of the expedition must be to overthrow the Bolsheviks. They would not have found it possible to believe that the government had arrived at its decision only by ignoring the very information which was most relevant to it.

The fact is that very few Americans, in the government or out of it, seem to have conceived of intervention as anti-Bolshevik in design. There is not much evidence, either, of a desire to reestablish an Eastern front, an objective favored by French and British experts. Nor was there evidence, for that matter, of a determination to thwart Japanese ambitions, which some historians have argued was the secret motive of American policy in agreeing to intervention, a motive which for reasons of diplomatic delicacy could not publicly be avowed. Fear of Japan was more often cited, when it was cited at all, as a reason for refusing than for agreeing to intervene. But if the press reflected popular opinion, most Americans had nothing but confidence in the good intentions of the Japanese.[45] Germany, not Japan, was the enemy to be defeated by sending troops to Russia. The one reason which was given again and again to justify intervention was the German penetration of Siberia. Senator King of Utah, introducing an interventionist resolution, claimed that German troops were advancing eastward "with a view to taking possession of . . . Siberia." [46] Senators Fall, Lewis, and Kenyon gravely warned that Germany "may make the seemingly impossible a fact by driving through Siberia and invading the United States and Canada through Alaska." [47] The New York *Times* announced that the West was confronted with "the most frightful menace conceivable," "a German-Russian Empire." [48] The Social Democratic League of America, an organization of prowar socialists, beseeched the government "to drive Germany and her allies out of Russia." [49] Even George Kennan, who, unlike most Americans, openly advocated the forcible overthrow of the Bolsheviks, also stressed the danger of German penetration of Siberia as a reason for military action.[50] So did Lansing, for a time.[51]

Occasionally someone admitted, as William Howard Taft wrote a few days after the first Allied landings at Vladivostok, that "we are now at war with the Bolsheviki." [52] But most people maintained the fiction that the Bolsheviks were not involved. David Lawrence explained that while the United States had no right to interfere in Russia's own affairs, it was bound "in self-defence" to "see to it that Germany does not reach out to the Pacific ocean." [53] The Milwaukee *Journal* declared that intervention "has no bearing on the internal situation [in Russia] but looks only to checkmate the common enemy, Germany." [54] The St. Louis *Post-Dispatch* assured its readers that inasmuch as "armies of Germans are already in Russia," Allied intervention offered no parallel, as many opponents of intervention were saying, to the interference of European royalists in the French revolution, which was motivated only by a desire to save the king.[55] The Philadelphia *Public Ledger*, Chicago *Daily News*, Des Moines *Register* and even the New York *Evening Post* all supported intervention on the grounds that "intervention," strictly speaking, was not contemplated at all.[56] Even the *New Republic* at first conceded that the Allies could not permit the Czechs to fall victim to the armed German prisoners of war; it asked only to be assured that the danger was as great as it had been made out to be.*

In the interventionist rationale Bolshevism had to be considered as a projection of Kaiserism. Hence the intense interest, in the United States, in the so-called Sisson documents, which purported to prove that the Bolsheviks were hired agents of

* *New Republic*, XVI (Aug. 31, 1918), 120.

Walter Lippmann and Charles Merz, "A Test of the News," *ibid.*, XXIII (supplement to Aug. 4, 1920), 14, break down 285 items from the New York *Times* in the period from April to Aug. 4, 1918, bearing on the question of intervention, as follows:

Japanese Intervention	69	The Red Peril	5
German Domination of Russia	49	Prisoners in Siberia Peril	3
Allied Intervention	48	Relief for Russia	3
Russian Anti-Bolshevism	34	Japanese in Peril	2
The Czechoslovaks	31	Guarding Stores	2
Anti-Intervention	13		

Puzzled by the fact "that the Red Peril should have played so insignificant a part in the news at a time when the debate over intervention in Russia's internal affairs was hottest," Lippmann and Merz concluded, rather irrelevantly, that "the notion of a fundamental antagonism between the Soviet government and the American is not insisted upon until after American troops are on Russian soil." What they were trying to prove by this is not clear. But one can hardly avoid agreeing with their observation that "the greatest reason for military action displayed in the news is the German domination of Russia."

It should be noted that the predominance of "Japanese intervention," "Allied intervention," and "the Czechoslovaks" mainly reflects the frequency with which these subjects were under offical discussion, and does not necessarily reflect any particular bias in coverage, except the eagerness with which the *Times* hailed every manifestation of an official willingness to intervene. Note also the emphasis on "Russian anti-Bolshevism," designed to create the impression that most Russians opposed the Bolsheviks and welcomed intervention. The important thing is that while "German domination of Siberia" was repeatedly urged as a reason for intervention, the "Red Peril" (that is, the terror) received hardly any attention; and the socialistic features of the regime, which presumably weighed so heavily with American capitalists, were not mentioned at all.

Germany. No other Allied country gave these documents the attention which they attracted in the United States. Only in the United States were they endorsed and published by the government. Only in the United States was their authenticity vouched for by eminent historians and accepted without question by most of the press. Elsewhere they were treated by governments and peoples alike with suspicion and scorn.

It must not be thought that the documents with which Edgar Sisson of the CPI came panting home from Russia in May, 1918, contributed anything new to the discussion of the revolution. The documents in one form or another had been knocking about Europe for months before Sisson got hold of them. Supporters of the Provisional Government at the time of the July uprising tried to persuade Kerensky to publish some of them in order to discredit the Bolsheviks.[57] A few months later they turned up in Paris and were published by the *Petit Parisien* on February 8, 1918. Several American papers at that time called attention to this fact and described the documents at some length. The *Evening Post* printed a detailed attack on them by the British correspondent of the *Russkoe Slovo*, an anti-Bolshevik paper.[58] Sisson in March, 1918, paid $25,000 for these "secrets," under the impression that he was making the most sensational scoop in the annals of modern journalism.

Neither the British government nor the American State Department was impressed by Sisson's discoveries, but George Creel found them "absolutely conclusive."[59] Wilson likewise professed to be "thoroughly satisfied" of their authenticity.[60] With the President's approval and without consulting the State Department, Creel released the documents to the press on September 15, 1918. After they had been serialized with great publicity in all the major dailies, he published them as a pamphlet, with an interpretive introduction by Sisson, under the imprint of the CPI. Not only conservative papers like the New York *Times* but most of the liberal-interventionist sheets accepted the documents as genuine, in spite of abundant evidence to the contrary. The *Evening Post*, however, subjected Sisson's texts to the most devastating analysis, pointing out discrepancies of dates which forced the reader to conclude either that the German General Staff was gifted with remarkable foresight, since it consistently referred to events in Russia which had not yet occurred at the time of writing, or that it dated all its communications, even those addressed to representatives in Switzerland and Sweden, according to the Russian calendar.[61] Such discrepancies suggested that the documents had originated not in Germany but in Russia, and that they were composed by someone enjoying the benefit of hindsight.

Other war liberals would not hear of such talk. The *World*, loyal, as always, to the administration, was scandalized to find that anyone questioned the word of Creel and Sisson that the documents were genuine.[62] Creel himself, his vanity stung, accused the *Evening Post* of having given "aid and comfort to the enemies of the United States." [63] But in order to lay all doubts to rest, he consented to have the documents professionally examined by impartial scholars, and he asked the National Board for Historical Research to appoint a committee of experts to investigate.[64] It came as something of a shock to those who looked forward to a really disinterested investigation of the evidence when the Board appointed Samuel Harper to serve on a committee of three with John Franklin Jameson and Archibald Cary Coolidge, for Harper was by this time an avowed apologist for the administration's Russian policy. When Harper and Jameson, after only a week's study of the documents, reported that most of them were undoubtedly genuine and that there was nothing in the others "that positively excludes the notion of their being genuine," anti-imperialists were quick to dismiss the verdict as that of a highly partisan jury.[65] Villard's *Nation* considered the investigation a "sham." "Must the reputation of

American scholars go by the board as a part of the wreckage of war?" [66]

It could be said in defense of Harper and Jameson that although they endorsed the authenticity of the documents themselves they pointedly avoided endorsing the conclusions which Sisson drew from them: that the Bolsheviks were mere hirelings who could be counted on to do Germany's bidding at all times; that they had no will of their own. Privately Harper confided to friends that "there was clear evidence in [the] documents . . . that Lenin constantly had in mind the possibility of double-crossing the Germans. . . . In other words he was ten times as dangerous as any German agent." [67] But mere abstention from comment on Sisson's inferences was no reply to them. That Harper himself was not very happy with his part in the affair, his attempts to excuse himself clearly show. In evaluating the documents, he wrote apologetically in his memoirs, he and Jameson were subjected by the administration to the most intense pressure to sustain Sisson's conclusions. At first, according to Harper, they refused to go any further than to say that by beginning a revolution in Russia at the height of the war the Bolsheviks had "objectively" aided the German cause, although that was not necessarily their object. But the historians were told "that such a statement would not help to promote that emotional upsurge necessary for the mobilization of all our resources to be thrown into the struggle." Harper's assertion, however, that "we stood our ground," falls somewhat short of the truth, for their silence, although it may have satisfied their consciences, was bound to be interpreted as an endorsement of the Sisson thesis.[68] "[M]ost people who read your report to Creel," as Bullard later reminded Sisson, "got the idea that you think these documents prove that Lenin et al. were a band of cheap adventurers who took the stand they did in order to earn German pay." [69] This impression Harper and Jameson did nothing to dispel. In the unpublished version of his memoirs Harper admitted that they had contributed to the "war spirit." [70]

It has been noted that not all advocates of intervention accepted the authenticity of the Sisson documents. Whether one accepted them or not depended not so much on one's feelings about the Bolsheviks as on his reasons for supporting the policy of intervention. Only those who were committed to the view that intervention was directed solely at Germany and thus did not constitute interference in Russia's internal affairs, that is, those who attempted to reconcile intervention with "self-determination," needed the Sisson documents to buttress their case. Those who had no qualms about intervening to overthrow a regime which was undesirable in itself, regardless of its alleged connections with Germany, did not have to prove the existence of a German-Bolshevik conspiracy. The attitude of the British is significant, in this connection: their refusal to publish the documents reflected not a nicer sense of propriety, but the fact that the British accepted intervention frankly as counter-revolution. A number of Americans, because they justified intervention on the same grounds, were likewise free to question the reality of the alleged German-Bolshevik conspiracy. Neither Harper, Bullard, nor Crane believed in it.[71] Neither did Lansing, who once he had finally accepted the necessity of intervention was not averse to regarding it as a means of getting rid of the Bolsheviks. It was no coincidence that the State Department, where anti-Bolshevism did not have to be reconciled with the rhetoric of Wilsonian internationalism, opposed publication of the Sisson documents, while Wilson and Creel pushed them on the public in order to explain the disparity between the principle of self-determination and the fact of intervention.*

* Those who believe that the publication of the Sisson documents was designed simply "to smother opposition to intervention," and that intervention, in turn, was designed simply to overthrow the Bolsheviks, find it hard to explain Wilson's approval of the publication of the documents. "Presumably," says Winton U. Solberg, "Impact of Soviet Russia on

It hardly needs to be said that the publication of the Sisson documents compounded the confusion regarding the nature of the Bolshevik revolution. In releasing the documents the government perpetuated a delusion of the most dangerous sort: that the Bolsheviks did not have to be reckoned with as a political force in their own right; indeed, that once the Germans were defeated, the Bolsheviks would disappear. But this was not all. The publication of these documents, the authenticity of which was so obviously open to question, discredited the case which could be made for the assertion that the Bolsheviks had taken German money, although for their own purposes. As Arthur Bullard once pointed out, "The statement that Bolshevist leaders received large sums from Germany does not rest solely on these documents." [72] Lenin's return to Russia from Switzerland by means of transportation furnished by the German General Staff was enough to warn anyone against easy conclusions of any sort; for in that instance it was clear enough that the Germans hoped to use the Bolsheviks to destroy Allied morale in very much the same way in which anti-imperialists hoped to use them to destroy German morale.

Documents from the German Foreign Office have recently come to light which make it clear that the Germans paid considerable sums to the Bolsheviks to help finance the revolution.*

American Life" (unpublished Ph.D. dissertation, Harvard, 1952), pp. 156–7, "he approved publication, and yet more than anyone else he knew that intervention was not designed to defeat Germany." As we have seen, that is exactly what he did not know.

If it seems preposterous that not only Wilson but most of his countrymen were absolutely convinced of the reality of the German menace in Russia, it should be borne in mind that most Americans are probably convinced that revolutionary movements in our own time are inspired and dominated by Soviet Russia.

* Z. A. B. Zeman, ed., *Germany and the Revolution in Russia, 1915–1918* (London, 1958). These documents also make it clear that the results of this policy were disappointing to the German High Command, in the long run. Thus Ludendorff complained of the "obscurity" of Soviet policy (as well as of the instability of the regime), on account of which it was necessary for Germany to look for "other Allies in the East." He regarded

These documents do not, of course, prove what Sisson wanted to prove, that the Bolsheviks kept faith with their employers; they do not prove that the Bolsheviks were "German agents" in the sense in which Sisson used the term. But they shed a great deal of light on the real character of the Bolshevik leaders: on the utter contempt in which they held all the governments of the decadent West, on the complete cynicism which enabled them to use any means to accomplish the end in sight. Such men, ruthless and desperate, were not the hired accomplices of any government; but neither were they the idealists the anti-imperialists made them out to be. Americans would have done well to have learned at an early date that the Bolsheviks were quite capable of taking "German gold"—or Allied gold, if it had been offered—and of using it to serve their own ends. But after the publication of Sisson's obvious forgeries it was difficult for reasonable men any longer to give serious consideration to such a possibility. After that it was possible to dismiss all suggestions that the Bolsheviks would stoop to such devices as war propaganda of the crudest sort. The government's wanton and irresponsible decision to release the documents was thus doubly disastrous.

It was not only the government, however, that contributed in this fashion to the misunderstanding of the revolution. The interventionist press, in its campaign on behalf of military action in Siberia, printed the most outlandish stories about the Bolshe-

"the dishonourable endeavours of the Soviet government with the gravest distrust." He concluded, "We can expect nothing from this government, although it lives by our mercy." Ludendorff to Kühlmann, June 9, 1918, *ibid.*, pp. 134–6. See also Mirbach to Kühlmann, June 25, 1918, *ibid.*, pp. 137–9. Ten days after writing this letter (July 6, 1918), Mirbach, the German ambassador to Soviet Russia, was assassinated in Moscow by Social Revolutionaries, as a protest against the "pro-German" policy of the Bolsheviks.

These documents from the German archives, it should be noted, are not the documents published by Sisson; the two sets of papers have nothing whatever in common.

viks, and with the same result: criticism of the Bolsheviks, because it evidently rested on deliberate misrepresentation of conditions in Russia, was quickly discredited. But whereas the government's propaganda was designed mainly to appeal to liberal opinion by preserving the fiction that intervention was directed not against the Bolsheviks but against Germany, the propaganda of the press was often openly anti-Bolshevik, particularly after the end of the war, when it became difficult to argue that intervention was directed solely against Germany.[73] Much of this propaganda originated in Russia, among the factions seeking the overthrow of the Bolsheviks, or among their American representatives. The Russian Information Bureau, under the direction of A. J. Sack, tirelessly devoted itself to the campaign for intervention. So did the diplomatic representatives of the Provisional Government, who remained in the United States although the government they represented had been overthrown. But much of the misleading news about Russia came, ironically, from Germany or from pro-German sources in Scandinavia. Thus the very people who so endlessly inveighed against the sinister influence of German propaganda and who took every opportunity to accuse their enemies of being tools of the Kaiser, when it came to reporting events in Russia, naïvely printed stories originating in Germany as if they rested on unimpeachable authority.

The manner in which news was distorted by interventionist papers was not arbitrary. It was deliberately designed to give the impression that Japanese intervention was imminent—indeed, that it was not so much a subject for discussion as an accomplished fact; that Siberia was overrun by German armies; that the Bolshevik regime was already in ruins; that apart from its weakness, which in itself was an invitation to intervention, it was thoroughly immoral and therefore ought to be destroyed by force of arms. It gave the impression, in short, that all signs pointed to the desirability of a quick and simple solution of the

Russian problem by means of Allied military action. Thus the interventionist press as early as December, 1917, reported, quite erroneously, that the Allies had appealed to Japan to land troops at Vladivostok to prevent supplies of war materiel from falling into "German" hands. A Japanese landing had already taken place, according to the New York *Times*.[74] In reality the object of Allied policy at that time, or at least of American policy, was precisely to prevent such action by the Japanese. Three months later Japanese troops, unbidden by the Allies, did make a landing at Vladivostok; but the American press, not satisfied with that, reported that they had marched 3,000 miles into Siberia to protect the seizure of Russian resources by the Germans.[75] It could be inferred from all this that Siberia was teeming with German military activity. But nothing in the campaign for intervention was left to inference alone; that Siberia was in imminent danger of conquest by Germany was explicitly pointed out, day after day.

All this time readers had to bear in mind that the Soviet regime was on the point of collapse. Late in April, 1918, it was widely reported that the Romonov dynasty had been restored and that all was well in Russia.[76] (The retraction of this story, on the other hand, was given very little play, although most readers were no doubt able to gather, from the fact that the Bolsheviks were subsequently referred to as if they were still in power, that the Romonov revival had been remarkably short-lived.) Shortly after the Czech uprising the *Times* received word by way of Berlin that Lenin was at last ready to resign.[77] A few days later came the encouraging news that a counter-revolutionary coup led by Grand Duke Michael had driven Lenin and Trotsky from the capitol.[78] In August the Bolsheviks, having mysteriously regained possession of the government, were again in flight; they had transferred their government to Kronstadt, it was reported.[79] On September 1, Lenin, still lingering inexplicably at Moscow, was shot by a young girl (which was true) and died of his wounds, according to the *Times*.[80] Max Eastman, hearing of this calamity, wrote a moving obituary in the *Liberator*.[81] Even the *Times* spared a few words of grudging admiration for the fallen leader: "Paid agent, political tool or plain fanatic there is no doubt of the man's ability." [82] It was embarrassing therefore for the *Times* to have to admit the next day: "Lenine Not Dead, Bolsheviki Announce." [83] But if he was alive, he was nevertheless in constant retreat. On September 13, his government "fell" again.[84] A little later Dosch-Fleurot, who now supported intervention, sent word that the Germans, having wearied of the Bolsheviks, intended to replace them with the Kadets.[85] The war ended before the Germans could complete these plans, but on November 28, the Bolshevik government fell anyway.[86] Thereafter it fell with a regularity that in time became almost tedious: on December 14, 1918, for instance; on May 23, 1918; and on October 18, 1919. [87] Altogether, if the New York *Times* was to be believed, it fell or was about to fall 91 times in a period of two years from November, 1917, to November, 1919.[88] The *Times* continued late into 1920 to announce the periodic collapse of Soviet authority.[89]

When they were not exposing the weakness of the Soviet regime, the interventionist papers, both liberal and conservative, dwelled on its diabolical cruelty. A case in point was the "nationalization of women," of all the rumors about the Bolsheviks one of the most persistent, probably because it appealed to a rather salacious curiosity. Like many of these rumors it sprang —insofar as it sprang from anything substantive—from the confusion of Bolshevism with anarchism. The period of the First World War was a time in which the idea of "free love" was avidly discussed in *avant-garde* circles in America, and actually put into practice (according to the Lusk committee, at any rate) in such anarchist communities as the Ferrer Colony in New Jersey.[90] It seemed reasonable to suppose, therefore, that the Bolsheviks, who were so often seen by Americans in the image of more familiar kinds of radicalism, also believed that women should be the property of the community. It was not surprising to discover that the Bolsheviks at Saratov on the Volga had issued a decree requiring all women over the age of eighteen to register with a "Bureau of Free Love"; after which they were parceled out among various husbands, an unlimited supply of women to each husband, with the single stipulation, as one paper breathlessly reported, that "men citizens have the right to use one woman not oftener than three times a week for three hours." [91] The instinctive association of such doctrines with anarchism was sound enough; it was an anarchist club in Saratov, according to reliable reports, which had issued the decree, although even the anarchists denied it. (Oliver Sayler, correspondent of the Indianapolis *News*, believed that the Bolsheviks might have posted the decree in order to discredit the anarchists.) [92] A similar decree had been issued in the town of Vladimir, according to some reports. Louise Bryant maintained that the Vladimir decree was nothing more than a practical joke on the part of a comic paper in Moscow, which invented the whole thing.[93] Whatever their source, the reports which presented these acts as Bolshevik policy were obviously fanciful. Nothing could have been less in keeping with the Puritanical spirit of Bolshevik morality than revelry and license.

Anti-Bolshevik papers at first hardly mentioned the terror; only after the end of the war deprived them of the German menace did they discover the Red menace. It is a curious fact, too, that while their accounts of the German penetration of Siberia, of the prisoner-of-war threat, of the impending collapse of the Soviet regime and of the nationalization of women were all largely fictitious, their coverage of the terror—which was intrinsically more fantastic—was surprisingly accurate, as the world now knows to its sorrow. But there was no way in which the rational reader of 1918 might have known this; the press had already been exposed in too many forgeries and falsehoods to be believed about anything concerning Russia, except by those who longed to believe against all the evidence of their senses. And even where the terror was concerned the anti-Bolsheviks overstated their case. Thus the New York papers told on October 31, 1918, how the Bolsheviks had designated November 10 as a day of mass terror, a "St. Bartholomew's eve" on which the bourgeoisie would be slaughtered without mercy; but only one paper (the *World*) called attention to the fact that St. Bartholomew's eve passed without violence—indeed, that the soviet chose that day to declare a general amnesty for all political prisoners. This obvious partisanship discredited the whole story, which in fact was based on reliable evidence.[94]

But the great obstacle to belief, in the case of the stories of the terror, was not so much the unreliable record of the press as the outrageous nature of the stories themselves. They were stories which Americans nurtured in the traditions of nineteenth-century rationalism, brought up to believe in the irresistible moral progress of the human spirit, simply could not bring themselves to believe. What experiences could have prepared Americans for the report from the Crimea, which happened to be true, to which the New York *World* treated its readers on the evening of March 21, 1918?

> The details now to hand of the latest massacres in Simferopol, in the Crimea, and in Sebastopol, are revolting beyond description. In Sebastopol, for instance, the sailors decided to execute a general massacre in the two streets inhabited by the best-to-do people in town.
>
> After the massacre, the bodies were thrown into the Black Sea. The widow of one of the murdered men asked a diver to bring up her husband's body. A few minutes after his immersion the diver hurriedly pulled his signal rope and was drawn to the surface. He was in a state bordering on insanity and for a long time could only mutter one word, "meeting," "meeting." The bodies of the murdered men had been thrown into the sea with stones tied to their feet and there was a throng, standing upright, swaying under water.[95]

The wonder is not that a few men doubted the truth of such reports but that a majority were evidently prepared to accept them without question.

Anti-imperialists never understood the nature of the mounting attack on the Bolsheviks. The propaganda campaign for intervention, the Sisson documents, the stories of violence and terror, all seemed to them to spring from one source: imperialistic fear of Soviet anti-imperialism; or, as the issue was sometimes stated, capitalistic fear of Soviet socialism. During the early period of the revolution Americans tended to emphasize the issues growing immediately out of the war, while after the war their interest shifted to the social and economic aspects of Russian communism; but the underlying issue was the same in either case.

Even Walter Lippmann and Charles Merz seemed to miss the point of their own investigations of the New York *Times*' coverage of Russian events: that a fear of socialism had nothing to do with the distortion of news. They did not, however, go to the other extreme of attributing all expressions of anti-Bolshevik sentiment to "Wall Street." But Evans Clark, an unreconstructed anti-war socialist, concluded flatly after making a study of news distortion: "The class war is neither an aspiration nor a dogma. It is the outstanding fact of today." [96] Upton Sinclair likewise dismissed the anti-Bolshevik stories as "propaganda" distributed by "our Wall Street newspapers and magazines." [97] The Socialist Labor party denounced the "vicious campaign of slander and vituperation carried on by the capitalist plunder bund against Soviet Russia." [98] It became fashionable among liberal theorists to explain the entire campaign for intervention as a manifestation of the economic tie between Allied capitalists and the old regime in Russia. Thus antipathy to the Bolsheviks could be traced (in the last analysis) to the international bankers—to those dark and sinister capitalistic conspiracies with which American radicals had been themselves embattled for years.[99] The same people who were fighting progress at home were fighting it in Russia. Intervention was "class war."

In vain did men like Arthur Bullard attempt to persuade their friends that the matter was more complicated than that. Bullard, complaining about Norman Hapgood's use of the "class-war" concept, found it "amusing that an old Socialist, like myself, should be arguing with you against this explanation of events in Russia." But the war, he said, had destroyed his ability "to see things happen as my theories had led me to expect." Reminding Hapgood that he had witnessed the events in question at first hand, he continued:

> In those first days of the Bolshevist regime, we were all dominated by the militaristic interpretation of history. I never chanced to hear a single one of the Allied officials curse out the Bolsheviki because of fear of the economic effects of their victory. The cursing—and there was a great deal of it—was based on fear of the military result.
>
> The economic motive, the class interest—Mr. Norman Angell's theories of war—do not, as far as I can see, work when blood is hot.

To this letter Bullard appended a note: "Not sent. Later articles of his seemed to make appeal to good faith impossible." [100]

The anti-imperialists, as good nineteenth-century liberals, believed that men act reasonably and intelligibly; they were no more able to understand what Bullard called the "militaristic interpretation of history" than Marx had understood nationalism. They assumed that the capitalist-imperialists who secretly controlled Allied policy wished to crush Bolshevism because it threatened their own privileges and prerogatives. They were sure that these same imperialists plotted to make peace with Germany in order to present a unified front to the challenge of Russian socialism. But in fact even out-and-out interventionists, as we have seen, were committed to the policy of "standing by" Russia. Class interest may have dictated the desertion of proletarian Russia in favor of peace with the German capitalists, as Lord Lansdowne advised. But the international bankers and the munitions-makers protested as vigorously as anyone else against the abandonment of Russia. They joined the liberals in demanding that Russia be saved from the menace of German militarism; saved for the West; saved (even if she had to be saved in spite of herself) for democracy.

V

The Bolsheviks as Anarchists

THE Bolsheviks, as we have seen, were consistently characterized in America as idealistic to the point of fanaticism; as doctrinaire, impractical, irresponsible, naïve. They were almost never spoken of, as we would speak of them, as forceful, ruthless, and imperious, fanatical only in their willingness to apply on a grand scale the philosophy that the end justifies the means. Their ends themselves, that is, their social and economic program, received very little attention in the United States. It was not as communists that they were approved of or despised, except as communism was regarded as a rather naïve and utopian, although otherwise unexceptional, program for the economic advancement of humanity. Their hostility to private enterprise was noted with disapproval, but it hardly constituted the burden of the complaint against them. Their alleged pacifism was far more objectionable.

The persistence of these attitudes toward the new masters of Russia explains why the controversy over how Russia might be restored to order went on for so long before it occurred to anyone that the Bolsheviks themselves might restore order—order more rigorous and more harshly enforced than anything Americans dreamed of. In the initial phase of the dispute over the revolution, both the Bolsheviks' sympathizers and their detractors assumed that the Bolsheviks alone would never be able to reestablish "normal" conditions in Russia. The anti-Bolsheviks looked for the eventual solution of the problem to a military dictator, while those who still continued to believe in "the revolution" hoped for the emergence of a coalition of the Left.

If the discussion of the early phases of the Bolshevik revolution seems to us to have about it an air of unreality, it may have been because Americans in the early twentieth century found it difficult to conceive of order and revolution except as opposites. That a revolutionary regime could exercise a high degree of central control was a notion for which recent history appeared to furnish no precedent. The French revolution still dominated political thought, and that event seemed to prove, if it proved anything, that order and revolution were irreconcilable. For conservatives it demonstrated in an unforgettable way what could happen when men's natural instincts were no longer held in check by authority—by church, state and tradition. Liberals likewise thought of the revolution as having freed the natural man from the bondage of artificial social restraints. Whether one preferred order or liberty, whether one was for the revolution or against it, depended on one's estimate of man's capacity for rational behavior. What concerns us here is that liberals and conservatives agreed that one could not have both order and liberty at the same time.

Wherever liberty appeared, throughout the nineteenth century, it appeared as the destroyer of order, the enemy of law; it dedicated itself to tearing down old institutions, to breaking the chains that bound the human spirit; and its utopia was not the perfect man-made state but the state of nature. Anarchism was implicit even in so mild a form of libertarianism as Jeffersonian democracy, whose prophet, after all, had proposed that one generation should not be allowed to bind the next. It was not so long a step from that to bomb-throwing. But it was a long step from the fear of the state as such, on the theory that all states in the nature of things, regardless of their original intentions, become oppressive, to the fear of the state only when it is controlled by a particular social class. For the Bolsheviks only the bourgeois state was oppressive. The workers' state by definition could not become an instrument of tyranny; therefore it could govern with an iron hand without fear of abusing its power. To be sure, even the workers' state was destined to wither away, and to the extent to which they conceived of the good society as a stateless society, the Bolsheviks revealed their eighteenth-century Western roots. But the fear of the state was at no time a very active ingredient in communist theory.* Engels, when confronted with Bakunin's theory of the state, expressed great amazement.

> Bakunin has a peculiar theory [he wrote]. The chief point is that he does not regard capital . . . as the main evil to be abolished. Instead, he thinks it is above all the State which must be done away with, and then capitalism will go to hell of itself. We, on the contrary, say: Do away with capital, the appropriation of the whole means of production in the hands of the few, and the State will fall away of itself. The difference is an essential one.[1]

It was a characteristic of the state established in Russia in November, 1917, that although its rigor was fully implied in Marx's doctrine of the dictatorship of the proletariat, this rigor had to be seen in action to be believed. Although Bolshevism, both in practice and in theory, is the very negation of everything anarchism stands for, Western anarchists themselves welcomed the Bolshevik revolution as the triumph of man over the state. Until one had seen at first hand the kind of control which this proletarian state intended to wield, it was difficult to overcome the initial impression that the Bolsheviks, like all radicals since Robespierre, were at bottom opposed to "order." References on the part of opponents of Bolshevism to Bolshevik "tyranny" should not mislead us. The anti-Bolsheviks were referring to the

* There are those who would deny that it was ever an ingredient at all. It is curious, however, and a fact worth noting, that every variety of nineteenth-century liberalism or radicalism looked upon the state as an engine of oppression, if only of a particular class, and conceived of Utopia as anarchy.

tyranny of "the mob." Like Burke and Tocqueville, they were troubled not by too little liberty but by too much.

Robert Lansing's hostility to Bolshevism is a case in point. Wilson's Secretary of State was convinced from the beginning that the Bolsheviks were "idealists" and "anarchists." [2] As early as February, 1918, he compared Bolshevism with Kaiserism and concluded that the latter was the lesser menace, representing at least an "intelligent despotism," while Bolshevism was a "despotism of ignorance," that is, of the mob. "One, at least has the virtue of order, while the other is productive of disorder and anarchy." [3] Nine months later Lansing wrote that Bolshevism was "the worst form of anarchism," [4] and a year after that he attacked communist economic theory on the grounds that it encouraged the ignorant to covet the rewards of enlightenment and virtue. "Because wealth unavoidably gravitates toward men who are intellectually superior and more ready to grasp opportunities than their fellows is that a reason for taking it away from them or for forcing them to divide with the improvident, the mentally inferior and the indolent?" [5] His premise that wealth gravitates to intelligence aside, Lansing's remark reveals a profound but very common misunderstanding of what was going on in Russia or, more broadly, of the nature of the Soviet threat to democracy. He was still attacking communism, as one hears schoolboys attack it today, as the rule of the rabble, as "ignorance" leading to anarchy.

It is no wonder that the men who attacked Bolshevism on these grounds soon found themselves looking with suspicion even upon efforts to extend democracy itself. Thus Lansing, in the same passage, goes on to deplore what he regards as President Wilson's indifference to the alarming spread of "communistic ideas" in the United States. Wilson, he says, erroneously believed that communism could be fought by removing the economic discontent from which it sprang. Lansing, however, by this time preferred repression to reform. Reform itself now seemed to him subversive, for it tended to destroy private property by denying its "exclusive use"; and "exclusive use," he thought, "is the fundamental idea of ownership."[6] The reformers, he thought, would encourage labor to throw off its chains only to find that labor, once free, would turn to Bolshevism. Lansing's analysis led naturally enough to the conclusion that it was safer in the long run to keep the chains securely in place.

Charles R. Crane tended toward the same position. After his return from Russia at the end of 1917, Crane wrote: "I feel that this year I have discovered two entirely new countries—Russia in revolution and America in evolution—and they are both overwhelming." That observation seemed to indicate a certain detachment; one might have expected it to lead to a consideration of why it was that progress in the two countries had to be achieved by such different means. But it led Crane only to the same threadbare conclusion to which it had led the Secretary of State: "I believe that the object lesson will be sufficiently convincing to the world for a long time of the futility of revolution as a means of progressing and the fearful disaster that may overtake a state and all of its citizens if it does not progress in orderly fashion."[7] In the light of that conclusion it was natural enough for Crane to become, much later, an apologist for Nazi Germany as the bulwark against "Jewish" communism.* "Order" was preferable to "anarchy."

* In 1933 he advised President Roosevelt on no account to "be drawn into any critical attitude toward Germany. She is the healthiest state of any country in Europe going along quietly minding her own business menacing no one the one power sincerely in favor of your disarmament policy. She is also the one Christian nation brave enough to make an uncompromising front against the flood of destructive influences and people coming out of Russia or in sympathy with them. She is the real political bulwark of Christian culture." Telegram, Crane to Roosevelt, Sept. 10, 1933, Edward M. House MSS, Yale University Library. In exactly the same language, twenty years before, people like Crane had spoken of "Holy Russia" as the bulwark against German "frightfulness." See also Crane to New York *Times*, letter dated May 19, 1933, in House MSS.

When those who, for whatever reason, repudiated Bolshevism seemed almost inevitably impelled to repudiate democracy as well, anti-imperialists found it all the more easy to believe that the Bolsheviks, in view of the kind of opposition they encountered, must in fact be fighting the good fight for liberty, equality and international brotherhood. They knew, of course, that the Bolsheviks were not democrats in an old-fashioned Jeffersonian sense. Their economic program was confiscatory, their rhetoric violently anti-capitalist. Was this democracy? "Not political democracy, as with us," anti-imperialists answered in the words of Lincoln Steffens; "economic democracy is the idea; democracy in the shop, factory, business." [8] For political democracy alone, the anti-imperialists themselves had little use; if the Bolshevik regime was not a mere political democracy, so much the better. "The great charge is that it is undemocratic," Walter Weyl mused. "From President Wilson down, down to John Spargo this is the charge." But those who made it, he reminded himself, referred only to "a political democracy"—"a democracy with as many holes in it as a Swiss cheese, but in which the holes are of the essence of the cheese." [9] Even some of the war liberals made the same point. Charles Edward Russell wrote: "[T]hese wise men that have so liberally condemned Russia to a state of hopeless ignorance have not themselves progressed a foot outside of the Jeffersonian realm of thought; to this day they can see nothing but political democracy." [10]

But if anti-imperialists were not content with "political democracy" alone, neither did they wish to abandon it; nor did they see any need of abandoning it. They conceived of "economic democracy" as merely an extension of "political democracy"—political democracy brought up to date, to cope with the realities of the machine age. That one should be achieved at the expense of the other was as inconceivable to them as it was obvious to the Bolsheviks (or for that matter to conservatives like Lansing). The Bolsheviks assumed that political democracy in the West had been achieved only by grinding down the worker; in their eyes democracy was as much a form of exploitation as feudalism. But to American anti-imperialists, economic equality and political liberty were inseparable. The whole progressive movement seemed to rest on that assumption. For if conservatives were right in maintaining that efforts to improve the condition of the worker undermined free institutions, then the progressive program of social reform would indeed have to be abandoned. Either that, or, as some anti-imperialists gradually began to suspect, "political democracy" would have to go by the board. As Walter Weyl put the question in August, 1919: "*Is our democratic Government adaptable & can it be made adaptable* (and unhindering) to a real Industrial Democratization such as the peoples want[?]" "*The ultimate Test,*" Weyl decided, "*is Survival.*" [11] But not many anti-imperialists had yet reached this point in their speculations.

They were not so simple as to suppose that Western parliamentary democracy could be transplanted in Russia as it was. They saw that parliamentary institutions were products of historical conditions peculiar to the West. The politics of consensus and compromise were not necessarily portable; as Harold Stearns wrote, "In a country [Russia] where the middle class are so numerically few as to make a compromise republic—as we know it in France, England, and America—impossible, no solution *is* possible but an extreme solution." [12] Or as Walter Weyl observed, in a mood more optimistic than the one in which he gave way to the reflections just quoted:

> We have no Czar, we have no large standing army to shoot us down, & other differences. . . . We shall develop, as we are at this moment, only we shall develop more rapidly in the future, by the unfolding power of the wage-earning class. We do not here need or want—as I see it at the present—a dictatorship of the proletariat.[13]

But the case of Russia was different.

Nevertheless anti-imperialists expected democracy eventually to take root in Russia—but in strange new forms. Unlike conservatives, they did not equate democracy narrowly with parliamentary institutions, many of which—the judiciary, for example—they were themselves attempting to reform. They did not regard the "rule of law" as indispensable to, or even compatible with, political freedom. They had no great faith in the structure of American political parties, or even in a two-party system as such. Many of them advocated some form of direct democracy, at once more primitive and more sophisticated than the prevailing system. They did not find it difficult to imagine, therefore, that the Russians, in their experiments with economic democracy, might discover promising new forms of political democracy as well. Indeed they believed that one of these forms was taking shape before their eyes: the soviet.

That institution inspired a vast amount of lyrical prose among friends of the revolution. "No political body more sensitive and responsive to the popular will was ever invented," exclaimed John Reed.[14] Arthur Ransome thought that it surpassed any other system in allowing centralization of authority without weakening local autonomy.[15] Evans Clark found the soviet, "unified, responsible, controlled by the masses at every point," far superior to the "congealed" institutions of American democracy, which were "frankly designed to check and to balance the popular will" rather than to give expression to it.[16] It was because they regarded the soviet as a sensitive instrument of popular government that American liberals were able to distinguish between the Bolsheviks and the soviets: when the Bolsheviks no longer expressed the will of the people, as reflected in the soviets, the soviets would turn them out.[17] "If the Bolsheviki are in power," wrote an admirer of the soviets, "it is . . . because the Soviets have accepted their program."[18] The fact that the Bolsheviks did not at first control the soviets encouraged people to think that they would not always control them in the future.

Much of the confusion regarding the soviets could be traced to the erroneous belief that they were indigenous institutions rooted in the Russian past. There was a widespread impression that they grew out of the *mir,* about which Westerners had entertained such romantic notions before the war. "[T]he Soviet is the natural form of government in Russia," wrote Frederic C. Howe, doubtless on the advice of Raymond Robins. "It is merely making constitutional the old community Mir." [19] Louis Edgar Browne of the Chicago *Daily News,* another disciple of Robins, did much to encourage this impression. The Soviet government was stable, he explained again and again, because it rested on the native, Slavic democracy of the *mir,* whereas Russian liberalism was weak because it tried to import Western institutions which could not flourish in Slavic soil.[20] Edward A. Ross also leaned to this view.[21] Even Albert Rhys Williams, who as a semiofficial propagandist of the Soviet government might have been expected to know more about its origins, declared that the soviet was "the outgrowth of . . . the Mir." [22]

The existence of the soviets was not necessarily an argument for active support of the Bolsheviks, but it was always an argument for keeping faith with "the revolution" in general, in the hope that the revolution would still produce a Russian democracy. Papers like the New York *Evening Post,* the Springfield *Republican* and the Des Moines *Register,* which could not bring themselves to advocate recognition of the Bolsheviks, nevertheless argued against Allied intervention on the grounds that it might be construed as an attack on the soviet form of government. Another paper, pointing out that "soviets existed long before the Bolsheviki and grew out of the old democratic communal councils of the Russian villages," hopefully concluded: "The soviet could just as well be the cornerstone of a representative democratic government as of the Bolshevist government. . . . The hope of all sincere democrats is that the soviets will see the folly of proletarian dictatorship and return to their original character as democratic institutions."[23] Edward A. Ross likewise advised the Allies to hesitate before proceeding against the soviets; if they were to come under the control of the Social Revolutionaries, he thought, "a very helpful democratic experiment might be worked out."[24]

The belief that the soviets might become the nucleus of an indigenous democracy, as opposed to a "democracy" imposed on Russia by the Allies, held out a last hope to men who could not admit to themselves that the revolution had failed. It was, however, an illusory hope. The soviets had no relation at all to the *mir*, and no roots in Russian history. They first appeared in 1905, as revolutionary organizations of workers (not peasants); they reappeared in March, 1917. They were the products of the revolution, not of Russian tradition. They were no more native to Russia than Marxism. They were the equivalents, not of the *mir*, still less of the New England town meeting, but of the Jacobin clubs or of the Paris commune, and their role was essentially negative and destructive—particularly after the February revolution, when their reason for being was simply to prevent the Provisional Government from functioning. They succeeded not because they commanded overwhelming popular support, but because the Provisional Government was too demoralized to exercise the powers which belonged to it. Once they had fulfilled the purpose for which they were called into being, the soviets had no particular reason for continuing to exist, and as early as 1918, far from being a portent of the future, they had already become obsolete. Almost as soon as the Bolsheviks seized power, effective authority gravitated to the central committee of the Bolshevik party, and the soviets were relegated to the passive role of merely approving decisions already made by the central committee.

Nor were the soviets at any time democratic, except perhaps in their internal organization, decisions being arrived at, as a rule, by majority vote. But they by no means represented the majority of the people. In the nature of things they represented a disciplined, determined minority. But to Western democrats the spectacle of the workers and soldiers of Petrograd deliberating grave questions of state was an inspiring example of grass-roots democracy in action.

Not only the outward appearance but the internal organization of the soviet system led Americans into mistaking it for a novel form of democracy. The idea prevailed that the soviet provided a new kind of representation—by occupation instead of by locality. "Our democracy is based on representation by areas," explained Ross. "The Bolshevik is suspicious of this amorphous structure . . . No, let the people group themselves by occupation when they choose their representative, and then he will really stand for something." [25] Admirers of the soviets dwelt on the obvious advantages of such a system. American legislative bodies, they pointed out, were not representative at all; lawyers, for instance, were greatly over-represented in Congress, while carpenters were not represented at all. Only in Russia were the trades and professions represented in proportion to their numbers. As a reader of the *Public* exclaimed: "The more I think it over the more it seems to me the Russian Soviet system is the only really representative one. Our Anglo-Saxon system of representation by localities certainly does result in most classes of the community not being represented at all, and is therefore subversive of true democracy." [26]

Since the soviets did indeed contain large numbers of workers and peasants, and very few lawyers, it is not difficult to see why anti-imperialists got the impression that representatives to the soviet were elected according to occupation. What is curious is why they should have considered such a system so vastly superior to their own. Their enthusiasm for the soviet system—or for what they imagined the soviet system to be—reflected their enthusiasm for an "economic democracy" of the plain people and their scorn of a merely "political" democracy, operated by lawyers. But as we have seen, they did not really believe that political liberty and economic equality were incompatible, although they sometimes talked as if they did. In the end they were not content to defend the government of the soviets as an experiment in "economic democracy" alone. On the contrary, they felt obliged to deal as well with the criticisms levelled against the soviets' disregard of political liberty.

This willingness to engage in an argument which from a more radical point of view—that of the Bolsheviks themselves, for instance—was altogether irrelevant was what distinguished liberal sympathizers with the revolution, like Raymond Robins or Herbert Croly or Oswald Garrison Villard, from out-and-out Bolsheviks like John Reed. It also distinguished one generation of American liberals from another: it was the older liberals, as a rule, who tried to reconcile Bolshevism with political liberty, while the younger ones appeared indifferent to the problem, or addressed themselves to it as if to some disagreeable chore, to satisfy their elders. Those who could not free themselves from liberal doubts envied the confidence and certainty of the young rebels, which they could not share. William Bullitt confessed to Colonel House, "I wish I could see Russia with as single an eye as Reed. I am unable to win through the welter of conflicting reports about the Bolshiviki [*sic*] to anything like solid conviction." At the same time he urged plaintively, "[W]e must get away from our present indecision." [27]

The radicals, for their part, could not conceal their contempt for the liberals' timidity. Bessie Beatty did not even attempt to explain to them how the Bolsheviks could be considered democratic when they disfranchised all holders of property, suppressed the freedom of the press and dispersed the Constituent Assembly. Liberals, she intimated, would never understand these mysteries; their "social vision stops with the guaranty of political rights, of free speech, free press and inviolability of the person." [28] Freda Kirchwey of the *Nation* was more charitable;

she conceded that liberals sometimes performed a useful function by getting a hearing for radical ideas. "A young comrade on the East Side demands the recall of troops from Russia, and is sent to jail for five years; Senator Johnson says the same thing, louder,—and lands on the front page of the New York Times. The moral is easy. Liberalism should be cherished." [29]

In spite of the derision with which radicals greeted their efforts, anti-imperialists persisted in trying to reconcile sovietism with political liberty. It was fitting that Villard's *Nation* should have played a leading role in this effort. Villard was the prototype of the older liberal, reared in a nineteenth-century tradition of laissez-faire, who struggled manfully to keep abreast of the increasing radicalism of his friends. He never quite succeeded —he admitted in 1929 that he was "still a Wilson Democrat on all domestic issues"—and he felt it necessary to apologize for his failure to become a real radical.[30] Thus he wrote wistfully to Hutchins Hapgood in 1919:

> I do not see how anyone could have stood still during the last four years who thinks at all. One must have either moved to the left or to the right and I have gone to the left; not so far as you, I fancy. I cannot embrace either the Socialist or the Communist doctrine, but I do feel . . . one must henceforth be either for or against the present political order. I do not wish my children to live in a world managed politically as the present world has been during the last five years. I realize fully the danger of my position as far as *The Nation* is concerned. It is that I shall fall between the two stools through unwillingness to go to the extreme left, but that I cannot help. Perhaps I am too well off and too happily situated in life—perhaps I haven't been close enough to the working people.

He added, in explanation of his failure to embrace socialism or communism: "Seeing the Soviet in Bavaria at work and watching the development of Lenin and Trotsky have not encouraged me. The reformers all turn to the same bad policies of those they eject." [31]

The *Nation*, until Villard acquired control of it in July, 1918, was an organ of ultra-respectable classical liberalism. Hapgood, who worked briefly for Villard in 1909, found the atmosphere in the *Nation* offices stifling and "old-maidish." [32] As the weekly edition of the *Evening Post*, the *Nation* reflected the views not so much of Villard, who owned both papers, as of Rollo Ogden, their chief editor, for the *Post* cherished a tradition of rigid separation of ownership and editorial policy.[33] Ogden was a disciple of E. L. Godkin, whose views he reproduced faithfully throughout his life. Until 1917, these were also the views of the owner. Toward the end of that year, however, Ogden's pacifism, which at first drew him close to Villard, grew more and more faint, until it finally dropped out of earshot altogether. His enthusiasm for the Russian revolution also waned, little by little; by September, 1918, the *Evening Post* was urging active support of the enemies of the Bolsheviks.[34] By that time Villard, saddened by what he regarded as the paper's decline, had sold the *Evening Post* to Thomas W. Lamont and had set about to convert the *Nation*, control of which he retained, into a radical weekly.[35]

The degree to which radicalism had become bound up with approval of the revolution was evident at once in the absorption of the new *Nation* in Russian affairs. Villard makes it clear in his memoirs that his *Nation* came into being in order to fight for a just peace and for "the freedom of the Russian people to control their own affairs"; and it may be added that in Villard's mind the two questions were inseparable.[36] The *Nation's* regular supplement of documents on international affairs gave great prominence to translations of Soviet documents—the decree on land, the Declaration of the Rights of Laboring and Exploited People, the Soviet Constitution of 1918. An able staff tracked down and remorselessly exposed evidence designed to discredit the policy of intervention; for example, a letter from Arthur Bullard to Colonel House which sharply criticized support of Kolchak's "experiment in reaction." "It was a terrible blow to the government to have [Bullard's letter] come out," Villard later gloated, for Bullard was a prominent official of the Committee on Public Information.[37] The *Nation* also made public the story of the Bullitt mission to Russia, well in advance of Bullitt's own disclosures before the Senate in September, 1919.[38] It published articles on Russia by Evans Clark, Villard, and Lincoln Colcord, who joined the staff in April, 1919. Editorially it hammered away, week after week, at the futility of the administration's policy in Russia. Meanwhile the *Nation's* circulation rose from about 7,000 in the summer of 1918, to 35,000 in the spring of 1919, "a spontaneous response," according to Villard, "to the liberal ideas we are preaching." [39] The *Nation* soon became "an absolute necessity," as H. L. Mencken put it, "to any man who desired to find out what was actually going on in Russia." [40] Albert Jay Nock thought that its success was "the first hopeful prospect" he had seen in years.[41]

The publication of the Soviet Constitution, on January 4, 1919, was the *Nation's* chief contribution to the anti-imperialist thesis that Russia had not sacrificed liberty in its quest for equality. The Constitution could be cited as documentary proof by those who argued that the Soviet system was the most responsible form of representation yet devised, "a pyramid of responsibility," as Evans Clark called it. As the Constitution showed, or seemed to show, the people elected the local soviets, the local soviets elected the provincial soviets, and the provincial soviets elected the All-Russian Congress of Soviets. What could be more logical or more democratic? Moreover the suffrage was remarkably broad: everyone over eighteen, regardless even of residence, could vote. Property-owners, to be sure, were excluded from the franchise, but Clark, for one, maintained that their exclusion worked no real hardship, since there were very few property-holders left to suffer from this restriction. "[E]ach month," he pointed out, "sees fewer and fewer in the property-owning class. The property-owners become workers and entitled to the franchise." [42] Others were not so enthusiastic about this particular feature of the Constitution. But even so cautious a paper as the Des Moines *Register* permitted itself to draw some comfort from an examination of the Constitution. The *Register* instructed a reader that the "obvious possibilities" of the Soviet system "as a representative governmental form" explained "why a good many people draw a distinction between the soviet government and bolshevik domination of it, saying that they are for the soviets but against the bolsheviki." [43] Previously the *Register* had had little use for this distinction.

Others found the Constitution puzzling and vaguely disturbing. "It represents, I understand, an intention rather than a fulfillment," wrote Walter Weyl. Nevertheless he was impressed with the symmetry of the system. "It is not an anarchic society," he declared in some surprise. Nor was it, on the other hand, despotic. "After all, whoever has actual control at present, the Constitution and the laws are intended for the benefit of the immense majority of the population. The abrogation of property rights is a transfer from the few to the many; the abolition of inheritance is the same." [44] A reading of the constitution brought to a head Weyl's determination to undertake a study of the soviets, a project which he had been considering for some time. An entry in his diary for July 29, 1919, shows, however, that he had not yet come to any very optimistic conclusions. He admitted that the soviet was "flatly opposed to our ordinary conceptions of Democracy." Yet it gained "millions of supporters." What did its success signify?

> Is it criticism of democracy as such, or of democracy as it has hitherto developed, or of formal democracy?
>
> Moreover, is it permanent? And if it is permanent, will it or can it, become more democratic in form and essence?
>
> And if it is not permanent, are there elements in it that will be permanent? Are there elements in it that are suitable for a non-proletarian government? [45]

Not even the editors of the *Nation* were ever able conclusively to answer these questions. As they became increasingly uncertain as to whether democracy would still flourish in Russia they attempted more and more to divert attention from the question by attacking American policy. But to prove that everything wrong with Russia could be blamed on America and the Allies did not, finally, conceal the fact that something was wrong with Russia. Nor was it much comfort merely to show that America was no nearer perfection than Russia, as when Evans Clark cited Charles A. Beard's studies to show that the Constitution of 1787, like the Constitution of 1918, was a class document.[46] The inevitability of class government was not, after all, what anti-imperialists had set out to prove. All their plans depended on the eventual disappearance of class conflict, in Russia as in America. Were their plans founded on an illusion?

Failing to resolve these difficulties, the *Nation,* like so many anti-imperialist organs of the period, early became merely irritable and quarrelsome, even a little tedious. Albert Jay Nock left the magazine in 1920 to start the *Freeman.* When the *Nation* in its columns welcomed the new magazine to the ranks of liberal journalism, Nock wrote to Villard: "I hate to seem ungrateful, but we *haint* liberal. We loathes liberalism and loathes it hard." "You make your appeal to Liberals," he said, "we make ours to Radicals." [47]

If the "radicals" found themselves increasingly impatient with the evasions and compromises of anti-imperialists, it was because they did not share the need to justify the soviet regime as a form of democracy. On this point they agreed with the most intransigent conservatives. Radicals and conservatives alike ridiculed the distinction between soviets and Bolsheviks, so dear to the liberals. John Reed declared in November, 1918, that to pretend to be in favor of the soviets but against the Bolsheviks was "an absurdity." The soviets were "the weapons of proletarian dictatorship, to which all anti-Bolshevik parties are bitterly opposed." [48] The ultra-interventionist correspondent of the New York *Times*, Harold Williams, heartily agreed that "the Soviets are distinctively Bolshevik institutions"—instruments of class tyranny. It was not dictatorship as such that he objected to, however, but a dictatorship of the proletariat. To Samuel Harper, Williams confided: "I think the first stage [in Russia's reconstruction] must be a wise military dictatorship." To hold elections "in the present state of the popular mind," he said, was simply to encourage "adventurers, of whom there are so terribly many." Russia was bound in the long run to emerge from its ordeal a democratic republic, "but it has not yet finished its education for democracy." [49]

Anti-Bolsheviks pointed to the dissolution of the Constituent Assembly, January 19, 1918, as a shining instance of Bolshevik contempt for democracy. If any body could ever have been considered representative, they contended, it was the assembly elected in November, 1918, under the only free elections ever conducted in modern Russia. Yet because they could not control it, the Bolsheviks were forced to dissolve it at gun's point. To this argument anti-imperialists were never able to make a very convincing reply. Radicals, on the other hand, did not feel it necessary to reply at all. They simply dismissed the Constituent Assembly as a "bourgeois" institution, taking their stand on Lenin's dictum that "when a revolutionary class is struggling against the propertied classes which offer resistance, that resistance has to be suppressed." [50] Albert Rhys Williams, addressing the Third All-Russian Congress of Soviets, which met four days after the dissolution of the Constituent Assembly, predicted that "this sort of parliamentarianism will also be adopted by us when the American proletariat makes up its mind to undertake a revolutionary struggle and to rise against its own bourgeoisie." [51] But the radicals were not alone in endorsing the Bolsheviks' high-handed and contemptuous action. At least one conservative paper, the Baltimore *Sun*, found the dissolution of the assembly a "rather refreshing . . . sign of masterfulness among the Russian mob of dreamers and debaters." The Bolsheviks, the *Sun* noted with approval, seemed "to possess the only iron hand left in Russia." [52]

Radicals and conservatives generally arrived at their distrust of democratic processes by different roads, of course. Radicals hated democracy because it was never "democratic" enough, conservatives because it had gone too far as it was. But some of the literary radicals were moved to radicalism in the first place by a deeply conservative impulse. The radicalism of H. L. Mencken, for instance, was really indistinguishable from the extreme conservatism of the Baltimore *Sun*, for which he wrote for so many years. Radicals like John Reed scoffed at the democratic process but loved "the people." Radicals like Mencken and Albert Jay Nock, on the other hand, made a point of despising the people. Mencken, in particular, professed to regard popular government as the worst possible form of tyranny. Nor did he and Nock draw distinctions, in respect to human folly, between the bourgeoisie and the proletariat. But insofar as the things they particularly disliked about the "booboisie" were associated with the rule of the middle class—and in America, where pretentiousness, prudery, and hypocrisy seemed to derive from the ascendancy of bourgeois respectability, the association was inevitable—these iconoclasts were drawn to the Bolsheviks as to any enemies of respectability. The fury of the propaganda campaign against them convinced Mencken that the Bolsheviks could not, at any rate, be more villainous than their detractors. The American press, with "its imbecile Sisson documents, its daily reports of the fall at St. Petersburg and its vast mass of palpable lies about the murder of Gorki, the socialization of women and the burning down of whole towns," first "irritated" and then "disgusted" him.[53] But it was not long before the Bolsheviks began to disgust him too. By the mid-twenties Nock and Mencken were bored with the revolution; the government of the proletariat, it appeared, was no more enlightened than that of the middle class. A friend tried without success to persuade Nock to visit Russia. "[A]ny one who knew the course of our republic's political history," he explained, "and knew the incidence of the laws which turned us into that course [statism] and kept us to it, had no need to go to Russia to see the same laws in operation there." [54]

Most of the anti-imperialists could not take even momentary refuge in the cynicism of Mencken and Nock. Committed to a belief in the ultimate triumph of the democratic principle, they could hardly rejoice in the Bolsheviks' repeated attacks on democracy, nor could they continue indefinitely to ignore them. Eventually they were forced to abandon even the distinction between the Bolsheviks and the soviets, which had stood them in such good stead. Thereafter they had either to look elsewhere for the nucleus around which to build Russian democracy or to look to the Bolsheviks themselves as saviors, in the hope that time would somehow contrive to make them more mellow.

Most friends of the revolution eventually chose the latter alternative. A few, however, managed for a time to convince themselves that the hope of the future rested with the Russian peasant cooperatives, which came to occupy the place in anti-imperialist thought once occupied by the soviets. The cooperatives too were regarded as a manifestation of grass-roots democracy. Nor was this optimism entirely without basis. The cooperatives claimed millions of members, mostly peasants; they owned, especially in Siberia, much of the land. They had some roots in Russian history, going back at least to the time of the emancipation of the serfs. As economic rather than political institutions they were free, moreover, from the bitter ideological wrangling which had so far characterized the history of the revolution; they were dominated by "practical" men. Americans who could no longer go along with the Bolsheviks but who were convinced that a return to reaction would be equally disastrous for Russia naturally looked to the cooperatives as "the foundation stone," as Arthur Bullard put it, "on which the regeneration of Russia must be built." [55]

The most persistent advocate of the cooperatives in America was Norman Hapgood, former editor of *Harper's Weekly*, now a sort of errand boy for Colonel House. Because he had been one of Wilson's first supporters in 1912, Hapgood, like Charles R. Crane, still commanded Wilson's respect, although he leaned to an anti-imperialist position with regard to the war.[56] With the help of Crane and Colonel House, Hapgood, in March, 1919, secured an appointment as minister to Denmark, from which vantage point he reported regularly to Wilson and House on the progress of the cooperative movement in Russia.[57] Hapgood had by this time decided that it was impossible to deal with the Bolsheviks.[58] On the other hand, he thought that to support Kolchak would merely drive all Russians into the arms of the Bolsheviks as a lesser evil. "There is only one institution in Russia that is a home growth," he told Wilson, "very large, and in active operation through the whole revolution; that is the United Cooperative Associations." [59] The Bolsheviks did not dare to attack the cooperatives, he said, because they knew that without them economic life would break down.[60] The Bolsheviks disapproved of them, however, as moderate, bourgeois institutions, and for that reason Hapgood was sure that the cooperatives could be counted on, in return, to oppose the Bolsheviks.[61] They could also be used, he thought, as agencies through which Allied economic aid to Russia might be administered, thus solving the chief problem associated with any program of aid.[62]

Wilson thanked Hapgood for his "very serviceable" letters and assured him that he would "try to keep in mind the whole aspect of the matter as you present it." [63] But nothing came of Hapgood's efforts. His appointment to Denmark was temporary in any case, since the Senate refused to confirm it. He returned to America greatly discouraged about Russia. But for a long time he remained convinced that the cooperatives offered the only hope of a democratic Russia.[64]

Many others at one time or another took up the cause of the cooperatives. Lewis Gannett argued for them in the *Survey*.[65] Both the *Nation* and the New York *Evening Post* favored sending economic aid to Russia through the cooperatives.[66] But even their admirers had to admit, with Arthur Bullard, that the cooperatives, like everything else, had been "sadly disorganized by the whirlwind of revolution." [67]

The last resort of the friends of the revolution was, inevitably, the Bolsheviks themselves. There seemed at last no question that the government of the Bolsheviks gave more promise of stability, or at least of permanence, than any of its competitors. No doubt the anti-imperialists, in their desire to get the Allies out of Russia, exaggerated its stability. Perhaps they also exaggerated the extent to which intervention, by rallying the Russian people to the Bolshevik government as the most effective resistance to foreign interference, had contributed to its stability. The fact remained, however, that the Bolsheviks not only beat off every threat to their power, but succeeded, moreover, in gaining new recruits from the non-Bolshevik parties of the Left. In theory it was still true that a dictatorship of the proletariat could never be imposed on a country of peasants, and that communism would not work in practice.[68] But history refused to listen to logic. A peasant republic, which Americans were told was the only kind of government which could survive in Russia, refused to materialize. The armies of Kolchak and Denikin retired in confusion. Bolshevism not only survived but showed signs of spreading to other countries. By the end of 1919, even some conservatives were beginning to concede that the Russian future, for better or worse, belonged to the party of Lenin and Trotsky.

In this very fact, however, there appeared to be a grain of hope. Was it unreasonable to expect that power might breed in the men who exercised it a sense of responsibility? Was it not barely possible that the test of practice would, not destroy perhaps, but modify the Bolshevik regime? The entrance into the government of the Mensheviks and the Left S-R's seemed a hopeful sign; surely these more moderate elements would influence the Bolsheviks as much as the Bolsheviks could influence them. The campaign against the anarchists, in the spring and summer of 1918, was another "edifying spectacle," as one paper described it (even though it accounted for the worst excesses of the terror), which strengthened the belief that "responsibility is apt to temper radicalism." [69] By the summer of 1918, some papers were convinced that the Bolsheviks were ready to abandon their "extreme socialistic notions" and "to entertain the idea of rational compromise." [70] The *New Republic* likewise believed that any government faced with the stark problem of putting a broken economy back together again would eventually have to "succumb insensibly to the custom of compromise." [71]

It was not until the winter of 1919 that anti-imperialists gained what they regarded as conclusive proof that their hopes were in the process of fulfillment. Proof came in the form of an interview with Lenin published by Robert Minor, a former cartoonist of the New York *World* and St. Louis *Post-Dispatch* and a dedicated anarchist. Minor, like so many anarchists, had welcomed the Bolshevik revolution as the triumph of man over the state, and set out for Russia in the spring of 1918 with the highest expectations. He was immediately and cruelly disillusioned by everything he saw. After nine months in Russia he concluded that the Soviet state was more despotic, more arbitrary, and more ruthless than the Tsarist tyranny. An interview with Lenin in January, 1919, capped his disappointment; Lenin, he thought, was willing to compromise with capitalist imperialism even to the point of introducing capitalistic techniques into Soviet Russia. Minor wrote three dispatches, burning with indignation, which Arno Dosch-Fleurot forwarded to the New York *World*, where they appeared on February 4, 6, and 7, 1919. Dosch-Fleurot, although he certainly did not share Minor's point of view, evidently thought the articles would be useful as anti-Bolshevik propaganda. He introduced Minor to the public as "no Bolshevik," although he did not mention Minor's anarchism. "Texan-born, of Virginia blood, he is aggressively democratic."

Minor's dispatches, if they had been read correctly, would have shed more light on the Bolshevik revolution than anything published in the American press up to that time. He began by depicting Lenin as anxious for respite from civil war and willing to compromise with the West in order to get it. At the same time Minor made it clear that the Bolsheviks had by no means abandoned hope of world revolution; he was surprised to find that Lenin confidently expected the revolution to flare up in America at any moment. Nor did Minor leave any doubt as to what Lenin thought of the West and in particular of Wilsonian diplomacy, which so many liberals regarded as fundamentally akin to the foreign policy of the Bolsheviks. Asked whether Russia intended to join the League of Nations, Lenin replied, according to Minor, "They are not forming a league of nations, but a league of imperialists to strangle the nations. President Wilson is a shrewd man," he added.

What especially impressed Minor was the evidence he saw in Soviet Russia of a return to capitalism. "[T]he so-called nationalization of Russian industry," he reported, "has put insurgent industry back into the hands of the business class, who disguise their activities by giving orders under the magic title of 'People's Commissaries.'" As he left the Kremlin after his interview, Minor saw "two smart limousines" pull up to the curb. From them alighted "several well-dressed men of the business type," obviously on their way to see some high Soviet official. These were the sort of men, Minor remarked bitterly, whom the Bolsheviks had formerly denounced as "bloodthirsty minions of predatory capital." Times had changed.

The business type ride in fine automobiles as before, live in fine mansions and are again managing the old industries, with more authority than ever before. Now they are 'People's Commissaries' . . . and the iron discipline of the army under the red flags has been developed in order to protect them again against all annoyance. A rose smells as sweetly to them under any other name.

Nor was labor any better off than before. Lenin pointed with pride to the growth of industrial unionism in Russia. Minor scoffed:

There is no more industrial unionism in Lenine's highly centralized institutions than in the United States postoffice. What he calls industrial unionism is nothing but nationalized industry in the highest degree of centralization . . .

Industrial unionism is a mere phrase in the Bolshevik dogma.[72]

Minor was the first Western observer to dwell on the disparity between Bolshevik rhetoric and Bolshevik practice. His second dispatch was explicit on this point. Revolutionary rhetoric, he contended, obscured the emergence of a new stage in the history of the revolution—the substitution of discipline for destruction, the beginnings of the long pull to modernize a primitive economy and to defend socialism in Russia from a hostile world. These developments were nevertheless attended by what Minor called the "war-whoop phraseology," which had become the "Russian state language." In one of his most penetrating passages Minor wrote:

I am convinced that such language has become more or less a permanent institution. So whoever wishes to discern the facts must see through the language. Perhaps none will rule eastern or central

Europe for a long time without using Socialist phrases. This does not necessarily imply great social changes; it is merely a matter of phraseology.[73]

The impact of Minor's articles on the American liberal mind was enormous, although hardly what Minor himself or Dosch-Fleurot must have intended. One or two papers cited Minor's interview as an argument for an anti-Bolshevik policy.[74] But most anti-imperialists drew from it a very different moral: that opposition to the Bolsheviks—intervention in particular—was a mistake, since it forced them into a posture of intransigence which if left to their own devices they would quickly shed. The very compromises that Minor deplored were greeted by anti-imperialists as evidence that the Bolshevik regime would become inevitably more moderate once it freed itself from outside pressure. Minor deplored the return of order and discipline; anti-imperialists welcomed it. As the *Nation* said: "It is easy to appreciate that an honest anarchist might well be irritated by a disciplined, integrated Government; but what is the rest of the world going to make of this last bit of anti-Bolshevik propaganda?" [75] Not everybody saw that Minor's articles were anti-Bolshevik in design; many people did not even know that Minor was an anarchist,[76] and most people would have been unable to see why an anarchist should attack the Bolshevik regime. But anti-imperialists and even many of the war liberals took his articles as an argument against military intervention, whether or not they were intended as such, and as an argument, more broadly, for hope.

What Bolshevism has wreaked upon Russia is often told [wrote the *World*]. Here, almost for the first time, we see Russia reacting upon Bolshevism. Little noticed, it may be, by its ignorant votaries, the system is being transformed, like many other radical experiments, by evolution and stern necessity. Analogy might require a Napoleon with his whiff of grapeshot.[77]

That the analogy was intended to flatter the new Napoleon, that is, Lenin, goes without saying. On the other hand, Trotsky, the proponent of world revolution, was now downgraded. A committee of anti-imperialists, including Nock, Paul Kellogg, Harold Stearns, Jane Addams, Amos Pinchot, and Lincoln Colcord, issued a statement declaring that "two conflicting policies" were contending for the mastery of Russia.

> Lenine, leading the more moderate Russian faction, has always expressed willingness to cooperate with the Western Powers . . . by redeeming the Russian loans, and confining activity to efforts at internal construction. Lenine's programme is that accepted by the Russian majority.
>
> Trotzky, on the other hand, has fought from the beginning for extreme policies. . . . He advocates class war throughout the world until all existing Governments are overthrown.[78]

The return of order was everywhere acclaimed with cries of great joy. "Lenine has shrunk back . . . to a policy of progressive Socialism," said the *Evening Post.*[79] Minor's articles made Lincoln Steffens see, more clearly than ever, that the Bolshevik government was "the most complete and all-embracing domination that there is in the world today." [80] With such a government, Steffens thought, Americans might literally do business. He advised his brother-in-law, an engineer, to apply for a job in Russian industry. The Bolsheviks, he said, realizing the importance of attracting Western experts, would be willing to pay him a high price.

> Only they want to hire him, not let him hire them. He can, and he does boss, but he gets the wage, not the workers. They'd make Jim rich if he'd build up a business or organize a mine, only they'd not let him own the plant. See? [81]

In the light of Minor's interview an article by Lenin entitled "The Soviet at Work," which appeared in *Pravda* in April, 1918, took on new importance. Ignored in America at the time of its first appearance, it was now translated and widely discussed, for it seemed to add to the impression that the Bolshevik system was undergoing drastic and fundamental modification. In this and in other writings of this period Lenin called upon Russian workers to apply themselves to the all-important task of the moment, that of increasing production.[82] He deplored the chaotic condition of Russian industry. He warned the proletariat that it would be expected in the future to submit to the most exacting discipline. "We must learn to combine the strong, energetic breaking of all restraints on the part of the toiling masses, with *iron discipline during work*, with *absolute submission* to the will of the person, the Soviet director, *during work*." [83] The managers themselves were to enjoy unusual privileges and high pay in the period ahead. In a passage widely quoted in America Lenin praised the Taylor system of scientific management.[84]

The new emphasis on order and obedience did not of course imply an abandonment of world revolution. But liberals were correct in sensing that the Bolsheviks would not be able to make much trouble elsewhere as long as the very survival of their experiment in Russia was in doubt. Where they went wide of the mark was in supposing that the return of discipline to Russia under Bolshevik rule was a hopeful sign of progress. Thus Alvin Johnson wrote, "If he remains in power long enough, [Lenin] is likely to compromise away most of what is usually meant by socialism," as though that in itself was tremendously reassuring, and William Allen White announced in September, 1919, that "the Bolshevism of a year ago" was dead.[85] But the return of the "business types," as Minor called them, the new emphasis on central planning, and the drive for "efficiency" were to prove no more auspicious than the rise of the Red Army. They were to prove, in their human effects, little short of catastrophic. And although anti-imperialists could hardly have been expected in 1919 to foresee the horrors of the Stalinist regime, the fact that they welcomed every step in the direction of order, stability, and discipline as steps toward the regeneration of Russia makes one wonder whether they did not go too far in attempting to convince American conservatives that the Bolshevik government had matters under control and, accordingly, ought to be recognized. What price stability? The anarchists, with their suspicion of political power in any form, were better able than the liberals to see in what direction Russia was heading.[86] Their advice, however, was disregarded.

Nor could even the anarchists always be depended upon to contribute a note of skepticism to discussion of the achievements of the Bolsheviks. The fate of Robert Minor himself was an ominous warning. A year after he published his bitter indictment of the Soviet regime, Minor returned to Russia and decided that he had been completely wrong in everything he had said. Exactly wherein he had been wrong, he was never able to say; nor did he ever retract his opinion that the Bolshevik government was the most dictatorial he could imagine. The fact simply ceased to trouble him. He slipped mysteriously beyond the boundaries of the ordinary world in which such questions as how a dictatorship can advance the cause of freedom, and how wars, however "revolutionary," can lead to world peace, are presumed to have reasonable answers.[87]

"That history repeats itself," the *Nation* once declared, "is one of the most ancient and obvious of platitudes." [88] The assumption, often unstated, that the Russian revolution could be expected in the end to recapitulate the history of the French revolution insinuated itself into every discussion of the future of Russia. Thus one paper was not surprised to hear, early in 1919, that Trotsky had ordered Lenin's arrest.

> The revolution [it declared] is running to form. The tendency of all such social convulsions is to devour their own offspring. Girondists destroy those of greater moderation, Jacobins destroy the Girondists and then a new faction in the war of classes destroys the Jacobins.[89]

Eventually the terror would bring about a reaction. "It is only a question of when the reaction will occur," said the *New Re-*

public, "and how far it can be kept under the control of sincere democrats." [90] Anti-imperialists also pointed to the French revolution to show that intervention from outside would drive the revolution to violent extremes. The *Nation* remembered that when Charles James Fox urged his countrymen to come to terms with the revolution, his advice was rejected. "What," cried Burke, "you would treat with regicides and assassins!" Burke prevailed, and what was the result? "France arose in a mighty unified effort against the armed forces of intervention," the *Nation* concluded, "Napoleon appeared, and for nearly two decades longer Europe was an abattoir." [91]

It was the assumption that revolutions "ran to form" that gave what appeared to be the sanction of history to the hope that Bolshevism would grow more moderate with the passage of time. The work of destruction, it appeared, was bound sooner or later to come to an end, and the work of reconstruction to begin, and the only question was whether the Bolsheviks themselves would preside over the period of consolidation and adjustment or whether they would give way to a military dictatorship. Most articulate Americans seemed to prefer the latter alternative. Anti-imperialists, however, could not bring themselves to support a counter-revolutionary regime. But their eventual support of the Bolsheviks—at which they arrived only after they had exhausted all the other available possibilities—was based on the premise that Bolshevism itself would gradually lose its revolutionary fervor. The belief that time would cool the ardor of the Bolsheviks in turn could be traced to the curious notion that radicalism sprang from an over-heated imagination; that is, that radicalism was utopian and would inevitably go to pieces when dashed against the facts of everyday life. To say that responsibility would bring sobriety to the Bolsheviks—and no metaphor was more tirelessly employed in discussing the subject—implied that the Bolsheviks were drunk, as the Jacobins had been drunk, with their own utopian fancies. It was with considerable condescension, therefore, that Americans applauded every sign of returning sobriety, of "the education of the Bolshevik mind," as one paper put it, "away from the rigor of formula to the realities of life." [92] That the "realities of life" were to prove immeasurably more terrible than the "formulas" which Americans found at once so dangerous and so absurd was left to later generations to discover.

VI

Getting Out of Russia: Withdrawal or Retreat?

THE persistence of the belief that Bolshevism if left alone would gradually grow more moderate explains why anti-imperialists, as time went on, were content merely to demand that intervention end, without specifying precisely what that step was expected to accomplish. It was as if the withdrawal of Allied forces offered in itself a final disposition of the Russian problem, instead of the necessary first step toward it. Granted the premise of anti-imperialist thought, it did. Others doubted whether so simple a solution of the question could be found—without, however, managing to explain why it could not. They saw too that the demand for the withdrawal of Allied troops from Russia, if not itself isolationist in inspiration, appealed strongly to those who wished the United States to withdraw from all foreign commitments of any kind. But their own position was no more satisfactory, since as the anti-imperialists pointed out, it compelled them ultimately to argue that the duty of the United States was to retain armies abroad, for an indefinite period of time, for the suppression of Bolshevism. Between repression and retreat, between a League of Nations which was in fact a Holy Alliance against revolution and no league at all, there seemed no middle ground.

The original argument against intervention, and to the end the most effective one, was that any interference short of a full-fledged military expedition would merely antagonize the Russian people while at the same time leaving the Bolsheviks as strong as ever. They would be stronger, in fact, since the mass of uncommitted Russians could be expected, in the face of foreign interference in their affairs, to rally to the Bolsheviks for purely patriotic reasons. On the other hand, a massive assault on Bolshevism would leave Russia in ruins, both economic and political; it would crush not only Bolshevism but all that remained of Russian democracy, clearing the way for a military dictatorship which would impose on Russia a tyranny worse than the one from which the revolution had delivered it.

Neither of the two possible answers to this argument was entirely convincing. It could be argued that the counterrevolutionists who aspired to succeed the Bolsheviks in power were more democratic than they appeared, but the fact remained that their governments depended for their existence on the presence of Allied troops in Siberia. The anti-Bolsheviks conceded the point when they argued for large-scale intervention. The second argument was somewhat more persuasive: that even a reactionary regime—that of Kolchak, for example—was better than a "dictatorship of the proletariat." That was Samuel Harper's reasoning; one suspects that it was also Arthur Bullard's, although in his book on the revolution Bullard tried to make a case for Kolchak's liberalism. Privately, however, he advised House, as we have seen, that Kolchak was "surrounded and dependent on the support of reaction[ary] elements whose principle of government is the reconquest of former grafts." [1] As for Harper, he confessed that he was "not altogether pleased with all that has happened around Kolchak. But it is a choice between him and Lenin," he said, "so I do not hesitate." [2]

In the eyes of Jerome Landfield, Harper's friend in the State Department, the undemocratic features of the Kolchak regime were not a liability but a virtue. "I am greatly heartened by the coup d'etat at Omsk," he wrote to Harper in November, 1918, "and I have great hopes that at last there will be a real military power in Russia that can restore orderly existence."[3] (Even Landfield, however, felt it necessary on occasion to insist that Kolchak was putting up a "splendid fight" against reaction.[4]) The Secretary of State was also untroubled by the issue of Kolchak's high-handed methods. The only thing which interested him was whether Kolchak was winning the civil war. It was because he was never convinced that he had "decisively beaten" the Bolsheviks that Lansing opposed recognition of Kolchak, which everyone else in the department favored.[5]

What these practitioners of *realpolitik* did not see was that Kolchak's military defeats were related to his lack of popular support, were in fact the direct consequence of it. When it came to giving or withholding support, the question of whether or not a regime was "democratic" was not, therefore, an airy abstraction, but a matter of great practical importance. The anti-imperialists were better realists when they insisted that it was impossible for any Russian government to stay in power unless it "accepted the revolution." It is possible in retrospect to see how a man like Kolchak might have succeeded for a time, with Allied military support, in holding back the flood of revolutionary energies released by Russia's social and economic breakdown. But it is difficult, with the example of recent dictators in mind, to believe that even a shrewd and resourceful man—and Kolchak was neither—could indefinitely have postponed a reckoning with the revolution. A people who, after having lived for centuries without hope, had finally caught a glimpse of a better life, were not likely to forget what they had seen. If the Russians submitted in the end to a dictator, he would be, as Robert Minor had foreseen, a dictator of the Left, a dictator who spoke the language of the revolution.

But the assertion that counter-revolutionary regimes could not in the long run command even the passive support of the population was not, after all, susceptible of immediate proof.

It is easy enough for us to see the force of the anti-imperialists' objections to Kolchak; but their contemporaries were not so readily convinced. The issue of Kolchak's success or failure remained in doubt until the end of 1919; after him, Denikin took up the fight, and after him Yudenitch and the Poles. It was possible well into 1920 for reasonable men to continue to hope for the overthrow of Bolshevism by the armies of the counter-revolution. Samuel Harper could say cheerily in the autumn of 1919, "The collapse of Kolchak does not worry me so much, for this leaves the field open to Denikin." [6] Only when all hope of a military victory of the whites had to be abandoned were men able to listen to those who argued that it was a mistake to have supported them in the first place. The opponents of intervention in the meantime had to devise other arguments against that policy, and these arguments, although more effective in arousing immediate opposition to the Allied expedition to Siberia, in the long run hopelessly confused the issue. In their eagerness to bring about the retirement of Allied troops from Russia, the anti-imperialists were willing to use whatever arguments came to hand and to accept support wherever it was offered. In the end those who believed that intervention was not the best solution of the Russian problem were swallowed up by those who were interested in putting off a solution indefinitely. Anti-imperialism was mingled with isolationism until the line between them became almost impossible to discern.

It was soon apparent that the most effective arguments against intervention were those which, far from pointing up its shortcomings, diverted attention from the entire problem. Intervention had been justified without reference to the Bolsheviks; it was now opposed in the same manner. It was argued, for instance, that Allied troops should be withdrawn from Russia because the purpose for which they were originally sent had been accomplished. Russia, that is, had been saved from the Germans by the Allied victory on the western front, and by the

Allies' insistence on German withdrawal from Russia as one of the conditions of surrender.* "The Germans either have withdrawn or are in process of withdrawing," Newton D. Baker advised Wilson.[7] Interventionists, still justifying intervention in the context of the German menace, tried to show that, on the contrary, large numbers of German troops still remained in Russia in violation of the armistice. Did the anti-imperialists really believe that the Germans would voluntarily withdraw? demanded Harper. "The Germans will not get out of Russia unless forced to do so." Moreover the Bolsheviks, as he reminded John R. Mott, were "largely dependent on German bayonets."[8] In this debate the advantage, for once, lay with the anti-imperialists. The American public, having been led to believe that the defeat of Germany would make the world safe for democracy, was in no mood to be told that there was any part of the world where the issue was still in doubt. The only trouble with citing Germany's defeat as a reason for Allied withdrawal from Russia was that it appeared to concede that the Allies had been justified in going in, in the first place.

Equally insidious was the argument that public opinion demanded withdrawal, indeed, that the troops themselves were clamoring to come home. Liberals might adduce evidence of disaffection among the troops in Russia as an instance of the unwillingness of men to fight for an unjust cause; but the same information also served as the basis for a demagogic appeal to isolationist opinion. The senators from Michigan, from which state most of the soldiers of the Archangel expedition came, rose to protest that the men were ill-fed and ill-clothed, and exposed

* It should not be forgotten that the Allies were under no obligation to save Russia from the consequences of Brest Litovsk. They could have made peace with Germany in the West without forcing Germany to surrender her conquests in Russia. That they scarcely considered such a course was another instance of the unanimity with which Westerners believed in "standing by Russia"—believed, that is, that unless Russia was made safe for democracy there could be no permanent peace made at Versailles.

to conflict with Russian forces outnumbering them fifteen to one.[9] These orators did not question the wisdom of intervention as such; they did not even concern themselves with its wisdom. They wanted nothing more than to bring the boys home. Medill McCormick demanded the recall of troops not only from Russia but from all Europe. Genuine anti-imperialists were puzzled at the drift of the debate; the *New Republic* thought McCormick's words "unfortunate." [10]

It was nevertheless with the active assistance of men like Robins, Colcord, and Villard that Johnson and Borah led the debate over intervention into a series of legalistic evasions. The most obvious of these was the assertion that military intervention was wrong because the United States was not technically at war with Russia; the most sophisticated, the proposition that whatever the desirability of restoring order in Russia, the Russians had a right to "work out their destiny for themselves," free from foreign interference. Of the first of these objections it is necessary to say only that its very simplicity explained its wide appeal. "Either we are at war with Russia or we are not. If we are at war, by whose authority are we at war? Congress alone has authority to declare that relation." [11] It is the second argument that commands our attention.

No principle was dearer to anti-imperialists than the inalienable right of "self-determination." The right of nations, particularly small, defenseless nations, to order their own affairs without fear of their more powerful neighbors was the heart of the proposed League of Nations, at least as anti-imperialists understood it. It was precisely because they attached such importance to the concept of self-determination that Russia had become for them the "acid test" of Allied good will. "We have not been fair to Russia," wrote Harold Stearns in November, 1918, "and it is high time to begin, if we wish the League of Nations to be a lasting reality. Because Russia presents typically, if in aggravated form, the kind of problem a League of Nations will constantly confront. Here is the test of our good faith and belief in the ability and right of peoples to determine their own destiny." [12] "If we really want to make the world safe for democracy," said Albert Rhys Williams, "we should . . . give Russia a chance to work out its own destinies." [13] Radicals in Seattle, where stevedores were causing a local sensation by refusing to load munitions on ships bound for Siberia, demanded of Wilson, "Why do you preach self-determination of peoples, and at the same time interfere with that self-determination in Russia by backing one faction in an internal conflict?" [14]

Self-determination was unimpeachable in theory. The only difficulty was that it seemed in practice to lead to the conclusion that the United States was not concerned with the outcome of the civil war in Russia, or that even if it was concerned with the outcome, it could do nothing to influence it. "[T]he Russian people have the same right to establish a socialistic state as we had to establish a republic," Borah argued.[15] "I agree with you," Amos Pinchot wrote to Johnson, who took the same position, "that the Russians are entitled to work out their own salvation; and if they want a Bolshevik form of government, a monarchy or anything else, they should have it." [16] The war liberals were quick to exploit this weakness of the anti-imperialist position. The New York *World* observed, "Senator Johnson's contention seems to be that, whether Russia is despotic or anarchistic [*sic*], we are not concerned." [17] The *World*, the *Evening Post*, the Springfield *Republican* and the Des Moines *Register* all pointed out that the Bolsheviks were not merely setting up a socialistic state in Russia, as Borah claimed; they were also attempting to overthrow established governments elsewhere. The *Register* urged supporters of the Johnson resolution for the withdrawal of troops to "bear in mind that bolshevism is a wildcat on democracy's back, which will neither get off itself nor permit anybody to push it off . . . The question of disposing of bolshevism has nothing in common with the granting to socialism of a fair chance to prove what it is good for." [18] The *New Republic* also objected at this time (although it later changed its mind) to an "immediate and unconditional" withdrawal from Russia. Such a policy, it thought, "would mean the resumption . . . of American isolation." [19]

To these objections the anti-imperialists replied, as Johnson put it, that the United States would have nothing to fear from international communism if it eliminated the poverty and misery on which communism thrived.[20] But the reply left something to be desired. If the United States might immunize itself against communism in this way, there were other parts of the world which were not so favorably situated—not, at least, as far as the immediate future was concerned. What about Germany, torn and shattered by four years of war? What would Johnson say, asked the New York *World*, if Germany and Austria "fell into the hands of anarchists [*sic*]?" [21] To this question Johnson never replied; it did not seem greatly to trouble him. It was precisely his apparent lack of concern that disturbed the war liberals, who believed that the United States, having assumed responsibilities to the rest of the world, could not renounce them without renouncing its moral leadership.

It was a question, however, whether all the advocates of "self-determination" for Russia were as unconcerned with the outcome of the civil war as they pretended to be. The genuine isolationists perhaps meant what they said when they professed indifference to the form of government finally adopted by the Russians. But it is hard to believe that such men as Robins were equally indifferent. Again and again, not only in public but privately as well, the friends of the revolution protested their neutrality. Thus Robins complained to Gumberg that the newspapers continually portrayed him as an "advocate and apologist for Lenin and Trotsky and the Bolshevik program," as if merely to repeat the charge was to expose its absurdity.[22]

Yet to this same Gumberg—who was certainly not neutral in the war between the reds and the whites; who was, indeed, frankly a propagandist for the former—Robins at other times wrote in a manner which makes one wonder whether the newspapers, for once, did not have a point. For Robins, communism in Russia was not simply an experiment which, in the interests of science, ought to be allowed to work itself out free from outside interference. The Bolsheviks were not always "they"; on occasion, they became "we." The American anti-imperialist was not always the dispassionate observer; he tended, without suspecting it himself, to become a participant in what at such times appeared to be a common struggle against the forces of ignorance and superstition. Thus when Robins learned in May, 1919, that the Allies intended to punish Germany for her "war guilt," his first instinct, perversely, was to rejoice. A punitive peace would drive Germany into the arms of Russia.

> I am much more hopeful [he wrote to Gumberg] . . . now that the peace terms are known. There will be as little disposition in Germany to trust to the allies as there has been in Russia & the union of Eastern Europe & the Black Sea littoral in a common defence seems reasonable. Neither England nor France can march armies against revolutionists who are defending their firesides from the effort to enforce a new economic slavery in the form of forcible indemnities & embargoes.
>
> If we can prevent the formal recognition of Kolchak & Lenin can maintain his front against the drive from the Urals the whole situation may be stabilized & the Russian Revolution end in the emancipation of half the world.[23]

William Hard, later Robins' admiring biographer, could insist that "the Russians ought to be left alone until at least they work out [their experiment] to its fullness so that I can go and take a look at it." [24] But when he was writing his series for the *New Republic* on "anti-Bolsheviks," under Gumberg's close supervision, Hard seemed more the apologist than the scholar. Something of the spirit in which he went about composing these polemics is suggested by the following query, one of a long list which he sent to Gumberg:

3. Many anti-Bolshevik papers going in May, 1918; *but we do not deny that papers were suppressed for fomenting outright destruction of Soviet State?* Is this right? For instance, in your list of papers in Moscow in May, there is no *Socialist Revolutionist* paper. Right? Or wrong? *Most* important.[25]

After weeks of work Hard was able to write to his tutor, "I think I have got everything right in the article now." But he also unburdened himself of a curious confession.

In all of these articles, I am taking the position that Lenin claims to be an anti-democrat and that Lenin's opponents in Russia, like Kolchak and Denikin, are actually grossly anti-democrats [*sic*], and that the US has no business backing any side in this struggle. I dare say you will think that my Americanism, as shown in my articles, is as sentimental as Robins's. But it cannot be helped. I have it. And, besides, it [the cry of "self-determination"] is the one thing which in the end can take America out of Russia.[26]

Thus Hard felt obliged to apologize for his "Americanism," for insisting that Americans should not take sides in the revolutionary struggle (just as liberals like Villard, when talking to radicals like Hutchins Hapgood, apologized for their liberalism). But the fact of the apology alone shows how precarious was the impartiality which it was intended to excuse. Neutrality, as Americans were beginning to discover, had become an uncomfortable, if not an untenable, position.

Neutrality, with all its implications, was the dilemma of the anti-imperialists. The "internationalists" in the meantime had to wrestle with a dilemma of their own. Granted that America had certain responsibilities to the rest of the world, where did the responsibilities end? At what point did Wilsonian "internationalism" become itself a kind of imperialism, as bad as the imperialism it was seeking to supplant? The New York *Evening*

Post, once a bastion of anti-imperialism, showed to what lengths "internationalism" might be carried when it declared impatiently at the end of the war that "the Allied interest demands the restoration of order, with democracy," in both Russia and Germany. At this time there was great apprehension in the West lest Bolshevism spread to Germany. The *Evening Post* demanded that it be kept out of Germany by force if necessary. Once Germany was made safe for democracy, Bolshevism could easily be attacked and stamped out in Russia.[27] Anti-imperialists immediately objected.

Your editorial [wrote Horace Kallen to the *Evening Post*] seems to assume that the Allied nations and the United States have now become the arbiters of democracy throughout the world . . . If the Allied armies are to be used to force a certain brand of democracy on great masses of people who firmly desire another brand, it would appear almost inevitable that the stage would be set for a long period of chaos and bloodshed.

He added that it was not the business of the United States to dictate to the Germans or to the Russians whether they should have "an old-fashioned parliamentary republic" or a "Soviet republic." [28] To Villard also, these Allied plans for "democratizing" the postwar world were "imperialism of the worst kind, which will make Prussian militarism a charming and attractive thing in comparison." He reminded David Lawrence that "a people's right of revolution is one of the most sacred that there is and no outsiders have a right to interfere with it." [29]

But neither Lawrence nor the editors of the *Evening Post* were disposed to retreat. The *Evening Post*, flatly opposing the demand for withdrawal from Russia, insisted that the Allies assembled at Versailles should guarantee the country "a republican form of government, broad civic liberties, and the land for the people, all to be worked out by a Constituent Assembly." On the basis of such guarantees, the editors believed that "the conscience of the world would approve a strong attempt to bring back order to Russia by the Allied arms and under Allied leadership, until such a time as the Russian people itself can take over the administration of a free, democratic government." [30]

This was the policy actually initiated by the Allies in May–June 1918, other expedients having failed: support of Kolchak ("a strong attempt to bring back order to Russia") on condition that he call a constituent assembly ("pledging to Russia . . . a republican form of government"). It is hard to say which anti-imperialists found more disturbing, the initial assumption that it was permissible to force democracy on Russia at the point of a gun, or the fact that the Allies were so easily satisfied by Kolchak's perfunctory assurances of good faith. It was bad enough to maintain that the United States could require Russia against her wishes to adopt a parliamentary form of government; it was twice as bad to prattle of democracy while foisting upon the country the unspeakable tyranny of Kolchak.

Kolchak found it easy enough to promise what the Allies, in their note of May 26, 1919, asked him to promise; he said that he would summon a Constituent Assembly based on free elections, refrain from restoring any class or government overthrown by the revolution, pay the national debt, and join the League of Nations. The Allies accordingly declared themselves satisfied.[31] Whether this meant that the Kolchak government was to be formally recognized as the *de facto* government of all Russia, or merely of Siberia, was not clear. Indeed it was not clear whether he was to be recognized at all, or whether the Allies were simply to continue to support him in the manner to which he had become accustomed.[32]

Most people assumed that Kolchak was about to be recognized and applauded the decision. "Our government has never had any doubt as to the liberal views of Admiral Kolchak himself," David Lawrence wrote; it wanted merely to be assured that he had surrounded himself with "men who favor the principles of the revolution as proclaimed when the czar was overthrown."[33] "Internationalists" were confident that he would shortly put the Bolsheviks to rout and proceed to set up a democratic government, although some papers later claimed to have opposed recognition all along.[34] The Des Moines *Register*, for instance, claimed in July, 1919, to have pointed out "again and again" that Kolchak had made no inroads on Bolshevik power, but in May the *Register* pictured the military situation as "certainly more favorable than at any time since the reds really got control of the country."[35] Among the organs of war liberalism only the Springfield *Republican* expressed strong reservations about Kolchak while he was still a contender for power.[36] Conservatives were likewise delighted with the "recognition" of the Omsk government. The Washington *Star* was confident that Kolchak would "rid Russia of the soviet in short order."[37]

It was not long, however, before Americans discovered that they had once again been taken in by counter-revolutionary propaganda. Kolchak's victories, it appeared, existed only in the imagination of his supporters. Thus it was reported on May 23, 1919, that his armies had penetrated deep into European Russia and that the "entire Bolshevik structure" was "crumbling." "Reds Begin Evacuation of Moscow," cried the New York *Times*.[38] But within a month it became clear that, far from driving the Bolsheviks from Moscow, Kolchak had been forced to evacuate his own capitol. By the end of August he was in full retreat; in January he surrendered what remained of his army, and on February 7, 1920, he was shot by a committee of Bolsheviks and Social Revolutionaries at Irkutsk.[39] When American liberals discovered that his armies had at no time been within a thousand miles of Moscow, they began to suspect that his entire campaign had been a "press agency fake," as the *New Republic* said, designed to prevent the Allies from reaching an accommodation with the Bolsheviks at Versailles.[40] The

New York *World* admitted that he had never had much popular support.[41] Even the New York *Globe*, a violently interventionist paper, declared that he had "failed to make the Russian people believe in him." [42]

Long before the fall of Kolchak the popular demand for withdrawal had already become almost impossible to resist. The Senate, goaded by Johnson and Borah, demanded to know what American boys were doing in Siberia and Archangel; why, if the war was over, they were not brought home as the boys in Europe were being brought home. By January, 1919, the attack had become "formidable," as Raymond Robins noted with satisfaction.[43] Norman Hapgood predicted that Johnson would win his fight. He warned Colonel House that the United States "absolutely must" get her troops out of Russia, "because the reasons for their being there, whatever those reasons may have been previous to the victory [over Germany], are now wholly shallow and unacceptable." [44] Frank Polk was "disturbed over the situation," as he cabled to Lansing. "It is obvious," he said, "that great difficulty would be encountered at home by any of the Allied Governments sending troops to Russia." [45]

Not only Congress and the public objected to keeping forces in Russia. The War Department, which had never approved of intervention, maintained a steady pressure on Wilson to withdraw from Russia. In January Polk reported in some alarm that General March, unless ordered otherwise, intended to "proceed with measures to withdraw . . . at the earliest possible opportunity." [46] On February 17, Secretary of War Baker, on his own authority, announced to Congress that American troops would be withdrawn as soon as warm weather came.[47] On both occasions Wilson intervened to stay the War Department's hand, but he must have found the task highly uncongenial, since he himself had reached the conclusion that the Allies should get out of Russia as soon as they could.

It seems likely that by the time he sailed for Paris in December, 1918, the President had made up his mind to fight for withdrawal at the peace conference. Beyond this, however, he seems to have had in mind no final or definitive solution of a problem with which, in spite of the persistent promptings of his conscience, he had never been able to come to grips. He could hardly have been unaware of the general feeling that it was impossible to make a permanent peace without Russia; it was a feeling he doubtless shared. He and his fellow statesmen, after all, had come to Paris to make peace, and half a dozen different wars were raging in Russia. These wars, too, had to be ended. Surely Wilson agreed with Lloyd George that "to pretend to make a permanent, endurable peace when Siberia and Russia were in a state of civil war would be a mockery." [48] But the immediate problem, and the one which absorbed all of Wilson's attention, was to put an end to the unhappy business of intervention. Perhaps Wilson, like other liberals, believed that if the Allies retired, the Bolshevik regime, unable any longer to cite the menace of foreign interference as a reason for keeping it in power, would "hang itself with its own rope," as William Allen White put it.[49] Perhaps he merely hoped that matters, if left to their own course, would solve themselves. Certainly he never conceived of the withdrawal of the troops as the first step toward an accommodation with Bolshevism, let alone recognition. For Wilson, the only desirable Russia was a Russia without Bolshevism. Of that much he could, upon occasion, speak with certainty. At the same time he was unable to envision any active steps by which such a result could be brought about. His policy remained as negative and as passive as that of Senator Johnson; indeed, the issue between them at times seemed to boil down to the question of whether it was proper for the United States to act unilaterally in the matter of retiring troops from Russia. Wilson, in this as in other matters, insisted that the United States could act only in concert with its Allies. But when it came to the question of precisely what withdrawal was expected to accomplish, the President was as vague as everybody else. Convinced that intervention was a mistake, he was ready to abandon it without being able to devise anything in its place.

Anti-imperialists, on the other hand, conceived of the retirement of Allied troops as the prelude to recognition of the Soviet regime; recognition, in turn, to be followed by a program of economic aid. They were profoundly convinced, as we have seen, that by ostracizing the revolution the West had again and again driven it into extremes which otherwise might have been avoided. It followed from this that a more tolerant and conciliatory attitude on the part of the Western nations might bring to the surface those elements of moderation and good sense which anti-imperialists still thought of as representing the "real Russia." Indeed, anti-imperialists thought the triumph of moderation inevitable. "As class dictators the Bolsheviks cannot survive," the *New Republic* declared.[50] But the anti-imperialists saw no reason why American diplomacy should not be used to hasten the collapse of proletarian dictatorship, first, by recognizing the Bolsheviks as a *de facto* government, and second, by putting into effect a program of economic aid (not only to Russia but to the rest of Europe as well) designed to eliminate the poverty and misery in which Bolshevism presumably took root. Some people insisted that it was not enough simply to send food; the *New Republic*, for instance, wanted "large and efficient commissions" sent to every capitol in central and eastern Europe to supervise a general "political and economic reorganization" of society.[51]

The idea of economic aid was not always associated with recognition of the Bolshevik government, however; it appealed to war liberals as well as to anti-imperialists. Almost all American liberals advocated sending relief and aid to Russia, if the choice lay between that and sending armies; but only a few of them were willing to recognize a government which rested on violence and which proclaimed the overthrow of existing governments everywhere as its leading objective. Yet most liberals had qualms about recognizing Kolchak. A program of economic aid gave them a way out of their difficulty, a means of avoiding altogether the problem of which government to recognize. It was because economic aid was regarded as a substitute for diplomacy of any sort that the idea was so appealing. It allowed American liberals to talk of "standing by" the Russian people while at the same time ignoring the various governments which claimed to represent them. But as people like Lansing repeatedly pointed out, and as events were again and again to show, a program of relief could not be undertaken—not officially, at any rate—until the attitude of the American government toward the Bolsheviks and their rivals had been clearly defined. The diplomatic question took precedence over any other. But when Lansing urged Wilson publicly to state "the attitude of the Government toward the Bolshevik authorities," Wilson told him that "the real thing with which to stop Bolshevism is food." Nothing was to be gained, he said, from "words and public statements in the matter of Bolshevism." [52]

Economic aid, insofar as it was regarded as an alternative to diplomacy, was only one of the many evasions into which Americans eventually retreated from the problem of Russia. And although the idea originated in an intuition of great importance—that revolutions "cannot be fought with guns"—it quickly degenerated into a cliché, grist to the cartoonists' mill: the "Square Meal" inevitably became "Poison to Anarchy." [53] But even this was doubtless better than the position of those who were content to demand a withdrawal of troops and nothing more. At least it conceded that the existence of Bolshevism created certain problems for the West. The demand for withdrawal did not even concede that. Those who simply demanded that the Allies get out of Russia, without considering the consequences of such a withdrawal, acted as if whatever problems may have existed had all been solved by the Allies' military victory over the Central Empires.

Merely getting the troops out of Russia was, to be sure, beset by difficulties. As Wilson observed, it was "harder to get out than it was to go in." [54] Since he took for granted the impossibility of unilateral action by the United States, he had to face the objections of the Allies, which were formidable. Although Lloyd George favored withdrawal, a majority of the British cabinet, led by Winston Churchill, opposed it, and the powerful Northcliffe press kept up a steady cry against any compromise with Bolshevism. The French wanted full-scale military intervention or, if that was impossible, vigorous support of the anti-Bolsheviks. But the greatest obstacle to withdrawal was the opposition of the anti-Bolsheviks themselves. In cooperating with Kolchak and others, the Allies had assumed obligations which it was impossible simply to renounce, especially inasmuch as all these factions had sent representatives to Paris, where they exercised an unremitting pressure on the peace conference. Never admitted to the deliberations, the Russians were never quite excluded from them. The merest rumor of an accommodation with the Bolsheviks roused them to Slavic fury, and their outbursts were fully recorded in the violently anti-Bolshevik press of Paris. The influence, out of all proportion to their power, which intervention gave to representatives of defunct or moribund regimes, was enough in itself to cast doubt on the wisdom of the whole policy.

Because of these circumstances it became necessary, if the Allies were gracefully to retire from Russia, to devise some formula which would appease the counter-revolutionaries and their supporters in the West, some arrangement, furthermore, which would leave Russia in at least a semblance of order. It was to this end that the British proposed on January 3, 1919, that following an armistice, to which all parties should agree, the various factions contending for mastery of Russia should be invited to meet under the benevolent supervision of the peace conference, to compose their differences. The French immediately announced that they would "make no contract with crime." * Lloyd George hastened to assure them that a "contract" was not contemplated. He proposed merely to hear the Russian contenders, not to recognize any one of them; he wanted only "to summon these people to Paris to appear before those present, somewhat in the way the Roman Empire summoned chiefs of outlying tributary states to render an account of their actions." [55] His metaphor perhaps revealed more than Lloyd George intended.

Wilson, independently of the British, had already made tentative overtures to the Bolsheviks. On December 24, 1918, Maxim Litvinov, on behalf of the Soviet government, begged the Western powers for an audience, and on New Year's Day, Wilson and House sent William H. Buckler to Stockholm to interview him.[56] Litvinov assured Buckler that the Soviet government was eager for peace.[57] On January 21, Wilson presented Buckler's report to the Council of Four as additional evidence in favor of the British proposal. Lloyd George thought the report "remarkable," "not," he hastened to add, "that it showed that the Bolsheviki were concerted [*sic*] to a realization of the error of their ways, but that it showed that they had at least seen that their plan would not do." Clemenceau, admitting that "sometimes in politics it is necessary to hold conversations with criminals," grudgingly assented to the British plan. At Wilson's insistence, the proposed place of meeting was moved from Paris, where the

* New York *World*, Jan. 12, 1919. The British proposal was sent through regular diplomatic channels. It was received in Washington but not forwarded to Paris, because Acting Secretary of State Polk assumed that it would be announced there as well. Lansing does not seem to have heard of the proposal until he read Foreign Minister Pichon's attack on it in the Paris papers on January 11. See Polk to Lansing, Jan. 12, 1919; Lansing to Polk, Jan. 11, 1919, Wilson MSS; and Polk's statement in New York *World*, Jan. 13, 1919.

French might be expected to dominate it, to the island of Prinkipo in the Sea of Marmora, near Constantinople.* Wilson drew up an invitation to all the "governments" of Russia; it was approved by the Council of Ten the following day and promptly communicated to all the Russian factions except the Bolsheviks. As Wilson explained, "to send an official communication would be tantamount to a recognition of the Bolshevik Government." The Bolsheviks learned of the invitation in the newspapers.[58]

It is difficult to know what Wilson and Lloyd George had in mind when they proposed the Prinkipo conference, since they made it clear that they did not plan to recognize the Bolsheviks. Perhaps they objected only to recognizing them as the government of all Russia, but were willing for practical purposes to recognize each of the various Russian regimes as a kind of *de facto* government of the area which it occupied. They were never very clear on this point. It seems unlikely, however, that they could have regarded a partition of Russia as a desirable arrangement. Wilson had once discussed the subject with House, who thought Russia "too big and too homogeneous for the safety of the world" and wanted "to see Siberia a separate republic, and European Russia divided into three parts." The President, according to House, emphatically disagreed.[59] That was in September, 1918, and there is no evidence that Wilson ever changed his mind. When in May, 1919, he and Lloyd George considered recognizing Kolchak's regime, it was as the government of all Russia, not of Siberia alone, that they proposed to negotiate with it.†

* Many American liberals erroneously believed that it was the French who insisted that the conference be held at Prinkipo, fearing the contamination of the working class of Paris if the Bolsheviks were invited there. See, *e.g.*, *Pearson's*, XL (March, 1919), 194; Tasker H. Bliss to Newton D. Baker, Jan. 21, 1919, Baker MSS.

† See Clemenceau *et al.* to Kolchak, May 26, 1919, Cumming and Pettit, *Russian-American Relations*, p. 338. In November, 1918, Wilson had objected to recognizing a "part of her" (Russia) by admitting dele-

But if the Prinkipo proposal was not intended to lead to a division of Russia, what was it meant to accomplish? Did the Allies expect all but one of the contending factions voluntarily to retire from the scene? There is no reason to think that these questions were even asked, much less answered. Torn between a dislike of Bolshevism on the one hand, and a desire to retreat from Russian commitments on the other, Wilson and Lloyd George devised a makeshift and tried to convince themselves that it was a real policy. Perhaps they did not expect the proposed "peace conference" to succeed but hoped merely to discredit whatever party refused to negotiate; having made a gesture at peacemaking, they could then retire from Russia and leave the Russians to fight it out among themselves. But when the anti-Bolsheviks by refusing to attend the Prinkipo conference gave them such an opportunity as they might have desired, neither Wilson nor Lloyd George showed any inclination to exploit it.

If these hypotheses as to the real purpose of the Prinkipo conference leave something to be desired, the official explanation is still more unsatisfying. When challenged by opponents of negotiations with the Soviet government, the adherents of Prinkipo replied that they were merely seeking information on which to base a decision. It was "not the intention of the American Government . . . to barter in matters of principle with the Bolshevik Government," as Lansing reassured Consul Poole at Archangel. "The purpose of the meeting is rather that of investigation in order that this Government may be in a position intelligently to direct its future policy in regard to all factions in Rus-

---

gates of the Omsk government to the peace conference. See Wilson to Lansing, Nov. 20, 1918, Wilson MSS, 7th series. Lansing noted that Wilson, as part of his policy of "an undivided Russia," refused to recognize Estonia, Lithuania, Georgia, the Ukraine, etc., as separate nationalities, in spite of the promptings of "self-determination." With Wilson's policy Lansing fully agreed. Robert Lansing, *The Peace Negotiations: A Personal Narrative* (Boston, 1921), pp. 99–100. Nevertheless Bakhmetev told Lansing that the "impression" was abroad "that [the] Allies intend to dismember Russia." Lansing MS Desk Diary, April 9, 1919, Feb. 26, 1919.

sia." [60] It is hard to believe that Wilson and Lloyd George really felt themselves handicapped, in formulating a Russian policy, by a lack of information. One must conclude either that they pleaded ignorance in order to postpone a decision or that they were seeking the sort of information which simply did not exist —information that would assure them that the Bolsheviks did not mean what they said when they talked of world revolution, that they had nothing but admiration for Western parliamentary institutions, that they intended as soon as possible to establish these institutions in Russia. If this was the information for which the Allies were looking, it was no wonder that they felt obliged to continue the search.

Feeble as the Prinkipo proposal may have been, it was hailed by American liberals as a stroke of great boldness and originality, "the only definite and intelligible Russian policy," said the New York *World*, "that any of the allied Governments has put forth since the revolution." [61] The Des Moines *Register* expected the conference to be "a very momentous affair"; the *Nation* called it "the dawning of a new day in diplomacy." [62] The plan appealed both to those who wanted to withdraw from Russia and to those who wished to "stand by." The *Nation* believed that in proposing such a conference the Allies were admitting their mistake in condemning the Bolsheviks to exile, and wondered only whether "an eleventh-hour recognition" would do any good.[63] Isolationists saw in Prinkipo the means by which the United States might back out of Russia altogether; the Chicago *Tribune* gave the plan its "unqualified approval." [64] Wilsonians favored it for precisely the opposite reason. When the Bolsheviks accepted the Allies' invitation, the New York *World* proclaimed their action "a fatal blow to Senators La Follette and Hiram Johnson, who insist that Bolshevism shall be let alone," and a vindication of those who had argued all along that a steady moral pressure would eventually bring the Bolsheviks to terms. "Weary of their own anarchy," the Bolsheviks, according to the *World,* were now "negotiating for a return to civilization on the best possible terms." [65]

The *New Republic* was more reserved in its enthusiasm. It believed that the Bolsheviks would accept the Allies' invitation but wondered what the proposed conference would accomplish. "It might have no positive results whatever," the editors warned, but because "it would open a means of communication between Russia and the western world," they supported it.[66] The Chicago *Daily News* shrewdly observed that in making the proposal the peace conference had committed itself to nothing. "It has not recognized the bolsheviki. It is seeking to obtain further information." [67] It was on these grounds, as we have seen, that Lloyd George and Wilson defended their policy before the Council of Ten.

Whatever the reasons for which it was called, the Prinkipo conference was scheduled to meet on February 15; William Allen White and George D. Herron, a war socialist then living in Geneva, were appointed as the American delegates. Both men were loyal Wilsonians, full of enthusiasm for "the revolution" but hostile to the Bolsheviks (Herron violently so, like most war socialists). They were good "internationalists" who had never wavered from the fervid conviction that the world had somehow, under the benevolent supervision of the Allied governments, to be made safe for democracy. Neither man had any particular qualifications for the mission he was to perform or even any very clear idea of what he was expected to accomplish. Both men, however, were enormously eager to be of service in restoring peace in Russia. Mrs. White told a friend that "this thing" meant more to her husband "than anything that has ever come into his life before." [68]

On February 4, the Soviet government not only agreed to attend the Prinkipo conference but offered to pay its debts, to grant concessions in mines and forests to citizens of Entente countries, and even to discuss the question of "annexations of

Russian territories by the Entente Powers." It did not, however, as the Allies had requested, set a date on which it would be willing to stop fighting. Instead it reminded the world that "the scope of the concessions to which the Soviet Government will agree will depend on its military situation with regard to the Entente Powers, and this situation is at present constantly improving." [69] Nevertheless it was clear that the Bolsheviks were willing to make certain concessions; nor is there any reason to doubt their sincerity in making them. The Red Army, as Chicherin said, was growing stronger every day, while its enemies grew weaker. The Bolsheviks were convinced that the counter-revolutionary movements would collapse at once if Allied support were withdrawn. They were therefore willing to negotiate with them, and even to recognize them as *de facto* governments, in the knowledge that any arrangements thus arrived at would prove to be of short duration. Time was on the side of the Bolsheviks, and worth bargaining for.

Only one contingency might upset these calculations: a full-scale assault on the Soviet Republic by the Allies. Lenin feared that having defeated Germany, the Allies would turn on Russia. "Now world capital will start an offensive against us," he told Chicherin at the time of the armistice.[70] Fanatically suspicious of the Western world, both as Marxists and as Russians, the Bolsheviks greatly exaggerated the desire of Western capitalism to crush the revolution by force of arms. The nightmare of being attacked by an army such as the one the Allies had hurled into Germany in 1918 could be dispelled by no amount of braggadocio. "What will you do," Robert Minor had asked Lenin, "if the Allies send big armies against you?"

"If they send anything short of very big armies," Lenin replied, "we will defeat them."

"And if they send very big armies?"

"Then they will make a very big war." [71]

What is striking is not so much Lenin's confidence in his

army as the assumption that a "very big war" was not at all unlikely. Assuming the imminence of a full-scale assault on Russia, to buy time, even if it meant parceling out Russian territories among the enemy, became a matter of the most desperate importance. The Bolsheviks could count on the international revolution to save them in the long run; and Lenin's belief that the war's end would be the signal for revolution throughout the West seemed to have been borne out, in the first months of the post-war period, by the revolutions in Germany (November, 1918), Hungary (March, 1919) and Bavaria (April, 1919). Any treaty signed under such circumstances might be expected to remain in force for no more than a matter of months. The Treaty of Brest Litovsk had lasted nine months. If Lenin's calculations were correct, the Treaty of Prinkipo would last no longer.[72]

Their willingness to negotiate did not, of course, mean that the Bolsheviks had abandoned any of their ultimate objectives, as American liberals supposed. It did not mean that any of the essential features of the Soviet regime had been modified. But one did not have to imagine that this was the case in order to advocate negotiations with the Bolsheviks. The case for negotiations properly rested on the consideration that however ruthless Lenin's intentions, and with whatever bad faith he signed a treaty, he would not find it as easy to break his agreements as he supposed. The Western nations, after all, could afford to gamble on the likelihood that they would survive the year without a revolution.

It was unfortunate that no one in America was able to bring himself to defend negotiations on these grounds. American liberals interpreted Lenin's overtures to the Allies as evidence of a change of heart, an admission of the error of his ways; and it was only with penitent sinners that they would treat. Lenin, said one paper, had as much as confessed that "Bolshevism will not last forever." [73] He was "less fanatical" than Trotsky, said another, and doubtless realized that "his colossal experiment is foredoomed to failure unless recognition is obtained by the soviet government." [74] Still another saw a multitude of signs that the Bolsheviks were "now more willing to abate their crazy pretensions, and to listen to reason." [75] The Springfield *Republican*, in view of the fact that the Bolsheviks were becoming "less fanatical and more practical and opportunist," ventured to predict that although the world might still have to live with a socialist Russia, "a moderate socialism need not provoke ill-will between nations if it minds its own business." [76]

For the next forty years every effort to negotiate with the Soviets was justified in just such language as this. Because Americans refused to converse with men they regarded as immoral, it was necessary to deny the immorality of the Bolsheviks, to insist that they had at last seen the light of reason, before negotiations could take place. Where expectations were so absurdly exaggerated, disillusionment inevitably ensued. Each round of negotiations discredited negotiations for years. There was no escape from this cycle of illusion and despair as long as Western democrats assumed that they could not live in a world which was not made safe, in some absolute and final sense, for democracy—as long as they clung to the dream of an earthly paradise from which doubt was forever banished.

The Bolsheviks' failure to name a day on which they would lay down their arms provided Kolchak, Denikin, and the rest with a plausible excuse for refusing to attend the Prinkipo conference. The French encouraged the recalcitrance of the anti-Bolsheviks. George D. Herron believed that French influence was decisive in their action. Representatives of the counter-revolutionary governments informed him "that officials of the French Government persuaded or commanded them not to go. It has become clear to me," Herron told Colonel House, "that the refusal of all of the parties except the Bolsheviks to participate is due to French intervention." [77] White and Bullitt were of the same opinion.[78]

February 15 came and went, and the Prinkipo conference failed to meet. The next few days were a period of great uncertainty and confusion. The interventionists renewed their efforts to send a large army to Russia. Emboldened by the temporary absence of both Wilson and Lloyd George, Clemenceau, supported by Sonnino of Italy, proposed to the Council of Ten on February 15 that the Allies abandon negotiation altogether and prepare to overthrow Bolshevism by force. Winston Churchill proposed a more subtle scheme. "The British Government wished it to appear that they had acted fairly by the Bolsheviks." Therefore it was necessary to make another gesture at negotiation, but a gesture calculated to come to nothing. The Allies should send another wireless: if the Bolsheviks ceased firing within five days, the Allies would then request their opponents to do likewise! He did not say so, but such a proposal could hardly fail to be refused, and could have been made with no other end in mind. If the invitation were rejected, Churchill continued, the Allies, having put the Bolsheviks in the wrong, could proceed with the business of raising an army and drawing up a plan of attack.[79]

All those present, even Colonel House, approved the substance of Churchill's telegram and therefore, by implication, the larger design behind it. House revealed "that he had never been in favour of the Prinkipo proposal [!], but it had been embarked upon, and therefore they must go along with it and, if eventually the Allies were compelled to embark on military operations, they would do so in a stronger and better [moral] position." [80] Perhaps he was only stalling for time; he was outnumbered, and Wilson was on the high seas, steaming toward America.

No action was finally taken on February 15. Two days later the Council considered the matter again. Unfortunately the minutes of the meeting of February 17 give none of the debate on Russia. House describes it as a turbulent meeting: "it was literally Balfour and myself against Churchill, the French and the Italians." Churchill "was persistent in pushing his plan for a military committee to examine into the question as to how Russia could best be invaded in the event it was necessary to do so." House claims to have "opposed this plan with some vehemence." [81] If he was more vehement than he had been on February 15, it was because just before the meeting, Philip Kerr, Lloyd George's secretary, had showed him telegrams from Lloyd George to Churchill, urging the latter to desist from his attempt to lay Prinkipo to rest.[82] Moreover, General Bliss, when asked for a military opinion, let it be known that American troops would under no circumstances be sent to Russia, as the United States did not consider itself at war with Russia.[83]

The interventionists were obliged to retreat. Balfour introduced in place of Churchill's proposal an innocuous resolution which, in effect, put off the whole matter indefinitely.[84] Whether it was adopted is not clear, but the strategy of watchful waiting had clearly carried the day. Kerr wired to London that the danger was past.[85] House sent similar messages to Wilson, who, like Lloyd George, had expressed great alarm at the drift the proceedings had taken in his absence. "It would be fatal," he wired to House, "to be led further into the Russian chaos." He thought he had made it clear that "he would not be in favor of any course which did not mean the earliest practicable withdrawal of military forces." [86] House assured the President that "Churchill's project is dead." [87]

Having beaten down the threat of military action, the adherents of negotiation were able to proceed with their plans for a revival, in slightly different form, of the Prinkipo proposal. It was in furtherance of this object that on February 17 or 18 House and Lansing, evidently without consulting their superiors, took the bold step of ordering William C. Bullitt to Moscow, where he was to ascertain exactly on what terms the Bolsheviks would be willing to negotiate.[88] Bullitt himself had advocated such a mission all along.[89] House first broached it to Lansing on February 16, even before the final disposition of Churchill's plan was assured; the Secretary noted laconically that they had "talked . . . about sending Bullitt to Russia to cure him of Bolshevism." [90] If this was their only object, it must be noted that the mission proved a complete failure.

The Bullitt mission has sometimes been interpreted as an abandonment of the Prinkipo idea in favor of direct negotiations with the Bolsheviks, from which the other Russian governments, because of their initial intransigence, were to be excluded.[91] But all the evidence suggests that at this stage of the conference those who were opposed to military intervention thought only of Prinkipo (or of taking no action at all, a policy probably favored by Lansing) as an alternative. Bullitt himself is quite clear on this point. "The idea in the minds of the British and the American delegation [was] that if the Allies made another proposal it should be a proposal which we would know in advance would be accepted, so that there would be no chance of another Prinkipos proposal miscarrying." [92] The Bolsheviks' acceptance of the first invitation was evasive enough to give their opponents an excuse for rejecting it. But if the Bolsheviks could be committed to definite and explicit terms, the counter-revolutionaries would have no choice but to fall in; or if they refused, their refusal might be made to serve as justification for leaving them to their fate. Some such reasoning as this must have prompted the decision to send Bullitt to Moscow. But House and Lansing were careful to leave a way out, in the event that some other policy were later taken up by the conference. Bullitt was clothed with no official power to negotiate; ostensibly he was merely "to proceed to Russia for the purpose of studying conditions, political and economic, therein." [93]

It happened that even while these events were in progress,

some of the anti-Bolshevik governments, prodded by Herron and White, and evidently reflecting on the moral disadvantage at which their refusal to hear of any meeting with the Bolsheviks had placed them, began to reconsider their position. On February 21, the day before Bullitt left Paris, Nicholas Tchaikovsky's North Russian government, according to Herron, agreed to attend a Prinkipo conference; and some of the others, Herron thought, showed signs of following his lead. These developments later enabled Herron, in a bitter post-mortem, to say that the Bullitt mission, dispatched at the moment when Prinkipo seemed most likely to succeed, was a deliberate attempt to sabotage the whole Prinkipo plan. "When we asked Hotel Crillon for information about this mission," Herron declared, ". . . we were met only with denial and evasion. Mr. Bullitt himself, the very hour in which he was on his way to the Embassy to arrange his passports, unaware that I knew he was starting to Moscow, vehemently assured me as to his fidelity to Prinkipo." [94] But there was nothing sinister, as Herron believed, in Bullitt's remarks, for Bullitt never conceived of his mission as anything but a means of reviving the Prinkipo project.

There is no denying, however, that Herron was met with "denial and evasion" at the Hotel Crillon. When he heard of Bullitt's mission he went to House for an explanation. But House "suddenly decided," according to Herron, "that he would not hear more of Russia until he had further information as to what England would do." [95] House refers to his conversation with Herron and White, which took place on March 1, in his diary. He "declined to discuss Russia with them at this time, telling them the matter could not well be brought up until after Lloyd George and I had had a discussion." [96] Lloyd George, in turn, hesitated to take action for reasons which he set forth in a memorandum to Kerr of February 19.[97] On that day Clemenceau had been shot by an unknown assassin, whom Lloyd George feared might turn out to be a Bolshevik. If that were the case, he wrote to Kerr, "you may take it that Prinkipo is off." But this indicates that until then, as far as Lloyd George was concerned, it was still on. A note in the Bullitt papers bears out this view. On February 18, according to Bullitt, "House & George [made an] engagement to meet on Feb. 24 Monday to concert plan for new P[rinkipo]. P[roposal]." [98]

Immediately after their conference with House—evidently on March 2—Herron and White were "unceremoniously informed by the chief clerk of the American Commission . . . that the Prinkipo proposition was dropped." [99] White later complained of having had no official notice of the abandonment of the project, and Wilson agreed that "it was shabby to treat you as you were treated in the matter of the Prinkipo conference," which seems to confirm Herron's statement that by this time the project had been given up.[100] But if Prinkipo had in fact been abandoned, it would seem to have been abandoned not, as Herron thought, in favor of negotiations with the Bolsheviks alone, but in favor of no negotiations at all. Lloyd George indicated such an alternative in his memorandum of February 19, in which he expressed the fear that the attempted assassination of Clemenceau had wrecked the Prinkipo idea. In view of that event, he told Kerr,

> we can for the moment only consider alternative policies. . . . No foreign intervention [that is, no *further* intervention] in Soviet Russia. No foreign troops to be sent to the aid of non-Bolshevik Russia unless volunteers choose to go of their own accord; but material assistance to be supplied to these Governments to enable them to hold their own in the territories which are not anxious to submit to Bolshevik rule.[101]

House sent this memorandum to Wilson on February 23, adding: "I do not think we shall have any difficulty reaching an agreement respecting our Russian policy after George arrives, inasmuch as his views apparently coincide with ours." [102] Thus the alternative to Prinkipo was not, as Herron believed, a more radical policy, but a much more passive and conservative one—a plan, incidentally, which reveals Lloyd George's continuing concern for the good will of those who were "not anxious to submit to Bolshevik rule."

Herron (who, it should not be forgotten, was strongly anti-Bolshevik [103]) concluded from his admittedly rather trying experiences that "so far as Hotel Crillon was concerned, the general movement and tendency was in favor of recognising the government of Lenin and Trotsky. I heard a good many voices in and around that unhappy hunting-ground, while the question of Prinkipo was held in the balance, and all the voices were in favor of an agreement with the Soviet Government, and not one voice was against it." [104] It is hard to know what voices he had been listening to. Not even all of the younger men on the American commission, who might have been expected to favor such a course, approved of recognition. David Hunter Miller and Gordon Auchincloss, to name only two influential members, were very much opposed to it. As for House, Wilson, and Lloyd George, whatever they had in mind, it was certainly not recognition of the Soviet government.

VII

Retreat and Resignation

ON February 25, 1919, Bullitt set out from Paris for Moscow, accompanied by Captain Walter W. Pettit, an army intelligence officer, and Lincoln Steffens. It was Steffens' second trip to Russia; he had already seen "a few chapters" of the revolution and had found them greatly to his liking.[1] But he was no more predisposed in favor of the revolution than his companions, even though they had not yet seen at first hand the conditions on which they were to report. Coming in on the train to Petrograd, Bullitt entertained the party, as Pettit noted, by attempting "to make a list of the lies which are told of the Soviet Government." [2] Normally the trip home from Russia, rather than the trip out, would have been a more suitable time for such activities. But Bullitt had come to Russia not to investigate (whatever Lansing and House might have thought about the purpose of his visit), but to negotiate with a government which he was already convinced was eager for a settlement. From Helsingfors he had wired to Joseph C. Grew in Paris that he was almost certain to have "definite propositions from the Soviet Government to transmit within a week or at most ten days." [3]

Bullitt carried with him two memoranda, one from House and one from Philip Kerr, setting forth the conditions on which the Allies would agree to negotiate with the Bolsheviks—or to be more precise, to renew the Prinkipo invitation. These documents agreed in substance. Kerr's was the more detailed. He proposed a bargain: the Allies to withdraw their troops from Russia, to restore commercial relations, to guarantee Soviet Russia access to railways and ports, and to postpone the question of the Russian debt; the Bolsheviks, in return, to agree to an immediate cessation of hostilities, after which all "de facto governments" were to remain "in full control of the territories which they at present occupy." [4] If the bargain was rather one-sided, the Bolsheviks receiving more than they were required to give, it was the price which Kerr, and presumably Lloyd George, were willing to pay in order to bring about a withdrawal of troops. House's views agreed, in the main, with Kerr's. It should be noted that neither of them demanded that the Bolsheviks pay their debts or promise to abandon revolutionary propaganda—the two points most generally agreed upon as the requirement of a satisfactory settlement. (House himself once told William Allen White that he "had just two things to ask of the Bolsheviks": that they stop fighting and "that they devote their propaganda to their own country." [5]) The unusual generosity of the terms confirms Bullitt's belief that the object of his mission was to make a proposal "which would certainly be accepted." [6] If the Bolsheviks would not accept these terms, it could fairly be concluded that they would accept no terms at all.

The question, however, was whether anyone else would accept them. As an academic exercise, designed to discover the lowest common denominator of agreement between Great Britain and the United States on the one hand and the Bolsheviks on the other, the Bullitt mission had a good deal to be said for it; but how its instigators were to persuade the French and the Italians, let alone the counter-revolutionary Russian governments, to settle with the Bolsheviks on these terms, was another matter. Indeed it is possible that the terms in question did not even reflect the thinking of Wilson and Lloyd George. It is possible that they reflected only the views of House and Kerr, of the more radical members of the British and American delegations, and in general of all those liberals (always a minority) who were willing to bring about a settlement with "the revolution" on almost any terms.

The Bolsheviks, as might have been expected, eagerly accepted the conditions which Bullitt laid before them. They agreed, that is, to meet with the Allies and with the other Russian governments and to recognize the latter as *de facto* governments of the territories they possessed, providing that Allied troops retired from Russia and that no further aid be sent to the anti-Soviet governments. On March 16, Bullitt wired the Soviet proposals to Paris from Helsingfors, adding:

> The Soviet Government hopes that [the] conference may be held in Norway. Its preferences thereafter are: first, some point on the frontier between Russia and Finland; second, on a large ocean liner anchored off Moon Island; third, on a large ocean liner anchored off the Aaland Islands; fourth, Prinkipos, to which the Soviet Government objects greatly.[7]

This statement makes it clear that House was thinking of another Prinkipo conference, not of a separate peace with the Bolsheviks, when he sent Bullitt to Russia.

Bullitt's telegram reached Paris on March 19, 1919. It was discussed on that day at a meeting of the American commission, which Wilson did not attend. Colonel House seemed impressed by what Bullitt had accomplished; he wanted to send a message congratulating Bullitt and asking him to get the Soviet proposals in writing. Lansing and Henry White demurred. David Hunter Miller, who attended this meeting, thought the Soviet note "very artfully drawn"; Bullitt, he said, "had been completely fooled by it."[8] Meanwhile Bullitt, Steffens, and Pettit were on their way back to Paris in high spirits. "[T]his gay boy did a man's work . . . after we got to Moscow," Steffens later wrote of Bullitt. "There was no more swank then. But then, again, on the way home, when the job was done, the pup played. It was bully."[9] Upon his arrival in Paris on the evening of March 25, Bullitt went straight to House, who was still excited about the results of the mission. "[A]t last I can see a way out of that vexatious [Russian] problem," House wrote that night in his diary.[10] Next morning Bullitt had breakfast with Lloyd George and other members of the British delegation. Both the Prime Minister and General Smuts agreed that the prospects of coming to some sort of understanding with the Bolsheviks were promising, although Lloyd George foresaw trouble in making a settlement palatable to the jingoes at home. As always, he was careful to commit himself to nothing.[11]

Bullitt next called on the American commissioners Lansing, Bliss, and White. He found them at first, he says, "mildly hostile, . . . but after two long sessions, they swung in behind the proposition in fine shape." [12] In view of their previous objections, it may be doubted whether they went as far as Bullitt thought they did. Lansing suspected him of misrepresenting conditions in Russia. He noted that Bullitt painted everything "rather rosily and praised the Bolshevik Lenine. Slid over terrible conditions and laid most [*sic*] everything on disorganized transportation." [13] Whatever Lansing or the other commissioners thought of Bullitt's report, however, it was not for them to decide whether it should be accepted or not. The future of the Bullitt report rested with Lloyd George and with Colonel House, to whom Wilson seems at this time to have turned over the whole question of Soviet-American relations.

House told Bullitt to draft a reply to the Soviet proposal.[14] Meanwhile he "tried out" the plan on Orlando. Perhaps because he realized that the Russian counter-revolutionists would never accept the terms agreed to by the Bolsheviks, he now went so far as to propose that the Allies negotiate with the Bolsheviks alone and leave the other Russian factions to shift for themselves. He "did not think we should make another Prinkipo proposal or try to have a meeting in some neutral country." He stressed the necessity of coming to terms with the Bolsheviks. "If we did not make terms with them," he told Orlando, "it was certain that as soon as we made peace with Germany, Russia and Germany would link up together, thereby realizing my prophecy that, sooner or later, everything east of the Rhine would be arrayed against the Western Powers." House believed that Orlando was impressed by this reasoning.[15]

House then telephoned Wilson, only to find the President too immersed in other matters to give any thought to the Russian problem. "As usual," House noted, "[I] find that his 'one-track mind' is against taking up this question at present." [16] By the time Wilson found time to talk with House, on the following day (March 27), another, and much milder, plan had been proposed—a plan to restore order in Russia by offering to feed the population on condition that hostilities cease. Evidently it was this project, rather than Bullitt's proposal, which occupied Wilson and House at their meeting on March 27, for Wilson instructed House to inquire of Herber Hoover whether a relief program, if decided upon, could be carried out. It was all "very difficult," House explained, "because no one wanted to deal with Lenine and Trotsky." [17]

It is not clear from House's diary who brought up the subject of sending provisions to Russia, Wilson or House himself. Nor is it clear whether House had yet abandoned the idea of negotiating with the Bolsheviks, which he had broached with such enthusiasm to Orlando. The day after his meeting with Wilson, he seems to have laid it before Lloyd George, who was still "sympathetic toward a settlement with Russia." [18]

The House-Bullitt plan, however, was dying a speedy death. As long as House was interested, it had some chance of success; but House was quickly losing interest. He could not have got much encouragement from Wilson, and it is not unlikely, although House does not say so, that Lloyd George had confided to him the same reservations which he had expressed to Bullitt at breakfast on March 26, that the Churchill-Northcliffe element was firmly opposed to an accommodation with the revolution. But what finally converted House to a more moderate plan than the one Bullitt proposed was not the coolness of Wilson or of Lloyd George but, it appears, the advice of his son-in-law, Gordon Auchincloss (by whose judgment House set great store), and Auchincloss' law partner, David Hunter Miller. On March 26, at which time he still favored a "treaty" with the Bolsheviks, House arranged to have "Gordon and David Miller look into the matter of such a treaty," evidently from the legal point of view.[19] He was perhaps surprised to learn that the very idea of a treaty appeared to them completely distasteful. They threw out the plan to negotiate with the Bolsheviks and proposed instead a scheme, evidently conceived by Herbert Hoover, to feed the Russians as Hoover had fed the Belgians.[20] The idea was not, of course, humanitarian, but political, for the feeding would take place only if the fighting stopped. Thus an offer of relief might serve as a roundabout way to peace which would not offend anybody and which would not involve dealing with the Bolsheviks. By March 29, House had been converted to the new plan.[21] Bullitt later testified: "Colonel House decided that it would be an easier way to peace if we could get there via the feeding plan under the guise of a purely humanitarian plan, if we could slide in that way instead of by a direct, outright statement inviting these people to sit down and make peace." [22] The very deviousness of the idea doubtless appealed to House's love of mystery and intrigue. Soon he was deep in consultation with Hoover as to the possibilities of "sliding in."

On April 3, Wilson, Lloyd George, and Clemenceau received a letter from Dr. Fridtjof Nansen, the Norwegian explorer and humanitarian, proposing that a commission of neutral nations undertake the relief of Russia. Presumably someone in the American commission inspired Nansen's letter. Bullitt believed that Hoover and Auchincloss had put him up to writing it, although Lincoln Steffens claimed that the Nansen letter was his idea.[23] In any case the letter was turned over to Auchincloss and Miller, who drafted a reply. They declared that while a relief program was eminently to be desired, it could be undertaken only following a complete cessation of hostilities "by Russian troops." Moreover they demanded that all Russian railroads be placed under the control of the neutral relief commission. Otherwise, they contended, there was no guarantee that supplies would be equitably distributed.[24] Bullitt predicted that the Bolsheviks would never accept a proposal which required them to cease firing but made no such demand of the Allied troops or those of the Finns, Estonians, Poles, etc., all of whom were to some degree involved in the civil war. The Miller-Auchincloss letter, Bullitt pointed out, did not even contain a guarantee that these troops would retire from Russian territory. Nor did it commit the Allies to abstain from sending further military aid to Kolchak. "You . . . go a long way," Bullitt told Auchincloss, "toward proving Trotsky's thesis: that any armistice will simply be used by the Allies as a period in which to supply tanks, . . . etc. to the various anti-Soviet governments." [25] Lansing also objected to the Miller-Auchincloss draft, which he found too "vague." [26]

Both he and Bullitt suggested replies of their own.[27] In style, the letter finally agreed upon followed Bullitt's draft rather than the long-winded and legalistic Miller-Auchincloss draft, but it resembled the latter in its evasiveness. Where Bullitt demanded the cessation of all hostilities "within the territory of the former Russian Empire," the final draft spoke of the cessation of hostilities "within definitive lines in the territory of Russia," without explaining what the "definitive lines" were to be.[28] No one seemed very happy with the final draft. Wilson, who signed it, later complained that it was unfair to ask Lenin to stop fighting without also putting pressure on Kolchak and Denikin to do likewise.[29] Clemenceau, still holding out for recognition of Kolchak, waited ten days before signing it.[30]

No sooner had he done so than Paris received word of a great offensive by Kolchak's army, which had carried him 100 miles to the west, resulting in the capture of Samara on the Volga. Actually Kolchak never did capture Samara, although he threatened it; and although he had made some progress during March and April, 1919, by the end of April, just when the Allies in Paris were beginning to wonder whether his success did not entitle him to recognition, Kolchak was once again in retreat. The city of Ufa, which he had captured on March 13, fell to the Bolsheviks on June 9; Ekaterinburg, 200 miles to the east, on July 14.[31] But information regarding the latest Bolshevik advance was slow to reach the assembled heads of state in Paris. Lloyd George could not understand the Bolsheviks' contemptuous rejection of Nansen's offer on the grounds that it prevented "the belligerent who has every reason to expect successes from obtaining them." [32] "To read this reply," Lloyd George declared, "gave the impression that the Bolshevists refused Dr. Nansen's offer because they did not wish to compromise their prospects of military success. All the information he had received, however, was that the Bolshevists were collapsing in a military sense." [33]

The Allies continued to proceed on the latter assumption.[34] On May 26, they notified Kolchak that he could expect their support on condition that he give adequate evidence of his good intentions. As Lloyd George pointed out, it would be "awkward" for the Allies to be "placed in the position of supporting a government that [they] did not believe in." But he doubted whether public opinion in the West would allow them to abandon Kolchak "even if he should establish a reactionary Government, because the world would say that the establishment of order was so important." [35]

Wilson agreed that it was impossible to abandon Kolchak, although it was clear that he would have liked to do so. He had wearied of the endless Russian wrangle. He admitted one day that he had always thought "the proper policy of the Allied and Associated Powers was to clear out of Russia and leave it to the Russians to fight it out among themselves."[36] Little remained of Wilson's determination to "stand by" Russia. The problem seemed to admit of no sane and moderate—that is to say, of no liberal—solution. The debate on Russia had become a struggle between those who wanted to recognize the Bolsheviks and those who wanted to beat them into submission, a struggle from which a moderate man could only retire in confusion.

Wilson and his followers made no further attempt to deal with the revolution. They could only plead that the League of Nations would eventually, no one knew how, put all wrongs to right. But for anti-imperialists, the League, as it finally emerged from the discussions at Paris, was the greatest disappointment of all, an engine of intolerable oppression designed to shore up decaying empires. The League of Nations Covenant seemed to commit the members of the League to the defense of all the inequalities and injustices which had been written into the treaty; to the defense of a "condition which is morbidly sick," as the *New Republic* put it, "with conflict and trouble." "Americans had nothing like this in mind when they acquiesced in the President's promises," the *New Republic* insisted.[37] It noted that Article Ten, which was the heart of Wilson's League and which required all members to combine in punishing "aggression,"

> was not even a part of that genuine league which [anti-imperialists] originally proposed. What they wanted . . . when they agitated for a League of Nations was a league of all the nations in which the legislators could find some representation [*sic*], in which the sanction of force was applied only to compelling peaceful adjustment of disputes. What they have got is an essentially secret committee of five executives who may use force not merely to compel peaceful adjustment but to compel adjustment in accordance with the status quo. Such a league is a caricature of what was anticipated.[38]

Walter Lippmann wrote privately to Colonel House in the same vein. "I hoped up to the very last," he said, "for a Treaty . . . that would not open the suspicion that the Covenant is a new

Holy Alliance." [39] All that palliated his disappointment was that the outcome was not altogether unexpected. As early as December, 1918, when, upon arriving in Paris, he found himself excluded from all the important work of the Inquiry, he had already become "bored" with the peace conference, and longed "to get away." [40] By February, 1919, according to friends, Lippmann was "almost a red." [41]

At that, Lippmann's disappointment matured more slowly than that of other anti-imperialists. Walter Weyl in August, 1918, was already so pessimistic as to the likelihood of Wilson's succeeding at Paris that Croly wondered whether he "would be able to write effectively & with enthusiasm for the N[ew] R[epublic]." [42] By the time the peace conference broke up, however, Croly himself was equally pessimistic about the world. Long before that, such radicals as Amos Pinchot and Oswald Garrison Villard were convinced that Wilson had "gotten himself into a position," as Pinchot put it, "where it [was] . . . impossible for him to make a real fight for open diplomacy and a liberal peace." In Pinchot's estimation the President had already laid for himself a "psychological foundation of failure." [43]

It was Lincoln Colcord who perhaps best struck the note of defeat and despair. And it was Colcord who, as always, brought the discussion back to the Russian problem, with which, as he had insisted all along, all the "larger issues" were "bound up." No one expressed as well as he the anti-imperialists' fear that the alternative to understanding and conciliating the revolution was the bloody suppression of it by an armed alliance of reaction. The triumph of reaction would in turn, Colcord thought, provoke another series of revolutions, more violent than the last, in which what little remained of Western civilization would go down in ruins. The "wrong peace," he predicted as early as July, 1918, would usher in "a quick and hideous era of world-wide militarism and imperialism, the reactionary forces apparently triumphant, reckless and arbitrary"—an era ending in "financial crisis," "industrial breakdown," and "social upheaval." "Then, instead of reconstruction, revolution and anarchy on every hand, and scenes to haunt men in dreams." [44] By November, 1918, Colcord was writing to Bullitt:

> The world is plunging on to revolution. They cannot stop it now. I anticipate a winter of terror and despair. When the Russian revolution was denied, civilization chose the alternative of self-destruction. I am for Wilson, but I have no hope. . . . It will be a tragic but splendid time, lit by the lurid light of chaos . . . Now the forces are gathering which were to be clearly foreseen a year ago. *The war has been driven a year beyond its appointed time.* To save the situation now it would be necessary for the President to go back through the past year and a half and pick up one by one his old errors. But were he great enough to do that, he would not have committed the errors.[45]

It could hardly be said, then, that anti-imperialists were unprepared for the disappointments of Versailles. The collapse of the Prinkipo conference and the quasi-recognition of Kolchak were, for them, only the latest in a long series of setbacks. Anti-imperialists had come to expect the worst as a matter of habit. Thus Colcord did not seem surprised to hear in March, 1919, that the Allies at last had "decided to invade Russia by way of the Black Sea region" with an army of 200,000 men.[46] Colonel House tried to reassure him that there was "absolutely no truth" in the report. On the contrary, he said, "we sent Bullitt and Steffens to Russia some weeks ago and they are back with their report. I am trying now to work something out that will be worth while." [47] But as we have seen, House had by this time turned his back on Bullitt and his proposal for negotiating with the Bolsheviks; whatever hopes he may have raised in Colcord were destined to be quickly disappointed.

Bullitt himself, ignored by Wilson, deserted by House, was "disgusted with life in general," according to Walter Weyl, and expected "to retire to Italy as soon as possible." [48] In a passionate letter he had warned the President that the Allies could not hope to make peace until they had "established a modum [*sic*] vivendi with the new Revolution." It was still possible, he insisted, for a wise diplomacy to "guide the Revolution into peaceful and constructive channels. . . . Draw the Russian Revolution into the paths of peace and constructive work and the remainder of the European people will follow it." He advised Wilson to take the "circuitous way to peace" offered by the Nansen plan, if he did not "dare . . . take the step" of negotiating directly with the Soviet government.[49]

Wilson never replied. Bullitt discovered that he and Lloyd George refused even to admit that they had sent him to Russia. When Lloyd George was asked in the House of Commons whether the Allies had been "approached" by the Bolsheviks with a proposal of peace, he declared:

> No; we have had no approaches at all. . . . I think I know what the right hon. gentleman refers to. There was some suggestion that there was some young Americans [*sic*] who had come back. All I can say about that is that it is not for me to judge the value of these communications. But if the President of the United States had attached any value to them he would have brought them before the conference, and he certainly did not.[50]

That seems to have been the first Bullitt knew of Wilson's absolute silence on the subject of his mission to Russia. Was it true, he demanded, that Wilson had never laid his report before the conference?[51] But to this question too the President did not see fit to reply.

On May 17, Bullitt resigned from the American Commission to Negotiate Peace. To Wilson he wrote:

> I was one of the millions who trusted confidently and implicitly in your leadership and believed that you would take nothing less than "a permanent peace" based upon "unselfish and unbiased justice." But our Government has consented now to deliver the suffering peoples of the world to new oppressions, subjections and dismemberments—a new century of war.[52]

Samuel Eliot Morison and Adolph A. Berle, Jr., also resigned from the commission.[53]

The circumstances surrounding the Bullitt mission were already becoming a matter of public knowledge, although the mission was intended to be secret. By the end of the summer the treatment of Bullitt was a major scandal in anti-imperialist circles, and Bullitt displaced Robins as the leading martyr of the cause. As early as March 24, 1919, even before Bullitt returned to Paris, American papers reported that Americans had been sent to Russia on a secret mission.[54] Villard wrote from Paris on April 3, that there was "no mystery" about the trip.[55] When Lloyd George denied any knowledge of the episode, the *Nation* reminded him that he had taken breakfast with Bullitt the morning after his return and was "as thoroughly familiar with the Bullitt report as are the members of the American peace delegations." [56]

It is possible that the very publicity which Bullitt's mission received helped to frighten Wilson away from it. On April 2, Wilson heard from Tumulty that the "proposed recognition of Lenine" had caused great "consternation" in Washington.[57] The State Department cabled to the same effect. E. Chappell Porter of the Russian-American Chamber of Commerce had warned the department that representatives of the Bolsheviks in America were "banking" on the hope that Bullitt and Steffens would bring back a report favorable to the Soviet government.[58] This was presumably enough to discredit such a report. Just how much weight these warnings carried with the President in Paris, it is impossible to know. Surely they could not have failed to add to his sense of the difficulties involved in getting out of Russia. Apparently the American people wanted nothing more than to get out. At the same time they opposed any effort to negotiate with the Bolsheviks. The most imaginative of statesmen would have found it difficult to reconcile the two.

In the face of the demand for information about the Bullitt mission Wilson preserved a strict silence. But anti-imperialists would not let the subject drop. They were aided in their search for information by the Soviet government itself, which in July made public the terms which Bullitt had brought to Moscow. The *Nation* promptly printed the Soviet dispatch.[59] But the *Nation* must have had access to other sources of information as well, for it referred also to events in Paris not mentioned in the Soviet dispatch. Regarding the Nansen plan, for instance, the *Nation* declared that "Mr. Bullitt himself drew up the Nansen correspondence with the Big Four with the exception of the reply of the Council of Four to the Nansen proposition, which the Big Four substituted for Mr. Bullitt's draft." [60] It should be remembered that Villard was in Paris throughout most of the peace conference. It does not seem altogether fanciful to suppose that Bullitt himself was the source of his information.

Frank Polk sent the *Nation's* exposé to Wilson, without comment, and Wilson submitted it for advice to Tumulty and to Gilbert F. Close, his confidential secretary. Close was indignant. He considered the article "amazing." He knew of "no such 'Allied terms' as are here quoted." He wanted the administration to demand that the *Nation* be compelled to show the evidence for its statements, which he was convinced were false.[61] That Close himself seems to have known nothing of the Bullitt mission suggests how much of the President's confidence his subordinates normally enjoyed. Tumulty knew better; he counseled silence. "Bullitt is discredited and no one pays any attention to the Nation," he said. Why should the administration advertise their charges by commenting on them? Wilson was convinced by this reasoning, and said nothing.[62]

Tumulty had astutely taken note of the possibility that the *Nation's* "slander" might eventually reach "Senators Lodge or Borah," who would make good use of it.[63] His intuition was correct. In September, 1919, Bullitt was invited by the Republican opponents of the Treaty of Versailles to testify against the treaty before the Senate Foreign Relations Committee. The incident dramatized the curious alliance of reactionaries and radicals against the treaty and the League of Nations—an alliance the irony of which the administration press never tired of pointing out. On every phase of national policy, and particularly on the question of what should be done about Russia, the views of Bullitt and of Senator Lodge could not have been much further apart. Men of Lodge's political outlook had only recently conducted a Senate investigation of Bolshevik propaganda in the United States, in which they not only aired the most absurd and hackneyed of the anti-Bolshevik canards, but managed to create the impression that American radicals, in imitation of the Bolsheviks, aimed at nothing less than the overthrow of their own government. Louise Bryant (who was to become Bullitt's wife in 1923) was treated with scorn and contempt when she testified before the Overman committee.[64] Nine months later Bullitt was treated by the Foreign Relations Committee as a distinguished diplomat to whom every courtesy was due. The contrast was illuminating if not edifying. Sympathy for the Russian revolution, insofar as it could be used to justify a policy of isolation in foreign affairs, had become, for the moment, eminently respectable.

Bullitt was camping in the Maine woods when he received the committee's summons; after his experiences in the Old World, he had evidently felt the need to reestablish contact with the natural beauties of the New.[65] Hastening to Washington on September 12, 1919, he told his story for the first time in full. He produced also the text of his report on conditions in Russia, together with that of Lincoln Steffens. Both of these documents stressed the "constructive work" of the revolution, toward which Bullitt and Steffens believed all the energies of the Soviet government were now directed. "The destructive phase of the revolution is over," Bullitt wrote.[66] The terror had ceased; order had been reestablished; the streets were safe. Effective opposition to the Bolsheviks had practically disappeared, except among the Left S-R's and the anarchists. The Bolsheviks themselves were ready for compromise with the West;

they needed peace in order to consolidate the gains of the revolution at home. Both Bullitt and Steffens, like Robert Minor before them, were evidently surprised to find that Lenin was not an anarchist. Steffens declared that the Soviet government was the "most autocratic" he had ever seen. Lenin, he said, was "farther removed from the people" than the Tsar had ever been.[67] Bullitt agreed that Lenin, "as a practical matter," stood "well to the right in the existing political life of Russia." According to Bullitt, he recognized "the undesirability, from the Socialist viewpoint," of compromise with capitalism, but he was nevertheless "ready to make the compromises." [68] The conclusions of Bullitt and Steffens, like those of so many anti-imperialists, rested on the unstated premise that communism was too ideal a system to work in practice, and that as it was modified in accordance with the exigencies of everyday life it would come more and more to resemble the evolutionary socialism of western Europe.

Bullitt was not content, in testifying before the Foreign Relations Committee, merely to give his own views on the peace conference. He also told of a conversation he had had with Lansing, just after Bullitt's resignation from the commission, in which Lansing had agreed with Bullitt's strictures on the treaty. It was probably this indiscretion, more than his comments on Russia, which brought down on Bullitt's head the full wrath of liberal orthodoxy. Lansing not unnaturally thought Bullitt's conduct "despicable and outrageous." [69] The secretary's widow later blamed Bullitt for precipitating the "break" between her husband and the President.[70] But neither she nor Lansing himself ever challenged the truth of what Bullitt said, either in public or in private. As a matter of fact Lansing printed in his own memoirs a memorandum which fully bore out Bullitt's remarks about his low opinion of the treaty.[71] Colonel House's opinion of Bullitt's testimony is also worth recording. The propriety of giving "to the enemies of the administration" private conversations with Lansing, House thought, spoke for itself. Nevertheless, he wrote in his diary, with particular reference to Lloyd George's blanket denial of all that Bullitt had said: "Candor compels me to record that in my opinion Bullitt told the truth." [72]

The orthodox, however, were not impressed. The Des Moines *Register* called Bullitt's story "preposterous"; the *Evening Post*, which all summer long had been challenging Bullitt to speak out, now dismissed him as a "well-intentioned and engaging young man" who took himself too seriously.[73] By the autumn of 1919, such papers had lost all interest in the possibility of an accommodation with Bolshevism. An accommodation such as Bullitt recommended seemed to the *Evening Post*, even at the time of the peace conference, "helpless surrender." On the other hand, the *Post* still objected to "a policy of bayonets and machine guns." What alternative was left? The editors hoped for a while to see Bolshevism challenged with "counter-ideas." Just as Wilson's "debates with the Central Powers" had helped to undermine German morale, so "a series of questions addressed publicly to Lenine" might undermine the Bolsheviks. "The Soviet rulers might be asked to state just what is their objection to a Constituent Assembly . . . They might be asked to state whether the peace they are asking for is indeed a peace or only a truce for the purpose of gathering strength for a new war against 'Western imperialism.' " [74]

But the advent of Kolchak put an end to such speculation. Simeon Strunsky, who wrote most of the *Evening Post's* editorials on foreign affairs, had already come around to the French plan of encircling Russia with a "wall of bayonets," according to Villard.[75] The *Evening Post*, like the New York *World*, the Philadelphia *Public Ledger*, the Des Moines *Register*, the St. Louis *Post-Dispatch* and the Chicago *Daily News*, all supported the decision of the peace conference to extend assistance to Kolchak in exchange for democratic guarantees.[76] The collapse of Kolchak left these papers high and dry. They could only take refuge in the vague hope that Wilson's League of Nations would somehow find the solution to the problem of how to get rid of the Bolsheviks without actually seeming to do so. Wilsonian "internationalism" was perhaps the most plausible of the various evasions into which American liberals retreated from the problem of Russia.

The anti-imperialists, lacking any faith in Wilson's League, gave themselves up to reflections of the gloomiest kind. Even so sanguine a prophet of the march of democracy and civilization as William Allen White was sobered by the spectacle of postwar Europe as seen from the perspective of Versailles. From the perspective of Emporia, White had seen the war, as so many liberals had seen it, as a clear-cut conflict between good and evil. A strong Allied partisan almost from the beginning, White was convinced that the "spiritual" principle represented by the Allies would inevitably triumph over the principle of brute force embodied in the German Empire, thus ushering in a new and better era in the history of mankind.[77] The Russian revolution seemed to him the first great tangible triumph of the "spiritual" principle. "In a middle class world," he exclaimed in January, 1918, "where, after all, business is business and profits are royal, what a specter of terror must the Bolsheviki be! They stand for something ahead of profit—humanity." [78]

A trip to Europe in 1917 under the auspices of the Red Cross had not shaken White's faith in the blessings the future had in store. Not until the spring of 1919 did he begin to understand the devastation, both moral and material, left by the war. Nor was it only suffering which had created the universal unrest among the "little peoples" of the world, which White began to sense was the war's chief legacy. Wilsonian diplomacy had encouraged people to throw off their chains. Wilson's appeal was designed for the ears of the people of the Central Empires, to be sure, but there was no way in which he could prevent others from hearing it too. The President, White decided, had not realized how "dangerous" his words were.

> For when you preach freedom to a people ridden by despotism, and when you exhort these peoples to rise—just because you happen to be fighting the particular despot who rules over these people . . . millions of other people living under what the Anglo-Saxon regards as highly moral government in a most exemplary fashion, may loathe the exemplary fashion and regard your exponent of orderly government as a despicable tyrant. And the man may be your best friend.[79]

It was no more possible to control the form assumed by the revolution than it was possible to control its geographical scope. What began as a democratic revolution had become a communist revolution, and the communist example, as White saw, would appeal mightily to underdogs everywhere. Bolshevism was "the strongest single idea in the world right now." [80] Meanwhile White's opinion of Bolshevism had drastically altered. Far from regarding it as a humanitarian movement, he now believed that Bolshevism was "a menace to progress and a step toward an era which will compare better to the Dark Ages, than to any other epoch in history." [81] His reflections on its growing strength therefore took on greater urgency. While Bolshevism was overrunning all of Europe, "orderly civilization" in Paris was "suffering from the indecision of anemia." [82] Failing to offer the masses an alternative to Bolshevism, White thought, the great Western powers would be obliged to oppose Bolshevism with force. Then they would be in the position of "sitting on the lid" of the revolution—an uncomfortable position, to say the least. Yet "one or the other must go down"; the world could not live "half Bolshevik and half capitalist." The struggle between the two systems, having been joined, could not be called off simply because one of them had tired of it. From it there could be no retreat, not even a retreat of the United States into isolation, for the future of the United States was now bound up with that of Europe. "Whether or not we like the League of Nations we are chained to it," White declared.[83]

Unwilling to see the United States retreat from her international commitments, White resigned himself, for the moment at least, to the role that the country seemed henceforth destined to play—a role analogous to that of Austria in the first half of the nineteenth century. Others preferred retreat to involvement in such infamies as the suppression, or at least the containment, of the revolution would necessarily involve. For as socialism spread from Russia throughout Europe, as it seemed to be doing in the spring of 1919, greater and greater efforts would be required to put it down: huge standing armies, crushing taxation, suppression of "self-determination" at home as well as abroad. The effort of policing the world would make police states of the Western nations themselves. Indeed the "red scare" of 1919 seemed to suggest that the process was already taking place.

Nobody seemed to doubt that the revolution was in fact spreading throughout the world. Even the peacemakers at Paris began to hear the ominous stirrings from below. Their deliberations became slightly hysterical in tone; nerves were frayed to the breaking-point. Lloyd George, badly frightened by the danger of a Bolshevik upheaval in Germany, backed down from his demand for revenge against the Huns; now he wanted to patch up a quick peace which would leave Germany intact as a barrier against Russia.[84] Lansing, after listening to Oswald Garrison Villard, who had just returned from Germany, feared that it was already too late to save Germany from revolution.[85] General Bliss agreed that the communization of Europe was almost inevitable. The war, he told the Council of Four, had raised throughout Europe "a universal feeling of dissatisfaction" with the old order. Governments of which the masses had once stood in awe had "crumbled to pieces"; as a result, respect for authority had disappeared. "The same spirit of revolution as existed one hundred years ago," Bliss declared, "is in the air everywhere," and no Holy Alliance could dispel it.[86]

Privately General Bliss expressed even greater misgivings. He heard from Marshal Foch that the French wanted to launch a massive invasion of Russia, financed, as Foch blithely informed him, by the United States. General Bliss was appalled. He had once predicted that when the peace conference had accomplished all that the Allies were aiming at, "western Europe would gasp with amazement and no little horror at finding itself face to face, without any intervening bulwark, with the Slavonic races backed by all the peoples of Asia." His gloomiest forebodings, he thought, had now come true. Under the circumstances, "the most humane thing" the United States could do was to withdraw its armed forces from Europe the moment peace was signed with Germany. "Without dabbling much longer in this mess over here, we ought to make sure of our ability to keep alive the spark of our civilization should it die out over here." *

General Bliss, in his disgust and alarm, repudiated Europe; others, doubting that even the United States could keep alive the spark of civilization as long as it was blinded by Wilsonian illusions, repudiated liberalism itself. Reinhold Niebuhr deplored the "gray spirit of compromise" that dominated the liberal approach to politics. Liberalism was "afraid to tear down old houses and build new ones." It lacked "the spirit of enthusiasm, not to say fanaticism, which is so necessary to move the world out of its beaten tracks."[87] William Bullitt complained that

* Bliss to Baker, March 4, April 3, 1919, Newton D. Baker MSS. It will be recalled that Norman Angell found it curious in 1914 that some of the military men were more fully aware of the Russian menace—and hence of the broad political implications of the war—than the civilians, who were more bellicose than the generals themselves. The same remarks apply to General Bliss; and in the Second World War, it may be added, to one or two generals, Stillwell in particular. It should be noted, however, that such men have always been in the minority among their military colleagues.

liberalism was "too delicate a plant, too entwined with the moral integrity of its prophet," to survive the great betrayal of Versailles. Bourgeois liberalism was dead. The "more courageous liberals" were now aligning themselves with "the parties which draw their strength from the labouring class," while the "less courageous" were "lapsing into an impotent faction scarcely distinguishable from the conservatives." [88] Anti-imperialists girded themselves for the "class war" which the betrayal of the workers' hopes at Versailles would inevitably provoke. Not many of them called themselves "Bolsheviks" or even approved of Bolshevism; all they were sure of was that liberalism was bankrupt and that labor was the hope of the world. "[T]he class division is coming," wrote Lincoln Colcord. "Within the next ten years the democratic and republican parties will merge in opposition to the new party of the proletariat." "[Y]ou and [Wilson]," he advised Colonel House, "are attempting the impossible—to maintain a bankrupt and outworn system." [89] Walter Weyl agreed that the "class war" was a reality and that liberalism, which denied the necessity of class conflict, was dead.[90] The editors of the *Nation* likewise believed that a "new political alignment, based on fundamental economic issues," was "bound to appear." [91]

When they looked back over the history of liberalism during the years of the war, anti-imperialists saw a long record of acquiescence and evasion. For years liberals had played the role of "suckers," said William Hard; even now, he pointed out, a meeting of Republican progressives in Chicago was striking what it regarded as a "progressive" note by insisting that if the United States intervened in Mexico it must promise also to get out. "But that is precisely the way in which liberals have made themselves into a tail to the imperialistic kite . . . everywhere," Hard observed. "What group of imperialists is not ready to promise to get out if only liberals and progressives will help them to get in?" [92] Charles T. Hallinan, a pacifist, was equally discouraged. The "wrath of the pacifists," he thought, had been as "short-lived and ineffective" as that of the war liberals. "Too many of us," he wrote to a friend, "are merely passivists, not pacifists. . . . [W]e go along meekly, 'getting behind the President' at every opportunity whether he does violence to our convictions or not." Having watched him sign his name to "the most imperialistic peace since Vienna," pacifists were now rushing "violently into mass meetings" to "ratify it as 'a step in the right direction!' " It was no wonder, he declared, that "the more radical wing" of the pacifist movement was "going over to Bolshevism." Pacifism, like liberalism, had lost its appeal, especially to the young.

> Whenever one talks to labor or radical groups against universal military training [Hallinan observed] he invariably encounters the young radical who declares that Bolshevism is right, that the working class can never recover power without the use of force and that they can never use force successfully until, like the Russians and the Germans, they have been shown how to use machine guns and hand grenades. Of course this isn't said openly to any great extent but it is said everywhere. Thousands upon thousands of men and women are deserting the movement because they have become so convinced that the labor movement is growing more radical very rapidly and that Bolshevism is the way out.
>
> You talk about work with children. No doubt it is important but things are moving so fast and apparently in such a revolutionary direction that the next generation seems a long way off.[93]

But the disillusionment of liberals with liberalism did not after all go very deep. What they attacked was not liberalism itself so much as Wilson's "betrayal" of it. They criticized Wilson for sacrificing his Fourteen Points to Allied greed, but they never criticized the Fourteen Points themselves. They attacked Wilson for failing to secure a repudiation of the secret treaties, but they still imagined that a redefinition of war aims would have been enough to save the world from the evils into which it had fallen.

Anti-imperialists understood well enough that the revolution, about which they had such ambivalent feelings, was the product of the continuation of the war, as Lincoln Colcord said, "beyond its appointed time." They saw in retrospect that the year 1917 was not only the decisive year of the war but one of the turning points of modern history.

> For in 1917 [wrote Colcord to Villard in 1922] certain decisions were taken—the decision to continue the war beyond its natural economic limit, and to refuse to face the Russian Revolution—which as time goes on will be seen to mark the beginning of a new era in civilization and the end of an old. The year of Versailles is relatively unimportant; but the year when the decision was taken to incur world-debts which cannot be paid, is the date of the beginning of the downfall of imperialism based on privilege and monopoly.[94]

What anti-imperialists never understood was the degree of their own complicity in the crime of prolonging the war, if that was a crime. They too were responsible for the social and political upheaval brought about by the war. If they were the first to understand that the defeat of Germany would inevitably enhance the influence of the East, a development which now led men like General Bliss to prophesy the imminent destruction of Europe by Asiatic barbarians, they were also the first to forget it. If they invented "peace without victory," they were among the first to abandon it in favor of the dream of total victory: the annihilation of autocracy everywhere. It was not only the rapacity of the Allies which had prolonged the war; it was also the American anti-imperialists' own insistence on revolution, in Germany as well as in Russia, as a condition of peace. And the outcome of the war, far from "betraying" liberal hopes, ironically fulfilled them: the revolution, which was to guarantee the safety of democracy in central Europe, became an indisputable fact. But the revolution which the New Diplomacy had helped into the world turned out to be no child of the Enlightenment, but a monster bent on its destruction. As Jerome Landfield wrote, "In making 'democracy' the aim of the war, we have started something, the end of which is impossible to foresee." [95]

When anti-imperialists transformed the war-aims question from a means of bringing about an early peace into a means of undermining German morale and at the same time of keeping Russia in the war—when Russia wanted nothing except to leave it—they contributed as effectively to the triumph of the Bolsheviks as if they had carried communist placards in the streets of Petrograd. Nothing but peace could have saved Russia for the West. But it was too soon after the event for anti-imperialists to understand that the Russian revolution had assumed an attitude more or less permanently antagonistic to the West. It still seemed only a matter of time before Russia would return to the company of "civilized" nations. The belief that the new rulers of Russia were impractical visionaries, and that their system could not conceivably work, led anti-imperialists to conclude that once the Bolsheviks had tested their theories against hard facts, they would have to abandon the theories. The belief that Russia had been driven to extremes in the first place only by the hostility of the West led anti-imperialists to think that once the West withdrew its troops and recognized the Soviet government, that government would become mild-mannered and law-abiding. They continued therefore to agitate for withdrawal and recognition with undiminished confidence that these measures would bring about changes of tremendous importance in the attitude of the Soviet Republic toward the rest of the world. If they became "disillusioned," it was only because they began to despair that the measures in question would ever be undertaken by the American government, not because they were uncertain as to what the measures themselves would accomplish. Disillusionment did not imply soul-searching, the reassessment of anti-imperialist assumptions about Russia, the revolution, and the world. It implied not doubt, but simply discouragement.

How little of their creed the anti-imperialists had given up became clear in the debates over recognition of Soviet Russia which followed the withdrawal of American troops in 1920. Withdrawal itself, of course, settled nothing; the inconclusiveness of the act was implicit in the way in which anti-imperialists had chosen to defend it. Their reluctance to argue the case against intervention on its merits allowed the government to withdraw from Russia without conceding the error of having gone in in the first place. Indeed the government, in the act of putting an end to intervention, reaffirmed the wisdom of that policy; it perpetuated the fiction that intervention had been designed solely to rescue the Czech Legion from the German prisoners of war. That having been accomplished, there was no reason for American troops to remain in Russia.

Withdrawal from Russia thus became part of the general retreat from Europe. As such, far from implying recognition of the Bolsheviks, it dictated a policy of having nothing to do with them at all. The State Department, now under the direction of Bainbridge Colby, took the position that as long as the Bolshevik regime rested on "the negation of every principle of honor and good faith," in Colby's words, the United States had no choice but to ignore its very existence.[96] Colby's successors faithfully adhered to the policy of nonrecognition, so characteristically Wilsonian in its underlying assumptions. Nor did the advocates of recognition challenge the appropriateness of the criteria Wilson and Colby had laid down. They merely challenged the accuracy of the government's description of the Soviet regime. They argued the facts of the case but not the principle itself.

Throughout the twenties the anti-imperialists, "disillusioned" as they claimed to be with liberalism, allowed the old liberal war-horses in the Senate to take charge of the debate, and once again these isolationists put the case on the worst possible ground. Senator Borah, backed by Robins and Gumberg, introduced a resolution calling for recognition of Soviet Russia on January 11, 1924. In defense of it, he did not point to the undeniable fact of the Soviet government's existence. He did not argue that whether or not the revolution threatened the security of the "American way of life," its existence could not simply be ignored. Instead he felt obliged to deny that its existence did, in fact, threaten anybody. The Soviet threat, he maintained, was an imaginary creation of American reactionaries eager to discredit an experiment in socialism. The Soviet government had not "in any way countenanced or urged or promulgated or indorsed or connived at any attempt to overthrow the American Government." There was no connection between the Soviet government and the American communists.[97]

Senator Norris, leaping into the debate, went even further. The Secretary of State, he conceded, "could not be blamed for refusing to recognize a government engaged in an attempt to overthrow our Government." But if he wished to base nonrecognition on these grounds, "he should have some evidence on which to stand." All the talk of a communist conspiracy was clearly no more than propaganda designed to create another red scare, "to pave the way for another crusade for deportations by which thousands and thousands of innocent people will be arrested . . . and pushed into ships and deported to a foreign country." [98] Remembering the wartime propaganda campaign against the Bolsheviks, liberals tended to discount anything that was said against them. "[M]ore anarchists [*sic*] are made around the marble-top desks of bureau chiefs," Norris scoffed, "than are made out in the world." [99]

The mistake of taking their stand on the nonexistence of a communist conspiracy against capitalism was at once brought home to the liberals. On January 7, 1924, Senator Lodge produced documents which showed that Russia was really governed by the communist party (not by the soviets); that the party itself was dominated by a few determined autocrats; and that the Russian communist party in turn dominated the International.[100] Further evidence to support these assertions was introduced by the State Department.[101] Norris and Borah backed down. Borah now argued that if the Soviet Union was indeed carrying on propaganda against the United States, the only way to prevent it from doing so was to recognize it.[102] He had worked himself into an impossible position. Having conceded that the United States could not recognize a government bent on its destruction, he was left without any ground to stand on when the government produced evidence that the Soviet Union was plotting the forcible overthrow of capitalism. The movement for recognition collapsed. Robins and Borah retired from the fray in some confusion; Alex Gumberg accused Robins in 1925 of having "lost interest in the Russian cause." [103] The recognition of the Soviet Union had to wait until 1933.

What is so interesting about the 1924 debates on recognition is that both sides agreed on an essential point: that it was impossible to have relations with Russia unless she paid her debts, promised to honor her agreements, and renounced the international revolution—unless the Soviet Union behaved as a "civilized" nation. Borah himself called attention to this underlying agreement: "We all desire apparently the same thing—settlement of the claims, adjustment of the debt, and abatement of propaganda if it exists. . . . No one advocates the recognition of the Russian Government without the adjustment of these controverted questions." [104] The only issue that remained, therefore, was whether these questions had already been settled; whether the Soviet regime had become so moderate, as its friends contended, as to be no longer a menace, or whether its existence threatened the security of the West. Neither side could bring itself to admit the necessity of living with an unregenerate Russia. The obvious answer to the State Department was not that communist propaganda did not exist, but that its existence was irrelevant to the question of recognition; but the advocates of recognition took their stand on quite different ground. Like their opponents, they assumed that the United States could have relations only with a regime which shared its own attitudes and assumptions about the world.

The belief that international intercourse was impossible between nations of radically different ideologies was perhaps the central theme of American diplomacy in the period of the First World War. Nor was it only with regard to American relations with Russia that Americans were misled by this peculiar conception of international affairs. The converse of this proposition —that just as opposite ideologies repelled, similar ideologies attracted each other—was responsible in the early years of the war for the fear of a rapprochement between militaristic Germany and Tsarist Russia; and the fear of such an alliance, as we have seen, was of fundamental importance in determining American attitudes toward the Russian revolution. It followed from this premise, furthermore, that if Tsarist Russia was irresistibly attracted to Germany, revolutionary Russia would be as irresistibly repelled by her. It was because they assumed that the new Russia was destined to be the natural enemy of the German Empire that American anti-imperialists believed that the Treaty of Brest Litovsk could not last. Russia's reentry into the war became a practical certainty; but even if she stayed out, some maintained, her influence in undermining German morale would be of even greater value than her military assistance. If it was true that German militarism could not live in amity with the revolution, it followed that Russia was to be treated as a friend. All these attitudes toward the revolution originated in the assumption that the ideological alignment of a nation dictated its foreign policy. Since these attitudes, in one form or another, persisted for decades, the importance of the original assumption can hardly be exaggerated.

Because of their fascination—one might almost say their

obsession—with ideology, anti-imperialists came to see the war as a competition of propagandas. As one of George Creel's associates in the CPI observed, "[T]his war is being fought in the minds of great masses of people as truly as it is being fought out on the battle fields of Europe." [105] Creel agreed that the American war effort was "the world's greatest adventure in advertising." [106] Victory over Germany was to be achieved, in the end, by weakening German morale. In the same way Allied propaganda was to make the Russians fight by convincing them of the justice of the Allied cause.

This attitude toward the efficacy of ideas was a curious blend of naïveté and cynicism. Anti-imperialists (and most of the war liberals as well) believed that men, being rational, could be stirred by appeals to the intellect. They believed that international disputes would some day be settled by discussion rather than by force. Yet they maintained that "ideas are weapons," as Max Lerner put it some years later, a proposition which seemed to imply that ideas had no intrinsic validity beyond their power to persuade. All ideas, ultimately, were propaganda—all but the Truth, which came from the People. It was this Truth, which they identified with their own civilization, on the assumption that people everywhere aspired to the same ideals which inspired Americans, that American liberals expected to conquer the world. At no other time in the history of the United States (unless it was during the 1840s and 1850s) were Americans more powerfully convinced of their messianic mission to other peoples. The force of the American example, they thought, would everywhere put tyranny to rout. In particular the spectacle of a great nation entering a war from which it had nothing materially to gain would persuade other nations to abandon their selfish ambitions. In March, 1917, the day of reckoning seemed at hand; the Russian revolution tolled the end of the old order. It was possible for Americans actually to see the new world taking shape before their eyes; and not only that, to take credit for bringing it into being. One paper could declare, without exaggeration, it seemed: "It was the American flag that has brought about the peaceable revolution in Russia. And it is the American flag that will bring about the revolution in Germany, peaceable or violent, for that revolution is bound to come. It is American ideals that dominate the world." [107]

This illusion was by no means abandoned, in spite of the discouraging events which followed. The revolution refused to conform to the American model; but Americans by no means gave up hope that the revolutionists would eventually admit the error of their ways. Only with the greatest difficulty could they imagine a future in which they would no longer inspire the rest of the world with the sheer splendor of their example. To set an example, after all, was their original reason for being. Other countries have had to give up empires—a painful task, but not as painful as giving up a long and splendid dream. The empires of the imagination are the last to fall.

Notes

Foreword

1. I have explored this subject in my honors thesis, "Imperialism and the Independents" (Harvard College, 1954), and in an article, "The Anti-Imperialists, the Philippines, and the Inequality of Man," *Journal of Southern History*, XXIV (Aug., 1958), 319–31.

2. (New York, 1955); see ch. 4.

3. Roosevelt to Archie Roosevelt, Feb. 2, 1918, in Elting E. Morison, ed., *The Letters of Theodore Roosevelt* (Cambridge, 1954), VIII, 1280.

I: The Russian Menace

1. Graham, "The Compensations of Illiteracy," *Living Age*, CCLXX (Sept. 30, 1911), 880. See also Stephen Graham, *The Way of Martha and the Way of Mary* (New York, 1915). For attacks on Graham see Michael S. Farbman, "Russia and the World," *Nation*, CVIII (Feb. 8, 1919), 188–90; and Nathan Shaviro, "Russia's Internal Foe," *ibid.*, CIV (Jan. 4, 1917), 9–11. Shaviro dismissed the *mir* as an "enslaving institution which has thwarted the development of the Russian people."

2. Sarolea in *Current Opinion*, LX (May, 1917), 341–2. This article originally appeared as "The Soul of Russia" in the London *Review of Reviews*. For an elaboration of these opinions see Charles Sarolea, *Europe's Debt to Russia* (London, 1916), especially ch. 6.

3. Havelock Ellis, "The Genius of Russia," *Contemporary Review* (London), LXXX (Sept., 1901), 420.

4. Crane to his wife, Berlin, May 28, 1900, Charles R. Crane MSS, Archive of Russian and East European History and Culture, Columbia University.

5. See Bernard Pares, *My Russian Memoirs* (London, 1931), pp. 92, 116.

6. Crane to Josephine Crane Bradley, April 5, 1916, Crane MSS.

7. Philadelphia *Public Ledger*, Dec. 6, 1920.

8. See, *e.g.*, Kennan, "The Ritual Murder Myth in Russia," *In-*

dependent, LXXVI (Nov. 13, 1913), 300–1. See also, for other non-Jewish attacks on Russian policy toward the Jews, editorials in *ibid.,* LXXI (Nov. 23, 1911), 1155–6; LXXV (Sept. 11, 1913), 807–10; LXXVI (Nov. 20, 1913), 327–8; and in *Outlook,* XCVII (Jan. 21, 1911), 104–5; XCVIII (July 1, 1911), 472–80.

9. Kennan in *ibid.,* CVII (July 18, 1914), 648.

10. Kennan to Lyman Abbott, Feb. 8, 1920, George Kennan MSS, Library of Congress.

11. Sydney Brooks, "Russia as a Great Power," *World's Work,* II (Oct., 1901), 1283.

12. A. Maurice Low, "Shall Russia Dominate the World?" *Independent,* LV (May 7, 1903), 1068–9. See also Poultney Bigelow, "The Spread of Russia," *ibid.,* LII (Dec. 20, 1900), 3021–5.

13. Graham, "Why Russia Is Fighting," *Collier's,* LIV (Jan. 23, 1915), 22. For a similar view see A. C. Alford, "Russia's Strength and Her Certainty of Ultimate Victory," *19th Century* (London), LXXVIII (Aug., 1915), 435–43.

14. Crane to Charles William Eliot, Dec. 15, 1914, Crane MSS.

15. *Outlook,* CXV (Jan. 10, 1917), 60.

16. *Independent,* LXXIX (Sept. 7, 1914), 324–5.

17. Harper to Charles R. Crane, June 21, 1916, Harper MSS.

18. Kennan, "The Spiritual Uplift in Russia," *Outlook,* CVIII (Oct. 14, 1914), 377–80; see also his "War Issues in Russia and the Far East," *ibid.,* CVIII (Sept. 2, 1914), 32–4.

19. Kennan, "Russia after the War," *Outlook,* CIX (April 14, 1915), 871–4.

20. Kennan, "Russia after the War," *ibid.,* CIX (April 28, 1915), 977–9.

21. Kennan, "Russia after the War," *ibid.,* CIX (April 7, 1915), 816–18.

22. Kennan, "Russia and Constantinople," *ibid.,* CIX (March 10, 1915), 567.

23. Percy Dearmer, "The Soul of Russia," *19th Century,* LXXVII (Jan., 1915), 77.

24. Norman Angell, *After All* (London, 1951), 182.

25. *Ibid.*

26. Crane to Wilson, Aug. 4, 1914, Crane MSS.

27. Crane to Charles William Eliot, Dec. 15, 1914, *ibid.*

28. House Diary, June 1, 1914, in Charles Seymour, ed., *The Intimate Papers of Colonel House* (Boston, 1926), I, 255.

29. House to Wilson, Aug. 22, 1914, in *ibid.,* 285.

30. House to Gordon Auchincloss, March 5, 1915, in *ibid.*, 388.

31. House Diary, April 28, 1917, in *ibid.*, III (Boston, 1928), 45–6. "Balfour, however, was more impressed with the German menace than he was by the possible danger from Russia."

32. House Diary, Sept. 19, Oct. 28, 1918, House MSS.

33. Brailsford, "The Empire of the East," *New Republic*, I (Nov. 7, 1914), 14–15.

34. Brailsford, "The Slavic Hope," *ibid.*, I (Jan. 9, 1915), 12–13.

35. *Ibid.*, IV (Aug. 14, 1915), 33–4.

36. "Peace without Victory," *New Republic*, IX (Dec. 23, 1916), 201–2.

37. *New Republic*, IX (Dec. 9, 1916), 136.

38. *Ibid.*, IX (Nov. 11, 1916), 36.

39. *Ibid.*, VI (Feb. 26, 1916), 99–100.

40. *New Republic*, X (Feb. 17, 1917), 60.

41. R. W. France to *ibid.*, X (March 10, 1917), 162–3. For similar views see Emily Greene Balch, "In the Balance," *Survey*, XXXVII (Feb. 17, 1917), 565–6; Paul U. Kellogg, "The Fighting Issues," *ibid.*, 572–7.

42. *New Republic*, IX (Sept. 25, 1915), 193.

43. Brailsford, "Russia in Transition," *ibid.*, IV (Oct. 9, 1915), 253.

44. Mary White Ovington to *ibid.*, IX (Jan. 27, 1917), 355.

45. Harold Goddard to *ibid.*, XX (Jan. 13, 1917), 298.

46. St. Louis *Post-Dispatch*, April 3, 1917; Des Moines *Register*, March 4, 1917; New York *World*, March 18, 1917. On Stürmer's treachery see also *Public*, XX (May 11, 1917), 453, citing a Roumanian authority, and Samuel H. Cross, "What Is Wrong in Russia?" *Nation*, CIV (March 8, 1917), 265–7.

47. On Protopopov see William Boyce Thompson, speech in New York, Jan. 28, 1918, William Boyce Thompson–Hermann A. Hagedorn MSS, Library of Congress. It is interesting to note that Protopopov's appointment in Nov., 1916, was at first taken as a "distinct setback to the German party"; see *Current Opinion*, LXI (Dec. 1916), 380–1. On Sukhomlinov see, *e.g.*, New York *Evening Post*, March 13, 1917; St. Louis *Post-Dispatch*, Sept. 4, 1917.

48. On the question of treason see Pares, *Fall of the Russian Monarchy*, pp. 345–7, 391–2; Florinsky, *End of the Russian Empire*, pp. 108–10; C. Jay Smith, *The Russian Struggle for Power* (New York, 1956), pp. 409–10.

Of an entirely different order of reliability were the so-called

"Willy-Nicky Letters," published by Herman Bernstein in the New York *Herald* in September, 1917. These letters between Wilhelm II of Germany and his cousin Nicholas II of Russia showed beyond question that during the period of the Russo-Japanese War the Kaiser had flirted with the possibility of a secret treaty with Russia against the West, and that the Tsar rather naïvely fell in with the spirit of these plans, although nothing came of them. By the time this correspondence was published the Tsar had been overthrown, and his treason, if any, was a dead issue, but the letters served retroactively to confirm the suspicions of the previous winter. Why this should have been so is hard to understand, for the correspondence referred to a period which recent events had made ancient history. A study of German intrigue in the court of Catherine the Great would have been as relevant to conditions in 1916 and 1917. For the letters, see New York *Herald*, Sept. 5–7, 1917. They were published as a book by Knopf in January, 1918. Bernstein sent a copy to Colonel House, whose opinion on the subject is unfortunately not recorded; see Bernstein to House, Dec. 20, 1917, House MSS. For comment see, *e.g.*, Des Moines *Register*, Sept. 7, 1917; also Sidney B. Fay, "The Kaiser's Secret Negotiations with the Tsar, 1904–1905," *American Historical Review*, XXIV (Oct., 1918), 48–72.

49. There are occasional instances of a real appreciation of Russia's social and economic weakness; see Gerald Morgan, "The Matter with Russia," *New Republic*, IV (Sept. 18, 1915), 175–6. But they become increasingly infrequent the longer the war goes on. Morgan himself later blamed Russia's ineffectiveness on the disloyalty of the "courtiers and bureaucrats." He claimed that the Union of the Russian People, a reactionary organization, was pro-German. As authority for this statement he cited articles in the *Journal de Geneve* (Switzerland) which he admitted were "evidently written by a Russian correspondent sympathetic to the Duma"! Morgan, "Russia's Door Ajar," *ibid.*, VI (April 1, 1916), 236–7.

II: The February Revolution

1. Hillquit to New York *World*, May 10, 1917.
2. St. Louis *Post-Dispatch*, March 16, 1917.
3. Des Moines *Register*, March 16, 1917.

4. H. N. Brailsford, "Russia and the Settlement," *New Republic,* X (April 21, 1917), 343; see also his "The President and 'Central Europe,'" *ibid.,* XIV (Feb. 16, 1918), 75–7.

5. According to one version of this story, the Tsar had actually signed a peace treaty with Germany, which the British ambassador, hearing of this subterfuge, demanded to see. Why the Tsar should have consented to show it to him was never made quite clear, but the advocates of this theory insisted that the interview had taken place, and that the British ambassador had torn the treaty to shreds before the Tsar's eyes. This episode presumably set the stage for the British machinations leading to the February revolution. George Foster Peabody to Emily Balch, May 3, 1917, Emily Greene Balch MSS, Swarthmore College Peace Collection. Sir George Buchanan, the British ambassador, had paid a visit to the Tsar, in which he implored the Tsar to grant reforms as the only alternative to "revolution and disaster." Sir George Buchanan, *My Mission to Russia and Other Diplomatic Memories* (London, 1923), II, 41–9. No doubt it was this interview which furnished the factual basis of Peabody's fancies.

6. Harper to Richard Crane, March 15, 1917; Crane to Harper, March 15, 1917, Samuel N. Harper MSS, University of Chicago Library.

7. Harper to Richard Crane, July 23, 1917, *ibid.*

8. New York *World,* March 18, 1917.

9. Springfield *Republican,* March 19, 1917; see also New York *World,* March 22, 1917.

10. Springfield *Republican,* March 19, 1917.

11. New York *Evening* Post, March 17, 1917.

12. Helena Dudley to Jane Addams, April 10 [1917], Jane Addams MSS, Swarthmore College Peace Collection.

13. New York *Evening Post,* March 16, 1917.

14. S[toughton]. C[ooley]. in *Public,* XX (March 23, 1917), 269. For this view see also Des Moines *Register,* March 20, March 21, March 28, 1917; New York *Evening Post,* March 16, March 19, 1917; Springfield *Republican,* March 21, 1917.

15. New York *World,* April 26, 1917. The *World* urged her probable defection as a reason why the United States should adopt all-out war measures, including conscription.

16. Frank Alfred Golder, *Documents of Russian History, 1914–1917* (New York, 1927), pp. 325–6.

17. See F. Seymour Cocks, *The Secret Treaties and Understandings* (London, 1918), *passim.* Arno J. Mayer, *Political Origins of the New Diplomacy* (New Haven, 1959), pp. 17–22, summarizes the contents of the treaties. See also C. Jay Smith, *The Russian Struggle for Power* (New York, 1956), *passim.*

18. For this reversal see N. N. Sukhanov, *The Russian Revolution* (London, 1955), p. 324.

19. As reported in Springfield *Republican,* May 4, 1917. For the full text see Golder, *Documents of Russian History,* pp. 333–4. See also Victor Chernov, *The Great Russian Revolution* (New Haven, 1936), pp. 198–200.

20. See Victor Murdock in Witchita *Eagle,* quoted in Emporia *Gazette,* May 17, 1917; also Springfield *Republican,* May 17, 1917.

21. *New Republic,* XI (May 12, 1917), 31; Springfield *Republican,* April 26, 1917.

22. Kennan to [Lansing], May 23, 1917, George Kennan MSS, Library of Congress.

23. Walling, " 'No Annexations, No Indemnities,' " *Independent,* XC (May 19, 1917), 327.

24. Kennan to Schiff, May 18, 1917, Kennan MSS.

25. Kennan to Lansing, June 16, 1917, *ibid.*

26. Kennan, "The Victory of the Russian People," *Outlook,* XCV (March 28, 1917), 547.

27. *New Republic,* XI (June 16, 1917), 171–2.

28. Philadelphia *Public Ledger,* May 21, 1917; Springfield *Republican,* June 10, 1917.

29. Sinclair, "A Socialist Peace," *Pearson's* XXXVIII (Aug., 1917), 82–3.

30. Colcord MS Diary, April 10 [1917], Lincoln Colcord MSS, in the possession of Mrs. Lincoln Colcord, Northampton, Mass.

31. *New Republic,* XI (May 19, 1917), 65–7. The withdrawal of Russia, the *New Republic* reminded its readers, "would constitute an irremediable disaster to the fighting resources of the Atlantic Powers—a disaster so irremediable that if their diplomacy does not prevent it the failure will constitute a confession of incompetence."

32. Brailsford, "The Russian Peace Formula," *New Republic,* XI (June 23, 1917), 207–9.

33. Beard to *New Republic,* XI (June 2, 1917), 137.

34. Steffens to House, June 20, 1917, Edward M. House MSS, Yale University Library.

35. *Cf.* also, for another expression of the same view, Isaac Don Levine, "The Russian Crisis," *New Republic*, XIII (Dec. 15, 1917). The Russians, according to Levine, were "by no means averse to fighting for democracy."

36. Colcord in Philadelphia *Public Ledger*, May 26, 1917.

37. New York *Evening Post*, May 28, 1917; see also, for comment on this dictum (all of it hostile), *New Republic*, XI (June 2, 1917), 119; New York *World*, May 29, 1917.

38. Russell to Lansing, n.d. [probably late May, 1917], Charles Edward Russell MSS, Library of Congress.

39. New York *World*, Aug. 9, 1917.

40. See *e.g.*, Russell to Wilson, Nov. 7, 1917, George Creel MSS, Library of Congress, and Wilson to Creel, Nov. 10, 1917, *ibid.*; Wilson to Russell, Nov. 10, 1917, Woodrow Wilson MSS, 2d series, Library of Congress.

41. See *Survey*, XXXVIII (Sept. 22, 1917), 558–9; and for an indication of how active the administration was in the formation of this organization, George [Creel] to Frank Walsh, Sept. 1, 1917; [Frederic] C. Howe to Walsh, Sept. 2, 1917; Walsh to Creel, Sept. 10, 1917, all in Frank Walsh MSS, New York Public Library.

42. New York *World*, Sept. 7, 1917.

43. Harold Ickes told Arthur Bestor of the CPI that Russell's appearance in Chicago was "probably the most profitable that has been held here . . . since we started our campaign of patriotic education here." Ickes to Bestor, Nov. 22, 1917, Russell MSS.

44. Kennan to Lansing, May 24, 1917, Kennan MSS.

45. Berger to William Kent, July 12, 1917, William Kent MSS, Yale University Library.

46. Frank Harris, "Russia's Revolutionary Appeal," *Pearson's*, XXXVIII (July, 1917), 24. See also the reply to a letter of Upton Sinclair, by either Harris or A. W. Ricker, *ibid.*, XXXVIII (Aug., 1917), 83, 87.

47. Trachtenberg, in *Report of the First American Conference for Democracy and Terms of Peace*, p. 27, Swarthmore College Peace Collection.

48. *Revolutionary Radicalism*, Report of the Joint Legislative Committee Investigating Seditious Activities, New York State Senate [Lusk Committee] (1920), Part I, vol. I, 1042.

49. Others included S. R. Bertron of the Russian-American Chamber of Commerce, James Duncan of the AFL, Basil Miles of the State Department, Cyrus H. McCormick of International Har-

vester, and John R. Mott of the YMCA. A complete list of the personnel of the mission may be found in the Elihu Root MSS, Library of Congress.

50. Kennan Diary, April 9, 1917, Kennan MSS; see also entry for April 10, 1917. Straus wanted Kennan to head the mission, but Kennan told him that "for many reasons" he would be unable to do so.

51. Typescript address to soviet, June 12, 1917, Russell MSS.

52. Typescript address at Hall of the Medical Academy, Petrograd, July 6, 1917, Russell MSS.

53. Francis to State Dept., cited in Ray W. McDuffee, "The Department of State and the Russian Revolutions" (unpublished Ph.D. dissertation, Georgetown University, 1954), pp. 58–9.

54. Lee to Hillquit, Dec. 17, 1918, Morris Hillquit MSS, State Historical Society of Wisconsin.

55. New York *World*, Feb. 22, 1918.

56. Lee to Hillquit, Dec. 17, 1918, Hillquit MSS.

57. McDuffee, "The Department of State and the Russian Revolutions," pp. 58–9.

58. Crane did not leave Petrograd until September; see Cyril Brown in New York *World*, Sept. 26, 1917.

59. Report of Root mission, n.d. [Aug., 1917], Root MSS.

60. Lansing Diary, Aug. 9, 1917, Robert Lansing MSS, Library of Congress.

61. Springfield *Republican*, July 28, 1917.

62. See, *e.g.*, Harper to a Mr. Stratton, Aug. 18, 1917, Harper MSS.

63. See Samuel N. Harper, *The Russia I Believe In* (Chicago, 1945), p. 107. For the optimism of the press see, *e.g.*, *Public*, XX (Aug. 31, 1917), 832; *Nation*, CV (Aug. 16, 1917), 166–7; New York *Evening Post*, Aug. 9, 1917; Philadelphia *Public Ledger*, Aug. 22, 1917; Springfield *Republican*, Aug. 9, 1917; New York *Sun*, quoted in *Literary Digest*, LV (Sept. 8, 1917), 16–18. The *New Republic*, XI (July 28, 1917), 342, was more measured in its optimism. It thought that Russia was out of the war in a military capacity, but doubted that she would sign a separate peace. The Emporia *Gazette*, Aug. 3, 1917, agreed with the New York *World* (see above, note 15) that it was unlikely that Russia would do any more fighting.

64. Harper, *The Russia I Believe In*, pp. 107–8. In retrospect Harper admitted that "we Americans were guilty of wishful think-

ing, grasping at mere details to support our picture of developing co-operation after an inevitable period of disintegration."

65. Bertron to House, June 18, 1917, House MSS. "The country is overrun with German propagandists," Bertron wrote, "who are preaching every possible wild doctrine in order to add to the general demoralization. The better and educated classes are frightened to death and are holding loose taking no part in the situation whatever. Therefore, the Workmen, who comprise less than 2% of the population, are really in control . . . The masses of the people are very kindly and very interested, but are mere children. They are a veritable kindergarten in the art of freedom." Under the circumstances, a dictator, Bertron thought, "may be a good thing." Nevertheless he did not think Russia would leave the war even if "a complete Socialist cabinet were installed." On the other hand he doubted whether she would "prosecute the war vigorously" unless the cabinet took "bigger steps."

In subsequent weeks Bertron's estimate of the situation remained unchanged.

66. Cyril Brown in New York *World*, Sept. 26, 1917. At the same time, however, Crane declared that although Russia needed peace, she was seeking not a separate but a general peace.

67. House to Wilson, Aug. 15, 1917, Wilson MSS, 2d series. Lincoln Colcord quoted House as saying at about this time: "What I am afraid of is that if we don't make a peace, and if the Russian situation gets worse and worse, there will be a world-wide reaction from democracy. I think that on this count alone, peace must be made this fall if possible." Colcord MS Diary, July 30 [1917].

68. House to Wilson, Aug. 15, 1917, Wilson MSS, 2d series.

69. Lansing to Wilson, Aug. 20, 1917, *ibid.*

70. See cable, House to Balfour, Aug. 18, 1917, Charles Seymour, *The Intimate Papers of Colonel House* (Boston, 1928), III, 154–5. House was conscious of "running counter to the President's own judgment" in favoring a conciliatory reply. He thought, however, that he had gained a friend in Frank Polk, counsellor of the State Department. See House MS Diary, Aug. 15, 1917.

71. House MS Diary, Aug. 18, 1917.

72. *Ibid.*

73. *Ibid.*, Aug. 19, 1917.

74. *Ibid.*

75. Lansing MS Desk Diary, Aug. 20, 1917. For the statement of the Russian embassy see Philadelphia *Public Ledger*, Aug. 21, 1917.

76. *Ibid.*, Aug. 22, 1917.

77. Bullitt's source was Lansing himself. See House MS Diary, Aug. 21, 1917.

78. House to Bakhmetev, Aug. 21, 1917, House MSS.

79. Colcord to House, Aug. 21, 1917, House MSS. See also House MS Diary, Aug. 21, 1917. For the headline in question see New York *Times*, Aug. 21, 1917.

80. House MS Diary, Aug. 22, 1917.

81. *Ibid.*

82. The *Literary Digest*, LV (Sept. 8, 1917), 11, noted that the President's note "was greeted by the American press with a most surprising unanimity of praise." See also Philadelphia *Public Ledger*, Aug. 29, 1917, which cites a great variety of editorial comments.

83. Croly to House, Sept. 7, 1917, House MSS. For the text of the note see Ray Stannard Baker and William E. Dodd, *The Public Papers of Woodrow Wilson* (New York, 1927), III, 96.

84. Lippmann to House, Sept. 10, 1917, House MSS. In a letter to the Secretary of War he had declared, " 'The world made safe for democracy' means concretely not a specific form of government for Germany . . . but a binding assurance that the future method of settlement between the powers shall be by a civil procedure." Lippmann to Newton D. Baker, n.d., Newton D. Baker MSS, Library of Congress.

85. See David Starr Jordan to William Kent, Oct. 29, 1917, Kent MSS, calling it a "masterpiece"; also Wilson to Max Eastman, Sept. 18, 1917, Wilson MSS, 7th series.

86. Emporia *Gazette*, Oct. 29, 1917. The Philadelphia *Public Ledger's* survey of press opinion, Aug. 29, 1917, indicates that the most common interpretation of Wilson's note was "no peace with Prussian autocracy."

87. *New Republic*, XII (Sept. 1, 1917), 116.

88. Sukhanov, *Russian Revolution*, p. 534.

89. See Des Moines *Register*, Sept. 21, 1917; New York *Evening Post*, Sept. 26, 1917. Both the *Register* and the *Evening Post* at this time deplored the search for a strong man.

90. See St. Louis *Post-Dispatch*, Sept. 12, 1917; New York *World*, Sept. 11, 1917.

91. St. Louis *Post-Dispatch*, Sept. 14, 1917. See also Springfield *Republican*, Sept. 11, 1917, Sept. 27, 1917. As long as the outcome was still in doubt, the *Republican* insisted that Kornilov was a Russian patriot, not a counter-revolutionist. After the rebellion fizzled out, the *Republican* took a much sterner view of the affair.

92. St. Louis *Post-Dispatch*, Nov. 19, 1917.

93. See *New Republic*, XII (Sept. 22, 1917), 202–3; *Nation*, CV (Oct. 4, 1917), 358, CV (Nov. 8, 1917), 501–2; New York *Evening Post*, Nov. 5, 1917.

94. New York *World*, Nov. 3, 1917.

95. Polk Diary, Nov. 2, 1917, Frank Polk MSS, Yale University Library; for the department's public statements see St. Louis *Post-Dispatch*, Nov. 3, 1917.

96. New York *World*, Nov. 3, 1917.

97. St. Louis *Post-Dispatch*, Nov. 3, 1917.

98. House MS Diary, Oct. 4, 1917.

99. *Ibid.*, Oct. 21, 1917; see also entry for Sept. 29, 1917, noting conversation with Bakhmetev, and for Sept. 16, 1917, in which House urged these views on the British.

100. Lansing to Francis, Nov. 2, 1917, in *Papers relating to the Foreign Relations of the United States*, 1917, Supplement 2, I, 286.

101. Mayer, *Political Origins of the New Diplomacy*, p. 259.

102. *Ibid.*, pp. 257–8.

103. Springfield *Republican*, Nov. 30, 1917.

III: The Judas of the Nations

1. St. Louis *Post-Dispatch*, Nov. 19, 1917; also *ibid.*, Aug. 21, Nov. 4, Nov. 11, 1917.

2. See, *e.g.*, *ibid.*, Nov. 11, 1917; Arno Dosch-Fleurot in New York *World*, Nov. 10, 1917.

3. See below, ch. 5.

4. St. Louis *Post-Dispatch*, Nov. 4, 1917.

5. *Public*, XX (Oct. 5, 1917), 954.

6. New York *Evening Post*, Nov. 10, 1917.

7. Emporia *Gazette*, Nov. 27, 1917.

8. Des Moines *Register*, Nov. 26, 1917.

9. Chicago *Daily News*, Feb. 14, 1918.

10. St. Louis *Post-Dispatch*, Feb. 16, 1918.

11. Springfield *Republican*, Dec. 15, 1917; see also *ibid.*, Jan. 12, 1918.

12. Milwaukee *Journal*, March 7, 1918.

13. Charles Edward Russell, *Unchained Russia* (New York, 1918), pp. 254–7. Earlier Russell was quoted as saying, "The bol-

sheviki are poor old dreamers, that's all." Milwaukee *Sentinel*, Jan. 1, 1918.

14. Des Moines *Register*, Nov. 20, 1918.

15. New York *World*, Nov. 26, 1917.

16. Lawrence to Villard, Feb. 18, 1918, Oswald Garrison Villard MSS, Harvard University Library. See also the *Evening Post's* very similar editorial, Feb. 16, 1918.

17. Des Moines *Register*, Nov. 9, 1917.

18. See *ibid.*, Dec. 15, 1917.

19. Pinchot to Creel, Nov. 14, 1917, Amos Pinchot MSS, Library of Congress.

20. New York *Evening Post*, Nov. 27, 1917. For Bonar Law's speech on war aims, see above, page 55.

21. Walter Weyl, *The End of the War* (New York, 1918), p. 177.

22. William Allen White, *Woodrow Wilson: The Man, His Times and His Task* (Boston, 1924), p. 364.

23. Arthur Bullard, *The Russian Pendulum* (New York, 1919), pp. 64–8. For other expressions of the theory that the Allies by refusing to revise their war aims undermined the Kerensky regime and prepared the way for the Bolshevik revolution—and one could cite hundreds of such expressions—see, *e.g.*, *New Republic*, XIII (Nov. 17, 1917), 60; XIV (Feb. 16, 1918), 68–9; XIV (March 2, 1918), 123–4; Isaac Don Levine, "The Russian Crisis," *ibid.*, XIII (Dec. 15, 1917), 525; Chicago *Daily News*, April 15, 1918; Louis Edgar Browne in *ibid.*, April 12, 1918; Arno Dosch-Fleurot in New York *World*, Feb. 22, June 2, 9, 23, 1918; Herbert Bayard Swope in *ibid.*, Feb. 25, 1918; Philadelphia *Public Ledger*, March 21, 1918; Lincoln Colcord in *ibid.*, Jan. 1, 1918; Colcord to Wilson, Dec. 3, 1917, Wilson MSS, 2d series; George Creel to Wilson, Dec. 27, 1917, *ibid.*; Des Moines *Register*, March 28, 1918; New York *Evening Post*, Nov. 24, 1917; Milwaukee *Journal*, Nov. 27, 1918; Edward A. Ross to Henry C. Stuart, Sept. 6, 1918, Edward A. Ross MSS, State Historical Society of Wisconsin; Raymond Clapper to his wife, Dec. 29, 1917, Raymond Clapper MSS, Library of Congress; Amos Pinchot to Frank Harris, April 11, 1918, Amos Pinchot MSS; Louise Bryant, *Six Red Months in Russia* (New York, 1918), p. 75; Charles Edward Russell, *Bare Hands and Stone Walls* (New York, 1933), p. 362.

24. For hostile comment see, *e.g.*, Springfield *Republican*, Nov. 25, 1917.

25. MS of address, Feb. 17, 1918, Amos Pinchot MSS.
26. *Nation,* CV (Nov. 29, 1917), 581.
27. New York *Evening Post,* Jan. 25, 26, 28, 1918. The treaties were reprinted in the Chicago *Daily News,* St. Louis *Post-Dispatch,* Milwaukee *Journal,* Philadelphia *Inquirer,* Pittsburgh *Press,* Baltimore *Sun,* Richmond *News Leader,* St. Paul *Dispatch,* Hartford *Times* and Buffalo *News.* See Oswald Garrison Villard, *Fighting Years: Memoirs of a Liberal Editor* (New York, 1939), p. 340–1. In England they were published by the Manchester *Guardian* beginning Dec. 12, 1917. Yet defenders of Wilson maintained to the end that the terms of the treaties were not widely known in the United States. See Ray Stannard Baker to Villard, March 1, 1922, and Villard's reply, March 6, 1922, in Villard MSS.
28. Nock to Villard, Jan. 26, 1918, Villard MSS.
29. New York *Evening Post,* Dec. 21, 1917.
30. Strunsky, "What the Bolsheviks Really Want," *Nation,* CV (Nov. 15, 1917), 530–2.
31. *New Republic,* XIII (Dec. 1, 1917), 105.
32. *Ibid.,* XIII (Nov. 17, 1917), 57–8.
33. House to Wilson, Nov. 28, 1917, in Charles Seymour, *Intimate Papers of Colonel House* (Boston, 1928), III, 281.
34. Colcord to House, Nov. 15, 20, 1917, Edward M. House MSS, Yale University Library, based on conversations with Bakhmetev on November 14 and 15. Bakhmetev had seen Lansing on November 14. "I asked him if he had urged this view of the Russian situation upon Secy. Lansing," Colcord wrote. "He said, 'I didn't try this time. Secy. Lansing does not understand.' "
35. Transmitted in cable, Maddin Summers to Lansing, Nov. 27, 1917, State Dept. file 861.00, vol. VIII, National Archives.
36. Bullard to House, Dec. 12, 1917, House MSS. "We all feel—excepting the Ambassador—that nothing should be done to gratuitously insult or offend the de facto government."
37. Bullard to Creel, Dec. 9, 1917, Arthur Bullard MSS, Princeton University Library.
38. Bullard, "Memorandum on the Bolshevik Movement in Russia," Jan., 1918, *ibid.*
39. Judson to his wife, Nov. 3, 1917, William V. Judson MSS, Newberry Library. For Robins' comment see Robins to his wife, Aug. 23, 1917, Raymond Robins MSS, State Historical Society of Wisconsin.
40. Judson to H. E. Yates, Dec. 11, 1917, Judson MSS.

41. George F. Kennan, *Soviet-American Relations* (Princeton, 1956), I, 128 on Judson's removal; see also New York *World*, Jan. 13, 1918.

42. Robins, "Some Considerations of the Present Condition in Russia," Nov. 20, 1917, Robins MSS.

43. Lamont, speech in New York, Dec. 6, 1918, William Boyce Thompson-Hermann Hagedorn MSS, Library of Congress.

44. House MS Diary, May 3, 1918; see also Lamont to House, [Jan. 2, 1918], April 5, 1918, House MSS.

45. Creel to Wilson, Dec. 31, 1917, Ray Stannard Baker MSS, Library of Congress. Two Baker collections are cited in this work, one in the Library of Congress, the other in the Princeton University Library. Unless otherwise indicated, the former is the one referred to.

46. For Thompson's visits see *ibid.*; also Lamont to House, April 5, 1918, House MSS; and Hermann Hagedorn, *The Magnate: William Boyce Thompson and His Time* (New York, 1935), pp. 251–60. For his interviews and articles see New York *World*, Jan. 10, 12, 1918; New York *Evening Post*, Jan. 18, 24, 1918; see also *New Republic*, XIII (Jan. 19, 1918), 325.

47. Roosevelt to Robins, Jan. 14, 1918, Robins MSS.

48. Peabody to Thompson, March 2, 1918, Thompson-Hagedorn MSS; New York *Herald Tribune*, Feb. 1, 1918.

49. Frank Polk MS Diary, Jan. 8, 1918, Yale University Library.

50. Henry S. Brown to Thompson, Feb. 19, 1918, Thompson-Hagedorn MSS. See also Thomas W. Lamont, *Across World Frontiers* (New York, 1951), p. 90.

51. Harper to Richard Crane, Feb. 22, 1918, Samuel N. Harper MSS, University of Chicago Library.

52. "Notes by Professor Harper," Feb. 7, 1918, *ibid.* There is a copy of these notes in the Charles Edward Russell MSS, Library of Congress.

53. Lippmann to House, Feb. 19, 1918, House MSS. See also Lincoln Steffens to George Creel, Sept. 7, 1918, Lincoln Steffens MSS, Columbia University Library: "I remember last winter how you and some of us wanted to communicate unofficially with Lenine, Trotzky and company, and how I searched for someone in New York whose mere word would go with these men. There was no such person then."

54. Robins to his wife, Nov. 11, 1917, Robins MSS.

55. Ross to Robins, Nov., 1917 [no day], *ibid.*

56. On Jan. 30, 1918 he wrote to the editor of *Century:* "There is a possibility I may be called to Washington to give my impressions and size-up of the Russian situation before long." Ross to Douglas Z. Doty, Jan. 30, 1918, Ross MSS. There is no record of any communication between Ross and Wilson before July, 1918, and a letter from Wilson to Charles R. Crane, June 28, 1918, Wilson MSS, 7th series, suggests that Wilson was not familiar with Ross' views. "Thank you for telling me about Professor Ross . . . and Professor Abbott. Would it be possible for you to suggest to them that a brief thesis from each of them on the aspects of the Russian situation which are most hopeful to them would be very warmly welcomed by me?" The mere fact that it was Crane who commended Ross to the President shows that by this time Ross was considered safe.

57. New York *World,* Nov. 4, 1917.

58. *Ibid.,* Jan. 5, 1918.

59. See *ibid.,* Jan. 3, 4, 1918.

60. William Henry Chamberlin, *The Russian Revolution, 1917–1921* (New York, 1935), I, 399–403.

61. Advertisement by Boni & Liveright in *Public,* XXI (Jan. 25, 1918), 98. See Trotsky, *The Bolsheviki and World Peace* (New York, 1918), with an introduction by Lincoln Steffens.

62. Chicago *Daily News,* Jan. 17, 1918. For serializations of the book see, *e.g.,* St. Louis *Post-Dispatch* and New York *World,* beginning Jan. 13, 1918; see also New York *Evening Post,* Jan. 22, 1918; Springfield *Republican,* Feb. 2, 1918.

63. St. Louis *Post-Dispatch,* Jan. 19, 1918.

64. New York *World,* Dec. 18, 1917.

65. St. Louis *Post-Dispatch,* Jan. 6, 1918.

66. House's manuscript diary is full of references to his concern with the *Public Ledger;* see, *e.g.,* entries for Jan. 10, 1917, Feb. 16, 1917, April 6, 1917, Aug. 22, 1917, Aug. 23, 1917. In the summer of 1917, when he was thinking of trying to publicize the war-aims question by arranging a debate between an American paper and the *Berliner Tageblatt* (an idea vetoed by Wilson), he considered selecting the *Ledger* before finally settling on the New York *World.* See Lincoln Colcord to House, July 4, 1917, House MSS.

67. Philadelphia *Public Ledger,* Jan. 13, 1918.

68. Philadelphia *North American,* March 20, 1918.

69. See Spurgeon to Lansing, April 6, 1918, Lansing MSS; Harold

Sudell to *Public Ledger*, March 21, 1918; Harold Evans to *ibid.*, March 22, 1918; Oswald Garrison Villard, *Some Newspapers and Newspaper-men* (New York, 1923), pp. 155–6.

70. For the New York *Times* see Walter Lippmann and Charles Merz, "A Test of the News," *New Republic*, XXIII (supplement to Aug. 4, 1920), 12.

71. New York *World*, Feb. 22, 23, 1918. This dispatch was widely reprinted and evoked approving comment even from papers previously indifferent to the war-aims question. See, *e.g.*, Des Moines *Register*, Feb. 28, March 28, 1918; Philadelphia *Public Ledger*, Feb. 23, 1918 (which pointed out with pride that Colcord had said the same thing at the time); Milwaukee *Journal*, Feb. 22, 1918; New York *Evening Post*, Feb. 22, 1918.

Colcord, Philadelphia *Public Ledger*, Feb. 25, 1918, claimed that Dosch-Fleurot's dispatch "had been smuggled past the [Allied] censor in manuscript."

72. New York *Evening Post*, Feb. 1, 1918.

73. House MS Diary, Feb. 1, 1918.

74. Philadelphia *Public Ledger*, Jan. 16, 1918.

75. *Ibid.*, Jan. 27, 1918.

76. Polk MS Diary, Jan. 8, 1918; but perhaps Polk himself was not in sympathy with Wilson's policy. Lamont, *Across World Frontiers*, p. 90, says that Polk favored the policy advocated by Robins and Thompson. But Lamont, in turn, may only have been repeating an erroneous impression which he had got from Thompson.

77. New York *World*, Jan. 11, 1918.

78. New York *Times*, Jan. 14, 1918.

79. Kennan, I, 271, refers to Creel's rebuttal but gives no source for it. I have been unable to locate it either in the *Times* or in the *World*.

80. Lansing MS Desk Diary, Jan. 15, 1918; Polk MS Diary, Jan. 14, 1918.

81. Walling, "The Chief Danger of Revolutions and Revolutionary Movements in Eastern Europe," enclosed in Wilson to Lansing, Feb. 13, 1918, Ray Stannard Baker MSS.

82. Wilson to Lansing, Feb. 13, 1918, *ibid.*

83. Lansing MS Desk Diary, Feb. 15, 1918.

84. Philadelphia *Public Ledger*, Jan. 9, 1918; see also his article in *ibid.*, Jan. 8, 1918.

85. Thomas H. Simpson to Amos Pinchot, Jan. 14, 1918, Amos Pinchot MSS.

86. Baltimore *Sun*, Jan. 9, 1918.

87. House MS Diary, Jan. 29, 1918.

88. Milwaukee *Journal*, Jan. 10, 1918.

89. New York *World*, Jan. 9, 1918. Harper to Mott, Feb. 7, 1918, Harper MSS, urged "a message to the constructive workers in Russia . . . over the heads of the Bolsheviki. This was the President's idea, I believe, in the message of January 8."

90. "As a harmonizer of discordant elements on war issues, Mr. Wilson has done astonishing work," said the Springfield *Republican*, Jan. 11, 1918. Everybody applauded the speech, for different reasons. By far the best contemporary analysis of it, which subjects its ambiguities to penetrating scrutiny, is an anonymous article by "Observer," New York *Evening Post*, Feb. 6, 1918.

91. John W. Wheeler-Bennett, *The Forgotten Peace: Brest Litovsk* (London, 1938), pp. 191–3, 226–8, 247–50.

92. *Public*, XXI (Feb. 16, 1918), 195–6.

93. *Ibid.*, XXI (Jan. 11, 1918), 36.

94. New York *World*, Feb. 26, 1918.

95. New York *Evening Post*, March 8, 1918.

96. Peabody to Pinchot, Feb. 23, 1918, Amos Pinchot MSS.

97. Peabody to Baker, Jan. 5, 1918, Newton D. Baker MSS, Library of Congress. After the resumption of the peace negotiations, however, people began to lose faith in the power of Russian propaganda to undermine German morale. "I expect Germany will in time disintegrate under the spread of democratic not Bolshevik doctrine," Peabody wrote to Pinchot, Feb. 23, 1918, Pinchot MSS.

98. See, *e.g.*, Springfield *Republican*, Jan. 3, 1918.

99. "They must have gone quite mad," Colcord exclaimed over one of their editorials. Colcord to House, Aug. 30, 1918, House MSS. For his departure from the *Public Ledger* see Colcord to House, Aug. 16, 1918, *ibid.*; and George P. West, "A Newspaper Tragedy," *Public*, XXI (Aug. 10, 1918), 1016–19. After serving briefly on the staff of the *Public* Colcord joined the *Nation* in the spring of 1919.

100. New York *World*, May 26, 1918.

101. Robins to his wife, April 14, 1918, Robins MSS.

102. Bullard to Creel, March 14, 1918, Bullard MSS.

103. Kennan, *Soviet-American Relations*, I, 492–3.

104. See Lockhart's memorandum of this conversation, March 5, 1918, Francis MSS. It is interesting to note that Lockhart stresses the importance of forestalling Japanese intervention and says almost nothing about military aid to the soviets.

105. Kennan, I, 503.

106. Gumberg's translation, in his hand, Alex Gumberg MSS, State Historical Society of Wisconsin.

107. *E.g.*, speech to League of Free Nations Assn., March 22, 1919, in *Nation*, CVIII (March 29, 1919), 453.

108. Sister Anne Vincent Meiburger, *Efforts of Raymond Robins toward the Recognition of Soviet Russia and the Outlawry of War, 1917–1933* (Washington, 1958), p. 57; William Hard, *Raymond Robins' Own Story* (New York, 1920), p. 215.

The State Department's apprehensions about Robins are succinctly stated in Lansing's MS Desk Diary entry for June 21, 1918: "[Basil] Miles on examining Robbins' [*sic*] baggage. Told him to make it thorough."

109. Robins MS Diary, June 28, 1918.

110. Croly to Robins, July 16, 1918, Robins MSS; Robins MS Diary, July 12, 1918.

111. Robins MS Diary, July 22, 1918.

112. See Croly to Robins, July 16, 1918; Robins to Croly, July 16, 1918, Robins MSS. For the article in question see Ransome, "An Open Letter to America," *New Republic*, XV (July 27, 1918), 371–7. The article contains no reference to Robins' negotiations with Trotsky.

113. Robins MS Diary, July 23, 1918.

114. Walter Weyl MS Diary, Aug. 2, 1918, in the possession of the Weyl family.

115. Robins to Roosevelt, Aug. 24 [1918], Robins MSS.

116. Clapper Diary, July 12, 1918, Raymond Clapper MSS, mentions meeting Robins.

117. Clapper to his wife, Dec. 8, 1918, Clapper MSS.

118. For Bullitt's connection with the State Dept. see William Phillips to Lansing, Dec. 26, 1917, William C. Bullitt MSS, Yale University Library.

119. His account, however, is garbled; according to Clapper, Bullitt, "a bolshevik himself," was the source of Robins' information that "the soviets were the natural indiginous form of local government" in Russia. Why Clapper thought that Robins, who

was in Russia throughout the early months of the revolution, should have had to rely for such information on Bullitt, who was in Washington the whole time, is a mystery. But it may be significant that Bullitt's name was mentioned in this context.

120. John Reed, "On Intervention in Russia," *Liberator*, I (Nov., 1918), 14–17.

121. *Upton Sinclair's* (Jan., 1919), p. 4.

122. *Liberator*, I (Oct., 1918), 25.

123. Harper to E. Chappell Porter, Dec. 13, 1918, Harper MSS. Harper held Robins "responsible for much of this loose thinking," but added that "in all justice to him, however, he is more frequently misquoted than correctly cited."

124. Roosevelt to Robins, Sept. 20, 1918, Robins MSS.

125. *Liberator*, I (Oct., 1918), 24–5.

126. *Nation*, CVII (Nov. 16, 1918), 574–5.

127. Colcord to House, Dec. 18, 1918, House MSS.

128. Johnson to Robins, Dec. 13, 1918, Robins MSS: "Will you please read the questions which I submitted, and, at your convenience, write me just what you have in support of the facts intimated in them." When Johnson next raised the question, he evidently had documents from Robins at hand; see Johnson to Robins, Dec. 20, 1918, Robins MSS. Raymond Clapper said that Johnson "got a copy of [Trotsky's appeal for aid] from Raymond Robbins [*sic*] . . . I imagine Johnson has heard everything that Robins [*sic*] could tell him by now." Clapper to his wife, n.d. [Jan., 1919], Clapper MSS.

129. *Congressional Record*, 65th Cong., 3d sess. (Dec. 12, 1918), 344–5.

130. Harper to William C. Huntington, n.d. [ca. Jan., 1919] in Samuel N. Harper, *The Russia I Believe In* (Chicago, 1945), pp. 112–13.

131. *New Republic*, XVIII (March 29, 1919), 262.

132. Colcord to Villard, Dec. 31, 1919, Villard MSS.

133. Harper to Jerome Landfield, March 22, 1919, Harper MSS.

134. Jameson to Harper, March 8, 1919, *ibid.*

135. Ransome, New York *World*, Feb. 22, 1918, incorrectly reported that Trotsky was for the treaty. But Trotsky's attitude was well known.

136. Kennan, I, 499–500, 516–17.

137. Francis to Lansing, March 12, 1918, *Foreign Relations*,

1918, Russia, I, 397–8. See also Francis to Lansing, March 9, 1918, Francis MSS, in which the ambassador warned the State Department that Trotsky and Lenin "may possibly request Allied assistance." "Cannot too strongly urge unwisdom of Japanese invasion now," Francis said. "Conference may ratify peace but if I receive assurance from you that Japanese peril baseless think conference will reject humiliating peace terms." See also a second telegram, Francis to Lansing, March 9, 1918, *ibid.*, to the same effect. The State Department could hardly have been as ignorant of the situation in Russia as Kennan (I, 516–17) believes.

138. C. K. Cumming and Walter W. Pettit, *Russian-American Relations, March, 1917–March, 1920* (New York, 1920), p. 88.

139. Kennan, I, 516.

IV: Standing by Russia

1. Norman Thomas to Lillian D. Wald, March 1, 1918, Norman Thomas MSS, New York Public Library.

2. Charles Seymour, *Intimate Papers of Colonel House* (Boston, 1928), III, 382.

3. New York *World*, Feb. 25, 1918.

4. *Liberator*, I (May, 1918), 5.

5. Address in Milwaukee, April 26, 1918, Milwaukee *Journal*, April 28, 1918.

6. Evans Clark to *New Republic*, XV (June 22, 1918), 234–5.

7. Chicago *Daily News*, Feb. 22, 1918; see also Des Moines *Register*, Feb. 22, 1918; Emporia *Gazette*, March 12, 1918.

8. Springfield *Republican*, April 11, 1918.

9. Milwaukee *Journal*, March 2, 1918; New York *Evening Post*, March 4, 1918.

10. *Liberator*, I (July, 1918), 5–6; A. W. Ricker in *Pearson's*, XXXIX (May, 1918), 43–4; *ibid.* (June, 1918), 108–9; *ibid.* (July, 1918), 184 ff.; Ricker to House, April 25, 30, 1918, Woodrow Wilson MSS, Library of Congress, 2d series; House MS Diary, May 16, 1918, Yale University Library.

11. New York *World*, June 28, 1918; New York *Times*, June 27, 1918.

12. Floyd Dell, *Homecoming* (New York, 1933), p. 321.

13. Thomas to Wald, March 1, 1918, Thomas MSS.

14. *Public*, XXI (Jan. 18, 1918), 67.

15. New York *Evening Post*, March 9, 1918.

16. White to Victor Murdock, Jan. 14, 1918, William Allen White MSS, Library of Congress.

17. American Association for International Conciliation pamphlets, no. 122 (New York, Jan., 1918), p. 8.

18. H. G. Wells, "The Question at Issue," *New Republic*, XIV (Feb. 9, 1918), 47–9.

19. Clapper to his wife, Feb. 12, 1918, Raymond Clapper MSS, Library of Congress.

20. Colcord to Wilson, Feb. 23, 1918, House MSS.

21. See above, pp. 83–84.

22. Ray Stannard Baker and William E. Dodd, *Public Papers of Woodrow Wilson* (New York, 1927), III, 206.

23. Baker to Polk, May 28, 1918, R. S. Baker MSS, Princeton University Library.

24. See Herbert L. Carpenter to House, May 11, 1918, and S. R. Bertron to House, May 20, 1918, House MSS; Bullitt to House, May 20, 1918, William C. Bullitt MSS, Yale University Library; Harper to Lippmann, May 7, 1918, Samuel N. Harper MSS, University of Chicago Library; Harper to Ross, June 14, 1918, Edward A. Ross MSS, State Historical Society of Wisconsin; House to Wilson, June 4, 1918, Woodrow Wilson MSS, Library of Congress, 2d series; Carpenter to Borah, Dec. 9, 1918, William E. Borah MSS, Library of Congress; *Survey*, XL (May 11, 1918), 164–5; David Lawrence in New York *Evening Post*, June 12, 1918.

25. House MS Diary, June 13, 1918; see also House to Wilson, June 13, 21, 1918, in Seymour, *Intimate Papers of Colonel House*, III, 409–10, 412–14.

26. House MS Diary, June 13, 1918; Hapgood to House, June 17, 1918, July 14 [1918], House MSS.

27. Frederic M. Corse to Harper, Aug. 2, 1918, Harper MSS. Corse attributed the suggestion to the *New Republic*.

28. Harper to Dixon, July 28, 1918, Harper MSS.

29. Porter to Harper, July 20, 1918, *ibid.*

30. Harper to Charles R. Crane, July 17, 1918, *ibid.*

31. Statement of Margaret Biddle, April 26, 1932, William Boyce Thompson–Hermann Hagedorn MSS, Library of Congress.

32. Lamont to House, April 5, 1918, House MSS; see also Thomas D. Thacher to Hagedorn, June 1, 1932, Thompson–Hagedorn MSS.

33. Proof of an article by Harper in *Union Labor Advocate*, en-

closed with George Hodge to Harper, May 10, 1918; Harper to Porter, n.d. [May, 1918], Harper MSS.

34. Harper to Corse, May 9, 1918, *ibid.*

35. Harper to Porter, July 4, 1918, *ibid.*

36. Harper to Richard Crane, June 30, 1918, *ibid.*

37. Harper to Mott, July 2, 1918, *ibid.*

38. Corse to Harper, May 6, 1918, *ibid.*

39. Harper to Corse, Aug. 10, 1918; Harper to Dixon, Aug. 11, 1918, *ibid.*

40. House to Wilson, March 3, 1918, Wilson MSS, 2d series; House MS Diary, March 2, 3, 4, 5, 1918; Polk MS Diary, Yale University Library, March 1, 3, 5, 6, 1918.

41. George F. Kennan, *Soviet-American Relations* (Princeton, 1958), II, 150–65, 294–320, gives by far the best account of the Czech revolt. See also John Albert White, *The Siberian Intervention* (Princeton, 1950), pp. 237–54.

42. Harper to Mott, July 13, 1918, Harper MSS.

43. Wilson to House, July 8, 1918, Ray Stannard Baker, MSS, Library of Congress.

44. See William B. Webster and W. L. Hicks to Robins, March 24, 29, 31, April 9, 1918; to Bruce Lockhart, March 30, April 1, 1918; to Robins and Lockhart, April 17, 1918; and their report, April 26, 1918, all in Raymond Robins MSS, State Historical Society of Wisconsin. See also Robins to Thompson, April 4, 1918, *ibid.*

45. On the question of whether American policy was really motivated by a fear of Japan, see my article, "American Intervention in Siberia: A Reinterpretation," *Political Science Quarterly*, LXXVII (June, 1962), 205–23.

46. New York *Times*, June 11, 1918.

47. *Ibid.*, June 20, 1918. For this view see also Columbus (Ohio) *Dispatch*, cited in White, *Siberian Intervention*, 353–4.

48. New York *Times*, June 8, 1918.

49. *Ibid.*, Oct. 28, 1918. At the meeting of Oct. 26, Charles Edward Russell was elected chairman of this organization, Henry L. Slobodin vice-chairman, William English Walling secretary and J. G. Phelps Stokes treasurer.

50. Kennan to Lansing, May 23, 1918, George Kennan MSS, Library of Congress, urged intervention "to help the Russians of the trans-Baikal to throw off the Bolshevik yoke."

51. See Lasch, "American Intervention in Siberia," *Political Science Quarterly*, LXXVII, 218–19.

52. Philadelphia *Public Ledger*, Aug. 22, 1918.

53. New York *Evening Post*, July 22, 1918.

54. Milwaukee *Journal*, Aug. 26, 1918.

55. St. Louis *Post-Dispatch*, Aug. 6, 1918.

56. Philadelphia *Public Ledger*, Aug. 5, 9, 1918; Chicago *Daily News*, Aug. 5, 1918; Des Moines *Register*, Aug. 8, 1918; New York *Evening Post*, Aug. 5, 1918.

57. Santeri Nuorteva in New York *Evening Post*, Sept. 21, 1918; George F. Kennan, "The Sisson Documents," *Journal of Modern History*, XXVIII (June, 1956), 130.

58. S. Poliakov-Litovzev in *New Europe*, reprinted in New York *Evening Post*, March 13, 1918. See also New York *World*, Feb. 9, 1918; Philadelphia *Public Ledger*, Feb. 10, 1918; Isaac Don Levine in *ibid.*, Feb. 19, 1918.

59. Philip Patchin to Creel, Sept. 20, 1918, in James R. Mock and Cedric Larson, *Words That Won the War* (Princeton, 1939), p. 319; Creel to Wilson, May 9, 1918, George Creel MSS, Library of Congress.

60. House MS Diary, Sept. 24, 1918.

61. New York *Evening Post*, Sept. 16, 17, 1918, Nov. 17, 1918. Most of the *Evening Post*'s criticisms, it should be noted, were borrowed from the analysis by Poliakov-Litovzev, cited above, note 58. The *Evening Post*, Oct. 2, 1918, reprinted his article. To the *Evening Post*'s objections as to chronology, Samuel Harper and J. F. Jameson replied that the documents were written in Russian, "and dated in accordance with the calendar currently used in Petrograd." New York *Evening Post*, Nov. 11, 1918.

For other attacks on the documents see Manchester *Guardian*, Sept. 19, 1918, reprinted in New York *Evening Post*, Oct. 5, 1918, and Santeri Nuorteva (head of the Finnish Information Bureau, a pro-Bolshevik propaganda agency), in *ibid.*, Sept. 21, 1918. The best modern criticism is the article by Kennan, cited above, note 57.

62. New York *World*, quoted in New York *Evening Post*, Sept. 18, 1918.

63. Creel to New York *Evening Post*, Oct. 2, 1918.

64. The *New Republic*, XVI (Oct. 5, 1918), 269–70, was perhaps the first to suggest this procedure.

65. For the Harper-Jameson report, Oct. 26, 1918, see New York

Evening Post, Nov. 11, 1918. For some reason Professor Coolidge took no part in the committee's investigation.

66. *Nation,* CVII (Nov. 23, 1918), 616–17.

67. Harper to Jerome Landfield, Nov. 15, 1918, Harper MSS. See also, for a later expression of the same view, Harper to S. R. Tompkins, Jan. 29, 1937, *ibid.*

68. Samuel N. Harper, *The Russia I Believe In* (Chicago, 1945), pp. 111–12.

69. Bullard to Sisson, n.d. [1919], Arthur Bullard MSS, Princeton University Library.

70. Draft of autobiography, Harper MSS. Kennan (I, 450–1) calls attention to the passage which Harper omitted in publication.

71. Harper's views have already been referred to. Bullard's are recorded in his memorandum, "German Gold," March, 1918, Bullard MSS. Crane stated categorically that Lenin was "not a German agent," although he added that he had done Germany "a far greater service . . . than any paid agent could possibly have done." New York *World,* March 1, 1918. George Kennan was also somewhat skeptical. He believed that the Bolsheviks numbered in their ranks "hundreds of Germans & German agents," but he never made this fact the burden of his complaint against them. Kennan to Lansing, May 23, 1918, Kennan MSS.

72. Arthur Bullard, *The Russian Pendulum* (New York, 1919), pp. 97–102.

73. "After the armistice intervention is justified by the Red Peril; before the armistice it is justified by the German peril." Lippmann and Merz, "A Test of the News," p. 14. The exodus of Allied correspondents from Russia in the summer of 1918 may have had something to do with the increasingly anti-Bolshevik tone of the reporting of events in Russia, for after their departure American papers were forced to depend more heavily than ever on questionable sources in Germany and Scandinavia. By Sept. 10, 1918, the New York *Times* itself admitted: "Bolshevist Russia now stands in absolute telegraphic isolation from the rest of the world, with the single exception of the outlet through Germany. . . . Consequently the Bolshevist wireless services and the German-censored and German-colored dispatches alone supply the outside world with Russian news." See also, on this point, Louis Edgar Browne, Chicago *Daily News,* July 3, 1918.

74. New York *Times,* Dec. 12, 1917.

75. New York *Herald,* March 6, 1918, quoted in *Public,* XXI (April 27, 1919), 533.

76. Springfield *Republican,* April 28, 1918, based on sources in Copenhagen and Stockholm.

77. New York *Times,* June 23, 1918.

78. Springfield *Republican,* June 29, 1918, New York *Evening Post,* June 28, 1918, based on German sources.

79. Springfield *Republican,* Aug. 13, 16, 1918; New York *Times,* Aug. 16, 1918, based on German sources.

80. New York *Times,* Sept. 2, 1918. The shooting itself was announced by *Pravda,* but the report that Lenin had died came from Copenhagen.

81. *Liberator,* I (Oct., 1918), 28–33.

82. New York *Times,* Sept. 2, 1918.

83. *Ibid.,* Sept. 3, 1918.

84. *Ibid.,* Sept. 14, 1918.

85. New York *World,* Oct. 9, 14, 1918.

86. Springfield *Republican,* Dec. 1, 1917.

87. New York *Times,* Dec. 16, 1918; *New Republic,* XIX (June 25, 1919), 228; Herman Bernstein in Washington *Post,* May 5, 1919; Louisville *Courier-Journal,* May 24, 1919; *New Republic,* XX (Nov. 19, 1919), 334.

88. Lippmann and Merz, "A Test of the News," pp. 10–11.

89. Lippmann and Merz, "More News from the Times," *New Republic,* XXIII (Aug. 11, 1920), 299–301.

90. Lusk Committee, *Hearings,* VI (June 26, 1919), 96–101.

91. Omaha *World-Herald,* May 17, 1919; see also New York *Times,* Oct. 26, 1918, June 7, 1918; Des Moines *Register,* Oct. 26, 1918.

92. Oliver M. Sayler, *Russia White or Red* (Boston, 1919), pp. 189–90.

93. Louise Bryant, "Are Russian Women 'Nationalized'?" *Liberator,* II (April, 1919), 20–21. See also Bessie Beatty in *Bolshevik Propaganda,* Hearings before the Subcommittee of the Committee on the Judiciary, U.S. Senate, 66th Cong. 1st sess. (1919), p. 708.

94. For the announcement of the impending massacres see New York *Times,* Oct. 31, Nov. 6, 8, 1918. For the retraction see the inconspicuous item in the New York *World,* Nov. 11, 1918.

Dial, LXV (Dec. 14, 1918), 563, admitted that there had been invitations to mass terror placarded about Moscow (at the instigation of Zinoviev, the *Dial* thought) and even that the words "St.

Bartholomew" had been used. See also *Liberator,* II (Jan., 1919), 6–7; *New Republic,* XVII (Nov. 16, 1918), 55. Algernon Lee to Morris Hillquit, Dec. 17, 1918, Morris Hillquit MSS, State Historical Society of Wisconsin, wrote: "There was just a grain of truth in the story about an intended Bartholomew's night on November 10. It seems that Zinovieff . . . did propose something like Danton's September prison-cleaning. The Council of People's Commissars promptly recalled him, putting Lunacharsky in his place, and replacing the latter with Gorky."

95. New York *World,* March 21, 1918, quoting a Petrograd dispatch to the London *Daily Telegraph.* See E. H. Carr, *The Bolshevik Revolution* (London, 1950–1953), I, 151–3.

96. Evans Clark, *Facts and Fabrications about Soviet Russia* (New York, 1920), p. 52. Clark dismissed even Arthur Bullard's *The Russian Pendulum,* a judicious account, as "anti-Soviet propaganda." *Ibid.,* p. 39.

97. *Upton Sinclair's,* Jan., 1919, p. 4.

98. Lusk Committee, *Hearings,* I (June 12, 1919), 66–7, quoting resolutions adopted by the National Executive Committee of the Socialist Labor Party, May 4, 1919.

99. Lincoln Colcord, "The Carving of Russia," *Nation,* CVIII (June 14, 1919), 940–41, accused the international bankers of conspiring to partition Russia and then to make Russia pay for the war.

100. Bullard to Norman Hapgood, March 16, 1920, Bullard MSS.

V: The Bolsheviks as Anarchists

1. Quoted by Dwight MacDonald in *Commentary,* XXIX (April, 1960), 292.

2. Robert Lansing MS Diary, Dec. 7, 1917, Library of Congress.

3. Lansing to Wilson, Feb. 15, 1918, State Dept. file 861.00/1333a, National Archives.

4. Lansing to R. S. Hungerford, Nov. 14, 1918, Lansing MSS.

5. Lansing MS Diary, Sept. 1, 1919.

6. *Ibid.*

7. Crane to Josephine Crane Bradley, Dec. 17, 1917, Charles R. Crane MSS, Archive of Russian and East European History, Columbia University.

8. Lincoln Steffens in *Treaty of Peace with Germany*, Hearings before the Committee on Foreign Relations, U.S. Senate, 66th Cong., 1st sess. (1919), p. 1282.

9. Walter Weyl MS Diary, Aug. 14, 1919.

10. Charles Edward Russell, *Unchained Russia* (New York, 1918), pp. 79–80.

11. Weyl MS Diary, Aug. 10, 1919. Italics in the original.

12. Stearns, review of Russell, *Unchained Russia, Dial,* LXV (Sept. 5, 1918), 158–60.

13. Weyl MS Workbook, undated entry [1918?].

14. Reed, "The Structure of the Soviet State," *Liberator,* I (Nov., 1918), 33.

15. New York *World,* Feb. 3, 1918.

16. Evans Clark, "Americanism and the Soviet," *Nation,* CVIII (March 22, 1919), 424.

17. See above, p. 105 ff. See also, *e.g., Independent,* XCVI (Dec. 14, 1918), 352–3; Oliver M. Sayler, *Russia White or Red,* pp. 279–80. But Sayler, unlike most of the writers on the subject, does not make the mistake of confusing the Soviet with the *mir.*

18. Moissaye J. Olgin, "To Make Russia Fight," *Asia,* XVIII (June, 1918), 447. See also Milwaukee *Journal,* April 27, 1919.

19. Howe, "Realpolitik in Russia," *New Republic,* XV (June 15, 1918), 202–3. Howe must have corresponded with Robins while the latter was in Russia, for in May, 1918 (a month before Robins' return) he told William Kent, who had grown skeptical about the revolution, that there were a "surprisingly large number of people" who disagreed with him. Colonel Thompson, for one, still regarded the revolution as a success. "And that is the impression I got from Raymond Robins as well." Howe to William Kent, May 20, 1918, Kent MSS, Yale University Library. Kent remained unconvinced. In 1924 he declared, as he had maintained all along, that the Bolsheviks had "set everything back for fifty years." Kent to Amos Pinchot, Nov. 18, 1924, *ibid.;* see also Kent to Charles R. Crane, Dec. 20, 1923, *ibid.*

20. Chicago *Daily News,* April 17, July 2, 1918. The *Daily News* accepted this interpretation in an editorial of July 2, 1918.

21. Ross, "Russian Character in Transition," *Asia,* XVIII (Sept., 1918), 762–4.

22. Williams, "The Soviet at Work," *Dial,* LXV, 531–3.

23. Milwaukee *Journal,* April 27, 1919.

24. Ross to Oliver M. Sayler, Oct. 8, 1918, Edward A. Ross MSS, State Historical Society of Wisconsin.

25. Edward A. Ross, *Russia in Upheaval* (New York, 1918), p. 205. This passage appears originally in his report to the Executive Committee and National Council of the American Institute of Social Service (which paid for his trip to Russia), March 30, 1918, Ross MSS.

26. Perly Doe to *Public*, XXI (Aug. 24, 1918), 1090.

27. Bullitt to House, May 20, 1918, Woodrow Wilson MSS, Library of Congress, 2d series.

28. Beatty, "Russian Bolshevism—Tyranny or Freedom," *Public*, XXII (Jan. 25, 1919), 84–6.

29. Freda Kirchwey, review of Bessie Beatty, *The Red Heart of Russia, Liberator*, II (April, 1919), 43–4.

30. Villard to Ray Stannard Baker, April 17, 1929, R. S. Baker MSS, Library of Congress.

31. Villard to Hapgood, May 19, 1919, Oswald Garrison Villard MSS, Harvard University Library. See also Villard, *Fighting Years* (New York, 1939), p. 461, where he takes credit for at least having outgrown, by 1919, "any merely smug liberalism and social blindness due to the ease and luxury of my upbringing."

32. Hutchins Hapgood, *A Victorian in the Modern World* (New York, 1939), pp. 259–60.

33. See New York *Evening Post*, Aug. 1, 3, 1918; Springfield *Republican*, Aug. 2, 1918. As the *Evening Post* was constituted in 1917, according to Allan Nevins (*The Evening Post: A Century of Journalism* [New York, 1922], 577), "Mr. Ogden decided all questions of policy [and] wrote almost all the leading political editorials." It may be added that the new owner, Thomas W. Lamont, exerted no greater influence over the policy of the paper than his predecessor.

34. New York *Evening Post*, Sept. 25, 1918.

35. For Villard's comments on the decline of the *Evening Post* see his *Some Newspapers and Newspaper-men* (New York, 1923). The divorce between the *Nation* and *Evening Post* became effective with the *Nation's* issue of July 6, 1918; the sale of the *Evening Post* to Lamont was completed Aug. 1, 1918.

According to Agnes Leach, a prominent backer of the *Evening Post*, Colonel House at one point made an offer to buy the paper. She said also that there was talk of Colonel William Boyce Thompson's coming in as co-owner with Lamont. Agnes Leach to Norman Thomas, June 7, 1918, Norman Thomas MSS, New York Public Library.

36. Villard, *Fighting Years*, pp. 352–3.

37. Villard to Max Eastman, Dec. 3, 1937, Villard MSS. According to Villard, *Fighting Years*, p. 469, it was Eastman who passed on to him the document in question; where Eastman got it, Villard was never able to ascertain. Eastman was in possession of other secret documents bearing on American policy in Russia, including a telegram from Frank Polk to Lansing, which he read before a mass meeting in New York. Springfield *Republican*, July 20, 1919.

Bullard's telegram is in *Nation*, CIX (July 19, 1919), 67. See also *Dial*, LXVII (July 26, 1919), 66.

38. For these disclosures see below, p. 201 ff.

39. Villard to Joseph P. Tumulty, Nov. 8, 1918, Villard MSS. Villard claimed that the issue of Nov. 8, 1919 consisted of 50,000 copies, while the corresponding issue of the previous year consisted of 11,773 copies. *Nation*, CIX (Nov. 8, 1919), 575. At that time he said that the *Nation* had added 4,750 readers since July. Villard to Tumulty, Nov. 8, 1918, Villard MSS. Thus the circulation in July, 1918, must have been around 7,000. The figure of 35,000 is from the Lusk Committee's report, *Revolutionary Radicalism*, Part I, vol. 2, p. 2005, dated April, 1920.

40. Mencken, "The Intelligentsia," clipping from Baltimore *Evening Sun*, March 16, 1920, in Villard MSS.

41. Nock to Amos Pinchot, June 26, 1918, Amos Pinchot MSS, Library of Congress.

42. Clark, "Americanism and the Soviet," *Nation*, CVIII (March 22, 1919), 422–4.

43. Des Moines *Register*, March 16, 1919.

44. Weyl MS Diary, July 20, 1919.

45. *Ibid.*, July 29, 1919.

46. "Americanism and the Soviet," *Nation*, CVIII, 422.

47. Nock to Villard, March 16, 1920, Villard MSS.

48. Reed, "The Structure of the Soviet State," *Liberator*, I (Nov., 1918), 34.

49. Williams to Harper, Sept. 4, 1918, Samuel N. Harper MSS, University of Chicago Library. Dosch-Fleurot, who now advocated active support of the counter-revolution, was likewise convinced that

the soviet form of government was no longer representative. The soviets were dominated by the Bolsheviks, he said, by means of physical terror. New York *World*, July 7, 1918.

50. Theses on Constituent Assembly, in E. H. Carr, *The Bolshevik Revolution* (London, 1950), I, 113–14. For American opinion see, *e.g.*, *Liberator*, I (March, 1918), 5–6; Bessie Beatty, "All Power to the Soviets!" *Asia*, XVIII (Sept., 1918), 756–61; Louise Bryant, *Six Red Months in Russia* (New York, 1918), pp. 89–103.

51. Quoted in George F. Kennan, *Soviet-American Relations* (Princeton, 1956), I, 359. The fact that the elections to the assembly went against the Bolsheviks only proved, according to Arthur Ransome, "An Open Letter to America," *New Republic*, XV (July 27, 1918), 374, that "in every country it is only a small minority that really concerns itself with politics"—a curious echo of Havelock Ellis' defense of Holy Russia (see above, p. 4).

52. Baltimore *Sun*, Jan. 22, 1918.

53. Baltimore *Evening* Sun, March 16, 1920, clipping in Villard MSS.

54. Albert Jay Nock, *Memoirs of a Superfluous Man* (New York, 1943), pp. 134–5.

55. Arthur Bullard, *The Russian Pendulum* (New York, 1919), p. 35.

56. He was president of the League of Free Nations Association, the anti-imperialist counterpart of the League to Enforce Peace. The fact that he opposed dismemberment of Austria-Hungary, which was advocated even by the *New Republic*, will offer some idea of his orientation. See Hapgood to *New Republic*, XVI (Sept. 21, 1918), 231.

57. For Hapgood's appointment see House MS Diary, Feb. 14, 1919; Hapgood to House, June 4, 1918, House MSS; Lansing MS Desk Diary, May 27, 1918.

58. See Frank Polk MS Diary, Jan. 13, 1919, Yale University Library: "Norman Hapgood: Discussed Russia. Said we made a mistake to have anything to do with Bolsheviks. Told him I could not agree with him." In his autobiography Hapgood says that he favored recognizing the Bolshevik government "as soon as its stability should seem reasonably probable" and advocated doing business with the cooperatives only as an "interim plan." Norman Hapgood, *The Changing Years* (New York, 1930), pp. 247–9. This hardly accords with his letters of the period. He did say in one letter

to Wilson that the Allies would have to treat the Bolsheviks with "tact" in order in help them "to a certain extent in saving their faces." Hapgood to Wilson, May 26, 1919, Wilson MSS, series 8-A. There is no evidence, however, that he advocated recognition of the Bolsheviks.

59. *Ibid.* 60. Hapgood to Wilson, June 30, 1919, *ibid.*

61. *Ibid.*

62. Hapgood to House, March 19, 1919, House MSS.

63. Wilson to Hapgood, June 20, 1919, Wilson MSS, series 8-A; and Aug. 1, 1919, *ibid.*, 7th series. For other letters in this correspondence see Hapgood to Wilson, June 21, 1919, *ibid.*, series 8-A; Hapgood to Wilson, July 27, 29, Aug. 8, 1919, *ibid.*, 2d series.

64. See Hapgood, "Who Speaks for Russia?" *New Republic,* XXI (Feb. 25, 1920), 378–9.

65. *Survey,* XLII (April 26, 1919), 140–3; XLII (Aug. 9, 1919), 709.

66. *Nation,* LVII (July 20, 1918), 55–6; New York *Evening Post,* May 16, 1918.

67. Bullard, *Russian Pendulum,* p. 35.

68. For the first objection see, *e.g.*, New York *Evening Post,* Sept. 10, 1918; *Public,* XXI(Sept. 21, 1918), 1199–1200; for the second, E. J. Dillon, quoted in New York *Times,* Nov. 3, 1918.

69. Springfield *Republican,* May 8, 1918.

70. Chicago *Daily News,* June 8, 1918.

71. *New Republic,* XVI (Aug. 24, 1918), 92.

72. New York *World,* Feb. 4, 1919.

73. *Ibid.*, Feb. 6, 1919.

74. See, *e.g.*, St. Louis *Post-Dispatch,* Feb. 4, 1919.

75. *Nation,* CVIII (Feb. 15, 1919), 239.

76. The *World,* for instance (Feb. 8, 1919), called him a "radical Socialist."

77. *Ibid.*

78. Unidentified newspaper clipping, n.d., George Creel MSS, Library of Congress. The organization referred to, the Truth about Russia Committee, was formed early in 1919; see W. J. Ghent in New York *Times,* Feb. 9, 1919.

79. New York *Evening Post,* April 12, 1919; see also *ibid.*, Feb. 4, 1919, and Springfield *Republican,* Feb. 5, 1919.

80. Steffens to Allen Suggett, June 14, 1919, Lincoln Steffens MSS, Columbia University Library.

81. Steffens to Mrs. J. J. Hollister, Dec. 6, 1919, Ella Winter and Granville Hicks, eds., *The Letters of Lincoln Steffens* (New York, 1938), I, 490.

82. See, *e.g.*, "The Immediate Tasks of the Soviet Government" (March–April, 1918), in V. I. Lenin, *Selected Works* (Moscow: Foreign Languages Publishing House, 1951), Vol. II, Part II, pp. 468–71.

83. Lenin, *The Soviets at Work* (New York: Rand School of Social Science, 1918), p. 38; italics in original. See also Springfield *Republican*, Sept. 26, 1919.

84. *The Soviets at Work*, p. 25.

85. Alvin Johnson, review of John Spargo, *Bolshevism*, *New Republic*, XIX (June 14, 1919), 231–2; Emporia *Gazette*, Sept. 17, 1919.

86. Alexander Berkman's Russian diary (1920–1922), *The Bolshevik Myth* (New York, 1925), is interesting in this light.

87. Theodore Draper, *The Roots of American Communism* (New York, 1957), pp. 121–6, is good on Minor's conversion to communism.

88. *Nation*, CVIII (Feb. 8, 1919), 181.

89. St. Louis *Post-Dispatch*, Jan. 9, 1919.

90. *New Republic*, XIV (April 6, 1918), 280.

91. *Nation*, CVIII (Feb. 8, 1919), 181.

92. New York *Evening Post*, March 20, 1918.

VI: Getting Out of Russia

1. Bullard to House, Jan. 25, 1919, in *Nation*, CIX (July 19, 1919), 67. See above, pp. 140–1.

2. Harper to Allen Carter, n.d. [Aug., 1919], Samuel N. Harper MSS, University of Chicago Library.

3. Landfield to Harper, Nov. 22, 1918, *ibid.*

4. Landfield to Harper, Aug. 19, 1919, *ibid.*

5. Lansing MS Diary, Oct. 9, 1919, Library of Congress.

6. Harper to Allen Carter, n.d. [Aug., 1919], Harper MSS.

7. Baker to Wilson, Nov. 27, 1918, Newton D. Baker MSS, Library of Congress.

8. Harper to Mott, Nov. 19, 1918, Harper MSS. See also Harper to Jerome Landfield, Nov. 29, 1918, *ibid.*

9. See Newton D. Baker to Wilson, Jan. 1, 1919, Woodrow Wilson MSS, Library of Congress, series 8-A.

10. *New Republic,* XX (Sept. 17, 1919), 185.

11. St. Louis *Post-Dispatch,* Feb. 3, 1919.

12. Stearns, "Will Russia Defeat Us?" *Dial,* LXV (Nov. 16, 1918), 397–9.

13. Williams, speech in New York, Dec. 27, 1918, in *Survey,* XLI (Jan. 11, 1919), 512.

14. Seattle *Union Record,* quoted in *Nation,* CIX (Sept. 27, 1919), 421.

15. Quoted in Springfield *Republican,* Jan, 12, 1919.

16. Amos Pinchot to Johnson, Dec. 9, 1918, Amos Pinchot MSS, Library of Congress.

17. New York *World,* Jan. 5, 1919.

18. Des Moines *Register,* Dec. 25, 1918.

19. *New Republic,* XVIII (Feb. 8, 1919), 37–9.

20. *Cong. Rec.,* 65th Cong., 3d sess. (Dec. 12, 1918), p. 345.

21. New York *World,* Jan. 5, 1919.

22. Robins to Gumberg, April 11, 1919, Alex Gumberg MSS, State Historical Society of Wisconsin.

23. Robins to Gumberg, May 14, 1919, *ibid.*

24. "I should hate to have it stopped," he told Gumberg, "before I had seen it with my own eyes." Hard to Gumberg, Oct. 24, 1919, *ibid.*

25. Hard to Gumberg, n.d. [July? 1918], *ibid.*

26. Hard to Gumberg, July 24, 1919, *ibid.*

27. New York *Evening Post,* Nov. 20, 1918.

28. H[orace]. K[allen]. to New York *Evening Post,* Nov. 23, 1918.

29. Villard to Lawrence, Nov. 12, 1918, Oswald Garrison Villard MSS, Harvard University Library.

30. New York *Evening Post,* Nov. 30, 1918; see also *ibid.,* Dec. 26, 1918, in which the editors argued that armed intervention was justified if it helped Russian democrats throw off Bolshevism.

31. For this correspondence see C. K. Cumming and Walter W. Pettit, *Russian-American Relations* (New York, 1920), pp. 337–43. Kolchak's note is dated June 4, 1919; the Allied reply, June 12, 1919.

32. See Polk to Lansing, June 19, 1919, Wilson MSS, series 8-A.

33. Springfield *Republican,* May 27, 1919.

34. New York *Evening Post,* June 13, 1919; Philadelphia *Public Ledger,* May 31, 1919; Chicago *Daily News,* June 14, 1919.

35. Des Moines *Register,* May 27, 1919, July 26, 1919. The *Register* admitted throughout, however, that Kolchak was a dictator and could not survive without Allied support. *Ibid.,* April 21, June 12, 18, 1919.

36. Springfield *Republican,* May 28, June 12, 28, 1919.

37. Washington *Star,* June 13, 1919; see also, *e.g.,* Omaha *World-Herald,* May 16, 1919.

38. New York *Times,* May 24, 1919.

39. John Albert White, *The Siberian Intervention* (Princeton, 1950), p. 107; William Henry Chamberlin, *The Russian Revolution* (New York, 1935), II, 202–3.

40. *New Republic,* XX (Aug. 6, 1919), 2.

41. New York *World,* Aug. 31, 1919.

42. Quoted in *New Republic,* XX (Sept. 10, 1919), 160.

43. Robins MS Diary, Jan. 30, 1919, State Historical Society of Wisconsin.

44. Hapgood to House, Dec. 18, 1918, Edward M. House MSS, Yale University Library.

45. Polk to Lansing, Jan. 11, 1919, Wilson MSS, series 8-A. See also Polk to Lansing, Jan. 24, 1919, *ibid.* Lansing passed Polk's cable along to Wilson; Lansing to Wilson, Jan. 15, 1919, *ibid.*

46. Polk to American Commission to Negotiate Peace, Jan. 8, 1919, Wilson MSS, series 8-A.

47. Springfield *Republican,* Feb. 18, 1919.

48. Notes of a Meeting of the Supreme War Council, Jan. 12, 1919, Wilson MSS, series 8-A.

49. Emporia *Gazette,* Sept. 17, 1919. *Cf.* Villard, "Peace Manoeuvres," *Nation,* CVIII (Jan. 11, 1919), 51: "the best way to get rid of Lenine and Trotsky is to let them hang themselves."

50. *New Republic,* XVIII (Feb. 15, 1919), 72.

51. *Ibid.,* XVIII (April 5, 1919), 288.

52. Lansing to Wilson, Jan. 9, 1919; Wilson to Lansing, Jan. 10, 1919, Wilson MSS, series 8-A; see also Polk to Lansing, Jan. 6, 1919, *ibid.*

53. *E.g.,* Brooklyn *Eagle,* reprinted in Springfield *Republican,* Jan. 19, 1919.

54. Wilson to Grenville S. MacFarland, Nov. 27, 1918, Wilson MSS, 2d series.

55. Notes, Council of Ten, Jan. 16, 1919, R. S. Baker MSS, Princeton University Library.

56. House MS Diary, Jan. 1, 1919.

57. "Notes by W. H. Buckler of Conversations with Mr. L[itvinov]. in Stockholm Jan. 14th to 16th, 1919," House MSS.

58. Notes, Council of Ten, Jan. 21, 22, Feb. 1, 1919, R. S. Baker MSS, Princeton.

59. House MS Diary, Sept. 19, 1918.

60. Lansing to Poole, Feb. 8, 1919, Wilson MSS, series 8-A.

61. New York *World*, Jan. 14, 1919.

62. Des Moines *Register*, Jan. 23, 1919; Villard in *Nation*, CVIII (Feb. 1, 1919), 166. See also, for other expressions of approval, New York *Evening Post*, Jan. 23, 1919; Springfield *Republican*, Jan. 23, 1919.

63. *Nation*, CVIII (Jan. 25, 1919), 110.

64. Chicago *Tribune*, quoted in St. Louis *Post-Dispatch*, Feb. 2, 1919.

65. New York *World*, Feb. 8, 1919.

66. *New Republic*, XVIII (Feb. 1, 1919), 9–10.

67. Chicago *Daily News*, Jan. 29, 1919.

68. Sallie White to Victor Murdock, Feb. 11, 1919, William Allen White MSS, Library of Congress.

69. Cumming and Pettit, *Russian-American Relations*, pp. 299–300.

70. Chamberlin, *Russian Revolution*, II, 155.

71. New York *World*, Feb. 4, 1919.

72. Chamberlin, *Russian Revolution*, II, 155–8, is good on Bolshevik motives at this time.

73. Des Moines *Register*, Feb. 21, 1919.

74. Chicago *Daily News*, Feb. 7, 1919.

75. New York *Evening Post*, Jan. 23, 1919.

76. Springfield *Republican*, Feb. 7, 1919.

77. Herron to House, Feb. 13, 1919, House MSS.

78. For Bullitt, see *Treaty of Peace with Germany*, Hearings before the Committee on Foreign Relations, U.S. Senate, 66th Cong., 1st sess. (1919), p. 1245; for White, see White to Mitchell Pirie Briggs, Aug. 24, 1929, in Briggs' *George D. Herron and the European Settlement* (Palo Alto, 1932), p. 145, n. 30; see also David Hunter Miller, *My Diary at the Peace Conference* (privately printed [1924]), IX, 178.

79. Notes, Council of Ten, Feb. 15, 1919, R. S. Baker MSS, Princeton.

80. *Ibid.* Balfour appeared to agree with this line of reasoning. He reminded the Council that there was a body of opinion hostile to intervention which could not simply be ignored; "it was necessary to take steps to put the Bolsheviks in the wrong."

81. House MS Diary, Feb. 17, 1919.

82. David Lloyd George, *Memoirs of the Peace Conference* (New Haven, 1939), I, 243–4; House to Wilson, n.d. [Feb. 19, 1919], Wilson MSS, series 8-A; House MS Diary, Feb. 17, 1919.

83. House to Wilson [Feb. 19, 1919], Wilson MSS; see also Lansing MS Desk Diary, Feb. 17, 1919.

84. House to Wilson [Feb. 19, 1919], Wilson MSS.

85. Lloyd George, *Memoirs,* I, 244.

86. Wilson to House, Feb. 19, 1919; see also Wilson to House [Feb. 20, 1919], Wilson MSS, series 8-A.

87. [House] to Wilson, Feb. 23, 1919, *ibid.*

88. Lansing to Bullitt, Feb. 18, 1919, in *Treaty of Peace with Germany,* p. 1234.

89. See, *e.g.,* Bullitt to House, Jan. 19, 1919, William C. Bullitt MSS, Yale University Library.

90. Lansing MS Desk Diary, Feb. 16, 1919.

91. See, *e.g.,* Briggs, *Herron and the European Settlement,* p. 147.

92. *Treaty of Peace with Germany,* p. 1245–6. William Allen White, for what his testimony is worth (and on a number of points his account of the Prinkipo affair is hopelessly garbled), took the same view. Bullitt and Steffens were sent to Moscow, White says in his *Autobiography* (New York, 1946), p. 562, "to find out whether or not Lenin and Trotsky and Tchicherin . . . would send delegates to Prinkipo."

93. Lansing to Bullitt, Feb. 18, 1919, in *Treaty of Peace with Germany,* p. 1234.

94. Herron to *New Republic,* XXI (Dec. 3, 1919), 25–6.

95. *Ibid.,* 26.

96. House MS Diary, March 1, 1919.

97. Lloyd George, *Memoirs,* I, 246.

98. Undated memorandum, in Bullitt's hand, of important peace conference dates, in an engagement book in Bullitt MSS. It is not at all clear whether these notes were made at the time of the con-

ference or later in preparation for Bullitt's appearance before the Senate. The fact that they were made in an engagement book seems to suggest the former, although it is hardly conclusive.

99. Herron to *New Republic*, XXI, 26.

100. See White to Wilson, April 2, 1919; Wilson to White, April 2, 1919, Wilson MSS, series 8-A.

101. Lloyd George, *Memoirs*, I, 246.

102. Charles Seymour, *Intimate Papers of Colonel House* (Boston, 1928), IV, 348.

103. "His hatred for the Bolshevists was lurid," said William Allen White, "What Happened to Prinkipo," *Metropolitan*, LI (Dec., 1919), 68.

104. Herron to *New Republic*, XXI, 26.

VII: Retreat and Resignation

1. Steffens to Brand Whitlock, Dec. 20, 1924, Lincoln Steffens MSS, Columbia University Library.

2. Pettit's notes of the trip, March 9, 1919, in Ann Garcia Gerhart, "The United States and the Problem of Russia at the Paris Peace Conference" (honors thesis, Bryn Mawr, 1956), p. 52.

3. Bullitt to Grew, March 6, 1919, in *ibid.*

4. Kerr to Bullitt, Feb. 21, 1919, in *Treaty of Peace with Germany*, Hearings before the Committee on Foreign Relations, U.S. Senate, 66th Cong., 1st sess. (1919), p. 1247.

5. White to Sallie White, Feb. 9, 1919, Walter Johnson, ed., *Selected Letters of William Allen White* (New York, 1947), p. 197.

6. *Treaty of Peace with Germany*, p. 1246.

7. Bullitt to Wilson, Lansing and House, March 16, 1919, in David Hunter Miller, *My Diary at the Peace Conference* (privately printed [1924]), VI, 445–50. Why they objected to Prinkipo is not clear. Presumably they objected because in order to get to that place their delegates would have had to pass through territory controlled by the armies of General Denikin.

8. Miller, *Diary*, I, 189 (March 19, 1919); Lansing MS Desk Diary, March 19, 1919, Library of Congress. "House seems favorable," Lansing wrote. "White opposed. I think that I must oppose."

9. Steffens to Ella Winter, Jan. 3, 1920, Steffens MSS.

10. House MS Diary, March 25, 1919, Yale University Library.

11. *Treaty of Peace with Germany*, pp. 1260–1.

12. Bullitt to Pettit, April 18, 1919, William C. Bullitt MSS, Yale University Library.

13. Lansing MS Desk Diary, March 26, 1919.

14. *Treaty of Peace with Germany*, p. 1261.

15. House MS Diary, March 26, 1919. See also *Treaty of Peace with Germany*, p. 1261.

16. House MS Diary, March 26, 1919.

17. *Ibid.*, March 26, 1919.

18. *Ibid.*, March 28, 1919.

19. *Ibid.*, March 26, 1919.

20. Bullitt to Pettit, April 18, 1919, Bullitt MSS. "At the last moment," according to Bullitt, just as the House-Bullitt plan seemed about to be adopted, "David Hunter Miller, who, as you know, is the blackest reactionary we have here, persuaded Auchincloss that such a proposal was excessively bad, and Auchincloss in turn persuaded House that something milder should be done at first."

21. House MS Diary, March 29, 1919.

22. *Treaty of Peace with Germany*, p. 1264.

23. "Hoover had made to House a proposition to feed the Russians. House had not been able to put over our whole proposition for peace direct and there was a hitch till Hoover came along with his humanitarian suggestion. Meanwhile I had had lunch one day with Nansen . . . and evidently I had stirred him up about Russia so that he had written a letter to the President. Our crowd . . . seized upon these two notions, Nansen's and Hoover's, put them together and were developing an American policy toward Russia." Steffens to Laura Suggett, April 8, 1919, in Ella Winter and Granville Hicks, *The Letters of Lincoln Steffens* (New York, 1938), I, 464–5.

24. Draft of reply to Nansen, April 3, 1919, Miller, *Diary*, VII, 433–4.

25. [Bullitt] to Auchincloss, April 4, 1919, Bullitt MSS.

26. Lansing MS Desk Diary, April 5, 1919.

27. *Ibid.*; Bullitt's redraft of Auchincloss-Miller letter, n.d., in Miller, *Diary*, VII, 440–1.

28. Reply to Nansen as sent, April 9, 1919, *ibid.*, pp. 442–3.

29. Notes, Council of Four, May 20, 1919, R. S. Baker MSS, Princeton University Library.

30. House MS Diary, April 14, 17, 1919; Miller, *Diary*, I, 254 (April 16, 1919).

31. William Henry Chamberlin, *The Russian Revolution* (New York, 1935), I, 189, 191–2.

32. Chicherin to Nansen, received in Paris May 15, 1919, in R. S. Baker MSS, Princeton.

33. Notes, Council of Four, May 19, 1919, *ibid.*

34. See Notes, Council of Four, May 7, 9, 10, *ibid.*

35. Notes, Council of Four, May 10, 1919, *ibid.*

36. Notes, Council of Four, May 9, 1919, *ibid.*

37. *New Republic*, XIX (May 24, 1919), 110.

38. *Ibid.*, XX (Sept. 3, 1919), 135–6.

39. Lippmann to House, July 19, 1919, House MSS; see also Lippmann to Baker, June 9, 1919, Newton D. Baker MSS, Library of Congress.

40. Weyl MS Diary, Dec. 28, 1918; Ralph Hayes to Newton D. Baker, Dec. 19, 22, 1918, Newton D. Baker MSS.

41. Weyl MS Diary, Feb. 23, 1919, citing Norman Angell and Frederic C. Howe.

42. Weyl MS Diary, Aug. 10, 1918.

43. Pinchot to Roy Howard, Jan. 23, 1919, Amos Pinchot MSS, Library of Congress; Villard to David Lawrence, Nov. 15, 1918, Oswald Garrison Villard MSS, Harvard University Library.

44. Colcord to Wilson, July 13, 1918, Woodrow Wilson MSS, Library of Congress, 2d series.

45. Colcord to Bullitt, Nov. 5, 1918, Bullitt MSS. Italics in original.

46. Colcord to House, March 8, 1919, Louis D. Brandeis MSS, University of Louisville Law Library. Colcord had probably read this rumor in the *Nation*; see its editorial, "A Russian Policy at Last," CVIII (March 8, 1919), 339.

47. House to Colcord, April 3, 1919, House MSS.

48. Weyl MS Diary, April 24, 1919.

49. Bullitt to Wilson, April 6, 1919, Bullitt MSS.

50. Clipping enclosed in Bullitt to Wilson, April 18, 1919, Wilson MSS, series 8-A.

51. *Ibid.*

52. Bullitt to Wilson, May 17, 1919, *ibid.*

53. Arthur M. Schlesinger Jr., *The Crisis of the Old Order* (Boston, 1957), p. 14. For Berle's views on Russian policy at the peace conference see his review of Cumming and Pettit, *Russian-American Relations*, *New Republic*, XXIII (June 16, 1920), 92–4;

for Morison's views see, *e.g.*, Morison to Isaiah Bowman, Feb. 24, 1919, House MSS.

54. New York *Tribune*, March 24, 1919. See also William Phillips to American Commission, March 28, 1919, Wilson MSS, series 8-A.

55. *Nation*, CVIII (April 16, 1919), 553.

56. *Nation*, CVIII (April 26, 1919), 643. For additional evidence see *ibid.*, CVIII (April 5, 1919), 488; Springfield *Republican*, March 27, April 5, 9, 1919; Washington *Post*, April 1, 2, 10, 1919; New York *Evening Post*, April 3, 1919; Des Moines *Register*, April 4, 5, 1919.

57. Tumulty to Wilson, April 2, 1919, Wilson MSS, series 8-A.

58. Phillips to American Commission, March 28, 1919, Wilson MSS, series 8-A; Porter to Harper, March 27, 1919, Samuel N. Harper MSS, University of Chicago Library. Porter was referring in particular to Ludwig C. A. K. Martens, head of the Soviet Bureau (which supplanted Nuorteva's Finnish Information Bureau in April, 1919 as the semi-official Bolshevik propaganda agency in America) and to George V. Lomonossov. The latter, a Menshevik, came to the United States in 1917 as a representative of the Provisional Government, but by the summer of 1918, he was advocating recognition of the Bolsheviks. See his article, "Recognize the Soviets," *Liberator*, I (Aug., 1918), 11–13; also "Russia at the Cross-Roads," *Nation*, CVIII (March 1, 1919), 321–2. For Martens see Theodore Draper, *The Roots of American Communism* (New York, 1957), pp. 161–2, and *Russian Propaganda*, Hearing before a Subcommittee of the Committee on Foreign Relations, U.S. Senate, 66th Cong., 2d sess. (1920), *passim;* for Lomonossov, see Rachelle S. Yarros to Helen Bones, July 11, 1918, Wilson MSS, 2d series; Gilbert E. Roe to Morris Hillquit, March 31, 1919, Morris Hillquit MSS, State Historical Society of Wisconsin.

59. *Nation*, CIX (July 12, 1919), 34.

60. *Ibid.*

61. G[ilbert]. F. C[lose]. to Tumulty, July 17, 1919, Wilson MSS, 2d series.

62. Tumulty to Wilson, July 17, 1919, with Wilson's "OK," Wilson MSS, 2d series.

63. *Ibid.*

64. *Bolshevik Propaganda*, pp. 536–7; see also Louise Bryant, "Louise Bryant before the Elders," *Pearson's*, XL (April, 1919), 246–7; Raymond Clapper to his wife, Feb. 13, 1919, Raymond

Clapper MSS, Library of Congress. It must be said, however, that Miss Bryant's tone was rather provocative, if not belligerent. As Samuel Harper observed, she "quite naturally used the occasion to tease the conservative senators." MS Autobiography, Harper MSS.

65. *Treaty of Peace with Germany*, p. 1161.

66. *Ibid.*, p. 1253. 67. *Ibid.*, p. 1280.

68. *Ibid.*, p. 1254. The original of Bullitt's "Memorandum for the President and the Commissioners Plenipotentiary to Negotiate Peace" [April 1, 1919], is in the Wilson MSS, series 8-A.

69. Lansing to Wilson, Sept. 17, 1919, Wilson MSS, 2d series; Lansing MS Desk Diary, Sept. 12, 1919.

70. Ray Stannard Baker, "Memorandum of a Conversation with Mrs. Robert Lansing," 1929, R. S. Baker MSS, Library of Congress. She herself admitted, however, according to Baker, "that Mr. Lansing was unwise in his action regarding that." Presumably she meant that he was unwise in giving his opinions to Bullitt in the first place, which he certainly was, if he expected them to remain confidential.

71. Memorandum, May 8, 1919, in Robert Lansing, *The Peace Negotiations: A Personal Narrative* (Boston, 1921), pp. 272–4. "It must be admitted in honesty," he wrote, "that the League is an instrument of the mighty to check the normal growth of national power and national aspirations among those who have been rendered impotent by defeat. Examine the Treaty and you will find peoples delivered against their wills into the hands of those whom they hate, while their economic resources are torn from them and given to others. Resentment and bitterness, if not desperation, are bound to be the consequences of such provisions." For additional evidence of Lansing's views see Bullitt's notes of the conversation in question, May 19, 1919, Bullitt MSS (presumably written immediately after the conversation), which agree with his testimony before the Senate; and Lansing's brief note, in his MS Desk Diary, May 19, 1919: "Bullitt on leaving service. Was complimentary on my work and attitude as to treaty of peace."

72. House MS Diary, Sept. 15, 1919.

73. Des Moines *Register*, Oct. 1, 1919; New York *Evening Post*, Aug. 1, Sept. 13, 1919.

74. *Ibid.*, April 4, 1919.

75. Villard, *Fighting Years* (New York, 1939), p. 448. Allan Nevins, *The Evening Post* (New York, 1922), p. 577, says that "international politics was left very largely to Simeon Strunsky."

76. New York *Evening Post,* May 26, 1919; Philadelphia *Public Ledger,* May 31, 1919; Des Moines *Register,* June 12, 18, 1919; Chicago *Daily News,* June 14, 1919. The Springfield *Republican* opposed recognition of Kolchak all along; *e.g.,* editorial of May 28, 1919.

77. See, *e.g.,* Emporia *Gazette,* Oct. 2, Nov. 5, 1918.

78. *Ibid.,* Jan. 23, 1918.

79. White in *ibid.,* June 2, 1919.

80. White in *ibid.,* April 25, 1919.

81. *Ibid.*

82. *Ibid.*

83. White in *ibid.,* May 17, 1919.

84. [Lloyd George], "Some Considerations for the Peace Conference before They Finally Draft Their Terms" [March 25, 1919], Wilson MSS, series 8-A.

85. Lansing MS Desk Diary, March 21, 1919.

86. "Remarks of General Bliss at the Meeting of the Council of Four," March 27, 1919, Newton D. Baker MSS.

87. R[einhold]. Niebuhr to New Republic, XIX (June 14, 1919), 218. It is possible that this letter ought to be attributed to Richard Niebuhr; but its tone seems more characteristic of his brother's writings of this period.

88. Bullitt, review of Keynes' *Economic Consequences of the Peace, Freeman,* I (March 17, 1920), 18–21.

89. Colcord to House, Jan. 1, 1919, House MSS.

90. See Charles B. Forcey, "Walter Weyl and the Class War," in Harvey Goldberg, ed., *American Radicals* (New York, 1957), pp. 265–76.

91. *Nation,* CVIII (March 29, 1919), 480–1.

92. Hard to Robins, Oct. 17, 1919, Raymond Robins MSS, State Historical Society of Wisconsin.

93. Charles T. Hallinan to Lydia G. Wentworth, June 10, 1919, Wentworth MSS, Swarthmore College Peace Collection. See also Hallinan to Wentworth, June 16, 1919, *ibid.*

94. Colcord to Villard, March 20, 1922, Villard MSS.

95. Jerome Landfield to Samuel Harper, Nov. 22, 1918, Harper MSS.

96. John Spargo, "Bainbridge Colby," in Samuel F. Bemis, *The American Secretaries of State and Their Diplomacy* (New York, 1958), X, 202–5. Spargo, it will be recalled, was an anti-Bolshevik socialist, hence an admirer of Colby's policy.

97. *Cong. Rec.,* 68th Cong., 1st sess. (Dec. 20, 1923), p. 449.

98. *Ibid.,* pp. 446–7.

99. *Ibid.,* p. 448.

100. *Ibid.* (Jan. 7, 1924), pp. 592–612.

101. *Recognition of Russia,* Hearings before a Subcommittee of the Committee on Foreign Relations, U.S. Senate, 68th Cong., 1st sess. (1924), pp. 161–205.

102. *Cong. Rec.*, 68th Cong., 1st sess., (Jan. 7, 1924), pp. 618, 621. Lenroot of Wisconsin chided Borah for his inconsistency. See *ibid.*, p. 623.

103. Quoted in Anne Vincent Meiburger, *Efforts of Raymond Robins toward the Recognition of Soviet Russia* (Washington, 1953), p. 100.

104. *Cong. Rec.*, 68th Cong., 1st sess. (Jan. 7, 1924), pp. 614–15.

105. Walter S. Rogers to Creel, Aug. 13, 1917, Wilson MSS, 2d series.

106. George Creel, *How We Advertised America* (New York, 1920), p. 4.

107. Des Moines *Register,* March 23, 1917.

Bibliography

1. In Marquis Childs and James Reston, eds., *Walter Lippmann and His Times* (New York, 1959), pp. 37–59.

2. Ernest R. May, *The World War and American Isolation* (Cambridge, 1959), p. 462.

3. See above, pp. 77–78, 88.

4. See above, pp. 139–40.

Acknowledgments and Bibliography

IN pursuing this study I have had more than once, like Tennessee Williams' Blanche DuBois, to rely on the kindness of strangers, to say nothing of the patience of friends. The obligation of which I am most immediately aware is to the Social Science Research Council, which awarded me a generous grant to enable me to complete this work. I am grateful also to those who at earlier stages of my research gave me encouragement less tangible but as urgently needed, and to those who offered advice and criticism as well as encouragement. Both my wife and William R. Taylor, who read the manuscript, or parts of it, were particularly free with their criticism. Mr. Henry Graff also read the manuscript and made many helpful suggestions. At a much later stage, Miss Joan Teitel edited the text with great sympathy and patience. William E. Leuchtenburg, who is chiefly responsible for my interest in the recent period of American history, has helped me more than I can possibly say, at every stage not only of this work but of my entire career.

Charles B. Forcey has been particularly generous in putting at my disposal his notes of the Walter Weyl Papers, access to which was granted by the late Mrs. Walter Weyl. I am grateful also to Frances Brooks Colcord for permission to consult the papers of Lincoln Colcord, in her possession. I should also like to thank the librarians at Columbia, Yale, Swarthmore, Princeton, the University of Chicago, the Newberry Library, the Missouri Historical Society, the State Historical Society of Wisconsin, the New York Public Library, the New York State Library (Albany) and, in particular, at the Library of Congress, all of whom have been extremely helpful.

Some of my obligations to George F. Kennan will be obvious enough to readers of this study, but I doubt whether Mr. Kennan himself knows the full extent of what all students of the period of the First World War owe to him. In particular, whatever understanding of the war-aims question I have achieved, I owe in no small part to a conversation with Mr. Kennan at Princeton in the autumn of 1959, and to his essay, "Walter Lippmann, the *New Republic*, and the Russian Revolution," [1] which has guided me through a most difficult subject.

MANUSCRIPTS

The Papers of Woodrow Wilson in the Library of Congress are the central collection for a study of this sort, containing not only letters to and from Wilson but a great variety of other correspondence which was brought to the President's attention by his advisers. The 2d series (general correspondence, both incoming and outgoing, chronologically arranged), the 7th series (carbon copies of letters from Wilson) and series 8-A (all material relating to the peace conference) were of special importance for this study. The Papers of Edward M. House, Yale University Library, are if anything even richer for the study of the war years; House's diary, which is in the process of being edited for publication, is indispensable. But the House Papers are only the core around which the Yale University Library has built a vast collection of other material relating to the history of the war: among other collections, those of Frank Polk, William C. Bullitt, William Kent, and Walter Lippmann. The Lippmann Papers, unfortunately, are not yet open to scholars.

The Samuel N. Harper Papers, in the Library of the University of Chicago, bear more directly on the subject of this work than any others, since Harper was preoccupied with Russia throughout his career. In addition, he was an indefatigable correspondent, so that the collection is quite large. It contains carbons of outgoing correspondence as well as letters to Harper. The Papers of Raymond Robins, in the State Historical Society of Wisconsin at Madison, are equally important. The Alex Gumberg Papers, in the same archive, supplement the Robins papers. The Edward A. Ross Papers, also at Madison, are blank for the period of Ross' Russian visit in 1917, when apparently he saved none of his correspondence; before and after that, they are very full. The State Historical Society of Wisconsin also holds the papers of DeWitt Clinton Poole, Seymour Stedman and John R. Commons; but the Poole and Stedman collections contain nothing earlier than 1920, and the Commons collection is made up of routine correspondence. The Society's collection of Morris Hillquit Papers, however, is of considerable interest.

The Papers of Oswald Garrison Villard, Harvard University Library, contain a high proportion of gold to dross; so do the Amos Pinchot Papers in the Library of Congress. The Papers of Walter Weyl are privately held by Mrs. Weyl. The Papers of Lincoln Colcord are also in private hands, as noted above. The Charles R. Crane Papers are deposited in the Archive of Russian and East European History and Culture at Columbia University; they are an excellent collection. The Lincoln Steffens Papers in the Columbia University Library, on the other hand, are somewhat disappointing. For the purposes of this study, so are the Randolph Bourne Papers in the same library. The George Kennan Papers in the Library of Congress contain only outgoing correspondence, but that is of great interest. The Papers of Raymond Clapper, also in the Library of Congress, are spotty and almost entirely without organization. For the period of the war the collection consists solely of letters from Clapper to his wife, but these are so frequent and so voluble as to be of great value. The George Creel collection is small, as is the Charles Edward Russell collection; both are housed in the Library of Congress. The Ray Stannard Baker collection in the Library of Congress is an assortment of Wilsoniana, collected by Baker while working on his biography of Wilson. It includes a number of items which appear neither in the Wilson nor in the House Papers. Some of Baker's Papers, also bearing on Wilson, are at the Princeton University Library, which also holds the small but important Arthur Bullard collection.

The William Boyce Thompson–Hermann Hagedorn Papers, Library of Congress, were collected by Hagedorn for his biography of Thompson, which, however, by no means exhausts them. The Papers of Robert Lansing, also in the Library of Congress, contain very little correspondence of interest, but Lansing's Diary (consisting of long, ruminative discourses on events, written from time to time) and his Desk Diary (consisting of daily entries summarizing the day's work) more than make up for this deficiency.

The Papers of Elihu Root were useful for this study mainly for a few items bearing on Root's mission to Russia in 1917. The Newton D. Baker Papers are more rewarding. The Papers of William E. Borah and of George W. Norris contain little material relating to Russia but a great deal on liberal attitudes toward the war in general. The William Allen White Papers are disappointing. The Ben B. Lindsey Papers are still closed. All these collections are in the Library of Congress.

The Swarthmore College Peace Collection, a vast storehouse, contains, among other collections, the papers of Jane Addams, Emily Greene Balch and Lydia G. Wentworth, and papers relating to the People's Council of America and the American Union against Militarism. The Princeton University Library holds a great collection of papers relating to the American Civil Liberties Union. The Lillian D. Wald Papers in the New York Public Library are useful mainly for letters to and from Jane Addams. The Norman Thomas Papers are more interesting, the Frank Walsh Papers much less so, for my purposes. Both collections are in the New York Public Library. Neither the William V. Judson Papers nor the Graham Taylor Papers in the Newberry Library, Chicago, are of much interest; nor, surprisingly, are the Robert Herrick and Robert Morss Lovett Papers in the University of Chicago Library. The Papers of David R. Francis in the Missouri Historical Society, St. Louis, are more helpful. The Papers of Louis D. Brandeis, University of Louisville Law Library, contain a number of items of interest to the student of liberal attitudes toward Russia. The Hiram Johnson Papers are in the University of California Library, Berkeley; I was unable to consult them for this study.

NEWSPAPERS AND PERIODICALS

It has been said that American newspapers are less useful to students of opinion than European newspapers, because while the latter often reflect the opinion of a party or a faction the former reflect only the opinion of the editor or publisher.[2] This generalization ignores the fact that American newspapers each make their appeal to a certain type of readership and are therefore subtly influenced, not only in their editorial opinions but in their treatment of news, by their own notions, at least, of what their readers expect of them, if not directly by readers themselves. The unsuccessful efforts of the Philadelphia *Public Ledger* to pursue a liberal editorial policy in opposition to a conservative clientele ought to dispose at once of the idea that publishers enjoy complete freedom in their choice of policies.[3] Nor can anyone read for long in the files of the

New York *Evening Post* without realizing that, in this case, the editors' point of view must have been shared by a great number of the paper's readers. The genteel pacifism of the paper (giving way as the war went on to an orthodox "internationalism"), its cautious advocacy of women's rights, its enthusiastic support of the New Freedom (especially tariff reform), its endorsement of prohibition, all reflect an identifiable point of view, that of the liberal mugwump. It would be a mistake to suppose that the paper's opinions reflected only those of Rollo Ogden, even though during his editorship Ogden dictated editorial policy to a degree rare on any paper. Clearly the *Evening Post* was the authentic voice of mugwumpery, and its editor spoke for thousands of people who shared his views.

The Springfield *Republican*, in these years under the editorship of Richard Hooker, and the Des Moines *Register*, edited by Harvey Ingham, saw the world from much the same point of view, although they retained their anti-imperialist leanings longer than the *Evening Post*. All of these papers, however, supported Wilson in his struggle with the Senate over ratification of the treaty. So did the New York *World*, which slavishly followed the administration at every turn. The St. Louis *Post-Dispatch*, controlled, like the *World*, by the Pulitzer family, pursued much the same policies. But if the *Evening Post* was the embodiment of mugwumpery, the *World* and the *Post-Dispatch* breathed the spirit of muckraking—muckraking no longer militant and tending increasingly toward orthodoxy in national and international affairs, but still priding itself on its crusading zeal. The Chicago *Daily News* and the Milwaukee *Journal*, although both Wilsonian in orientation, were somewhat more conservative. The Emporia *Gazette*, a classic case of a one-man paper, nevertheless spoke, in a general way, for all those midwestern Republican progressives who, like William Allen White, eventually enlisted under the banner of Woodrow Wilson. All these papers can be called "liberal"; none was in any sense radical.

In addition to these journals, which I have followed day by day throughout the period embraced by this study, and in addition to the New York *Times*, which, consulted for information, proved to be a fruitful source of misinformation as well, I have examined, in less detail, the Omaha *World-Herald*, the Louisville *Courier-Journal*, the Washington *Post*, the New York *Tribune*, the Baltimore *Sun* and the Philadelphia *North American*, in ascending order of conservatism. The *North American,* a Roosevelt-progressive organ, was a particularly vicious and intemperate sheet.

The following secondary works are helpful to the reader of newspapers: Frank Luther Mott, *American Journalism: A History of Newspapers in the United States through 250 Years* (New York, 1941); Allan Nevins, *The Evening Post: A Century of Journalism* (New York, 1922); Oswald Garrison Villard, *Some Newspapers and Newspaper-men* (New York, 1923); James W. Barrett, *The World, The Flesh and Messrs. Pulitzer* (New York, 1931); Gerald W. Johnson *et al., The Sunpapers of Baltimore* (New York, 1937); Richard Hooker, *The Story of an Independent Newspaper: One Hundred Years of the Springfield Republican* (New York, 1924); Ralph O. Nafziger, "The American Press and Public Opinion during the World War, 1914 to April 1917" (unpublished Ph.D. dissertation, University of Wisconsin, 1936).

Among periodicals, the *New Republic* and the *Nation* are by far the most important for a study of liberal attitudes toward Russia. The *Nation* underwent a change of ownership in July, 1918, and must be read with that in mind.[4] The *Dial* devoted itself to literary subjects until its removal from Chicago to New York in the summer of 1918, whereupon, under the editorship of Harold Stearns and others, it became for a brief time predominantly political in content. Under Stearns the *Dial,* in both format and policy, resembled the post-1918 *Nation.* The *Nation,* in turn, was decidedly more radical than the *New Republic.* The *Public,* on the other hand, which also moved from Chicago to New York at about this time, although controlled by prominent single-taxers, was more conservative on war issues than any of the others. Like them, however, it opposed ratification of the Treaty of Versailles. The main interest of the *Survey,* edited by Paul U. Kellogg, was the social work movement. In international affairs its contributors tended toward pacifism. Because the magazine had no editorial policy of its own, it is of slightly less interest than the others.

To the left of these journals were *Pearson's Magazine,* edited by Frank Harris and A. W. Ricker, and Max Eastman's *Liberator,* founded in 1918 as a successor to the *Masses. Upton Sinclair's,* founded in April, 1918 ("A Monthly Magazine for a Clean Peace and the Internation" [*sic*]), and *Reconstruction,* founded in 1919, were edited by "loyal" socialists. Albert Jay Nock's *Freeman,* anarchistic rather than socialistic, was founded in 1920, too late to be of much use here.

Asia, the monthly publication of the American Asiatic Association, contains a good many articles on the Russian revolution. Insofar as the magazine itself had a policy, it was one of opposition to intervention.

I used the *Independent* and the *Outlook* chiefly for the early years of this study, and the *Metropolitan*, *Literary Digest*, and *Current Opinion* only intermittently.

BOOKS AND ARTICLES

Only articles of unusual interest are mentioned here; for the rest, readers may consult the footnotes in the text.

Russia before the Revolution

The works of Stephen Graham are voluminous. The most important are probably *The Way of Martha and the Way of Mary* (New York, 1915); *Changing Russia* (London, 1915) and *Undiscovered Russia* (London, 1912). In addition Graham published articles on Russia in numerous periodicals, both English and American, throughout the early years of the war. Other examples of Russophilia include Charles Sarolea, *Europe's Debt to Russia* (London, 1916); E. J. Dillon's regular contributions to the *Contemporary Review* (London), 1900–1917; Donald Mackenzie Wallace, *Russia* (New York, 1877) and *Our Russian Ally* (London, 1914); and, of special interest, H. G. Wells' curious apology for Russia, "The Liberal Fear of Russia," *Harper's Weekly*, LIX (Sept. 19, 1914), 268–70. For more critical comment see George Kennan, *Siberia and the Exile System* (New York, 1891) and Kennan's contributions to the *Outlook*, 1900–1917; William English Walling, *Russia's Message: The True Import of the Revolution* (New York, 1908); and the various articles cited in the notes to chapter I.

Among secondary works on this period of Russian history, Bernard Pares, *The Fall of the Russian Monarchy* (London, 1939); Michael T. Florinsky, *The End of the Russian Empire* (New Haven, 1931); and C. Jay Smith, *The Russian Struggle for Power* (New York, 1956) are all outstanding. On the question of Tsarist-

German relations, as well as on political divisions within Germany, see John W. Wheeler-Bennett, *Wooden Titan: Hindenburg in Twenty Years of German History* (New York, 1936); Klaus Epstein, *Matthias Erzberger and the Dilemma of German Democracy* (Princeton, 1959); and Karl Schorske, *German Social Democracy* (Cambridge, 1955). One who reads neither German nor Russian finds the primary sources on this subject necessarily limited. Theobald von Bethmann-Hollweg, *Reflections on the World War* (London, 1920), is very thin, and Erich von Ludendorff, *Ludendorff's Own Story* (New York, 1919), 2 vols., confines itself largely to military matters. It is a pity the General did not follow this wise practice in life as in literature. Von Jagow left no memoirs, but those of Alfred von Tirpitz, *My Memoirs* (New York, 1919), 2 vols., and Erich von Falkenhayn, *The German General Staff and Its Decisions, 1914–1916* (New York, 1920), are illuminating, if only to show how difficult it is, in the case of Germany, as in the case of the United States, to make a correlation between ideology and war aims. The collection of German documents translated and edited by Z. A. B. Zeman, cited below, helps to make up for the absence of other sources. See also Ernesta Drinker Bullitt, *An Uncensored Diary from the Central Empires* (Garden City, 1917), which, however, is more helpful in understanding American opinion than German. For the correspondence between the Kaiser and the Tsar see Hermann Bernstein, *The Willy-Nicky Correspondence* (New York, 1918); also Sidney B. Fay, "The Kaiser's Secret Negotiations with the Tsar, 1904–1905," *American Historical Review*, XXI (Oct., 1918), 48–72. Sir George Buchanan, *My Mission to Russia and Other Diplomatic Memories* (London, 1923), 2 vols., is useful.

The War

Walter Weyl, *The End of the War* (New York, 1918); Walter Lippmann, *The Political Scene* (New York, 1919); Horace Kallen, *The Structure of Lasting Peace* (Boston, 1918); Frederic C. Howe, *The Only Possible Peace* (New York, 1919); and Norman Hapgood, *The Advancing Hour* (New York, 1920), all bear more or less directly on the war; but all these works represent unsatisfactory attempts to deal at length and in detail with a political situation which was changing too rapidly to yield to such treatment. The most revealing comments on the war and on the question of war aims, as on the Russian revolution itself, remain imbedded in newspapers, periodicals and manuscripts.

Of secondary works dealing with liberal attitudes toward the war, Arno J. Mayer, *Political Origins of the New Diplomacy* (New Haven, 1959), is easily the best; but see also Laurence W. Martin, *Peace without Victory: Woodrow Wilson and the British Liberals* (New Haven, 1958). Ernest R. May, *The World War and American Isolation* (Cambridge, 1959) is a much more conventional treatment, which in its interpretations follows what is still the standard authority, Charles Seymour, *American Diplomacy during the World War* (Baltimore, 1934). Arthur Link, *Woodrow Wilson and the Progressive Era* (New York, 1954), also follows Seymour, although in this volume (but not in some of his later writings) Link is more critical of Wilson than either Seymour or May. None of these writers seems to me to grasp either the importance or the difficulty of the war-aims controversy, for an appreciation of the subtleties of which one must consult the works of Mayer and Martin and the sketch by George F. Kennan, "Walter Lippmann, the *New Republic* and the Russian Revolution," cited above, p. 263, n. 1.

Frederick C. Paxson, *American Democracy and the World War* (Boston, 1936–1948), 3 vols., covers everything without getting beneath the surface of anything; but James R. Mock and Cedric Larson, *Words that Won the War* (Princeton, 1939) is a thorough study of the Committee on Public Information that raises broader questions than the subject might seem to imply. Walton E. Bean, "George Creel and His Critics: A Study of the Attacks on the Committee on Public Information, 1917–1919" (unpublished Ph.D. dissertation, University of California, 1941) is an unconvincing defense of Creel. Creel's own apology is his *How We Advertised America* (New York, 1920), the title of which speaks for itself. Creel's *The War, the World and Wilson* (New York, 1920), a somewhat broader survey, is interesting chiefly for the dexterity with which the author confuses issues and blurs distinctions. Robert K. Murray, *Red Scare: A Study in National Hysteria, 1919–1920* (Minneapolis, 1955), examines roughly the same subject, as its sub-title indicates, as the study by Mock and Larson, but in a somewhat later period. On the movement for a League of Nations see Ruhl J. Bartlett, *The League to Enforce Peace* (Chapel Hill, 1944). The League of Free Nations Association has not received comparable attention.

Sidney Kaplan, "Social Engineers as Saviors: Effects of World War I on Some American Liberals," *Journal of the History of Ideas*, XVII (June, 1956), 347–69, and Selig Adler, *The Isolationist Impulse* (Buffalo, 1959), bear indirectly on the subject of this study. Henry F. May, *The End of American Innocence* (New York, 1959), is much broader, dealing not only with the war but with the whole drift of American culture in the period just before the United States entered the war. It is an indispensable book.

On the peace conference, see David Hunter Miller, *My Diary at the Peace Conference of Paris* (privately printed, [1924]), 21 vols.; Robert Lansing, *The Peace Negotiations: A Personal Narrative* (Boston, 1921); and David Lloyd George, *Memoirs of the Peace Conference* (New Haven, 1939), 2 vols. Mitchell Pirie Briggs, *George D. Herron and the European Settlement* (Palo Alto, 1932), based on 13 volumes of Herron MSS in the Hoover Library, is important for the Prinkipo proposal; see also William Allen White, "What Happened to Prinkipo," *Metropolitan*, LI (Dec., 1919), 68 ff. On the Bullitt mission see Bullitt's "The Tragedy of Versailles," *Life*, XVI (March 27, 1944), 98 ff., and, more important, Ann Garcia Gerhart, "The United States and the Problem of Russia at the Paris Peace Conference" (honors thesis, Bryn Mawr, 1956), which draws upon notes made by Walter W. Pettit, unavailable elsewhere. John Thompson has written a study, "The Russian Problem at the Conference of Versailles," (unpublished Ph.D. dissertation, Columbia University, 1960), but he has withdrawn it from circulation pending publication. For a brief summary of the subject see George F. Kennan, "Russia and the Versailles Conference," *American Scholar*, XXX (winter 1960–61), 13–42. Broader secondary works on the peace conference include Paul Birdsall, *Versailles Twenty Years After* (New York, 1941) and Thomas A. Bailey, *Woodrow Wilson and the Lost Peace* (New York, 1944).

The Revolution

Arthur Bullard, *The Russian Pendulum: Autocracy—Democracy—Bolshevism* (New York, 1919) and Oliver M. Sayler, *Russia White or Red* (Boston, 1919) are the most judicious of contemporary accounts. Much more partisan are Louise Bryant, *Six Red Months in Russia* (New York, 1918); Arthur Ransome, *Russia in 1919* (New York, 1919); Bessie Beatty, *The Red Heart of Russia*

(New York, 1918); M. Phillips Price, *My Reminiscences of the Russian Revolution* (London, 1921); Louis Edgar Browne, *New Russia in the Balance* (Chicago, 1918); and, of course, John Reed, *Ten Days that Shook the World* (New York, 1919), all of which favor the Bolsheviks; and John Spargo, *Bolshevism: The Enemy of Political and Industrial Democracy* (New York, 1919), *The Psychology of Bolshevism* (New York, 1919), *The Greatest Failure in All History* (New York, 1920), and *Russia as an American Problem* (New York, 1920); William English Walling, *Sovietism: The ABC of Russian Bolshevism* (New York, 1920); and E. J. Dillon, *The Eclipse of Russia* (New York, 1918), all of which vigorously denounce them. Alexander Berkman, *The Bolshevik Myth* (New York, 1925), also denounces the Bolsheviks, but from a very different point of view. Edgar Sisson, *100 Red Days* (New Haven, 1931), also hostile, was written somewhat later and is cast more in the form of a memoir than these other accounts. Charles Edward Russell, *Unchained Russia* (New York, 1918), is surprisingly restrained; Edward Alsworth Ross, *Russia in Upheaval* (New York, 1918), shows the influence of Robins. Isaac Don Levine, *The Russian Revolution* (New York, 1917); Moissaye J. Olgin, *The Soul of the Russian Revolution* (New York, 1917); and Michael Farbman, *The Russian Revolution and the War* (London, 1917), all date from the pre-Bolshevik period of the revolution, and all are written from a point of view favorable to the soviet as opposed to the Provisional Government. Samuel N. Harper, "Forces behind the Russian Revolution," in Alexander Petrunkevitch *et al.*, *The Russian Revolution* (Cambridge, 1918), pp. 25–43, stresses the Tsarist-German conspiracy.

Walter Lippmann and Charles Merz, "A Test of the News," *New Republic*, XXIII (supplement to Aug. 4, 1920), examines the bias in the New York *Times*' coverage of the revolution. Evans Clark, *Facts and Fabrications about Soviet Russia* (New York, 1920), surveys news distortion in general. Meno Lovenstein, *American Opinion of Soviet Russia* (Washington, 1941) also stresses the distortion of news. Both this work and Winton U. Solberg, "The Impact of Soviet Russia on American Life and Thought, 1917–1933" (unpublished Ph.D. dissertation, Harvard, 1952), rely for evidence of American press opinion chiefly on the *Literary Digest*, a procedure made necessary by their effort to cover more ground than can be treated with any care. Beth Alene Roberts,

"A Study of American Opinion regarding Allied Intervention in Siberia" (unpublished M.A. thesis, University of Hawaii, 1938), is more modest, and more persuasive. Paul H. Anderson, *The Attitude of the American Leftist Leaders toward the Russian Revolution* (Notre Dame, 1942), a doctoral thesis, suffers by the indiscriminate use of the word "leftist" to mean anyone to the left of, and including, Herbert Hoover and Samuel Gompers. Stephen Richards Graubard, "The Russian Revolution in British Labor History, 1917–1924" (unpublished Ph.D. dissertation, Harvard, 1951) touches the subject of this work only indirectly. The same thing is true of Theodore Draper's important study, *The Roots of American Communism* (New York, 1957).

On the history of the revolution itself N. N. Sukhanov, *The Russian Revolution* (London, 1955), is perhaps the most illuminating of the Russian sources available in English, although it deals only with the period from March to November, 1917. Sukhanov, as a member of a small dissident faction of the Menshevik party, was committed to none of the major parties engaged in the struggle for power; therefore he was free to criticize them all. None of the other observers was so detached. Victor M. Chernov, *The Great Russian Revolution* (New Haven, 1936) is the work of a Social Revolutionary (although highly critical of Kerensky), as is Alexander Kerensky, *The Crucifixion of Liberty* (New York, 1934), the thesis of which is evident in the title. Leon Trotsky, *The History of the Russian Revolution* (New York, 1932), 3 vols., naturally shows a Bolshevik bias; on Trotsky see also the excellent biography by Isaac Deutscher, of which the first volume, *The Prophet Armed* (New York, 1954), covers the period of the revolution. Lenin's *Selected Works* are available in English in a two volume edition (Moscow: Foreign Languages Publishing House, 1951).

The best general survey of the revolution is still William Henry Chamberlin, *The Russian Revolution* (New York, 1935), 2 vols. E. H. Carr, *The Bolshevik Revolution* (London, 1950–53), 3 vols., is more detailed but highly partisan. Louis Fischer, *The Soviets in World Affairs* (Princeton, 1951), 2 vols., a detailed study of Soviet diplomacy, is also biased in favor of the Bolsheviks. It benefits, however, from the author's close association with Chicherin and Litvinov. John W. Wheeler-Bennett, *The Forgotten Peace: Brest Litovsk* (London, 1938), is a masterly account. Studies of Soviet-American relations are legion. George F. Kennan, *Soviet-American Relations, 1917–1920* (Princeton, 1956–1958), 2 vols., is easily the best, but still incomplete, ending at August, 1918. Robert Paul Browder, *The Origins of Soviet-American Diplomacy* (Princeton, 1953), is a brief survey. Thomas A. Bailey, *America Faces Russia* (Ithaca, 1950), and Stefan T. Possony, *A Century of Conflict* (Chicago, 1953), are somewhat more extended but also thinner. William Appleman Williams, *American-Russian Relations, 1781–1947* (New York, 1952), the better part of which is an extension of Williams' dissertation on Raymond Robins, favors the Robins point of view. Among more specialized studies Leonid I. Strakhovsky, *The Origins of American Intervention in North Russia* (Princeton, 1937), is the only one to deal with that subject. Histories of the Siberian intervention, however, abound. John Albert White, *The Siberian Intervention* (Princeton, 1950), attempts to defend intervention as a maneuver directed against Japan. Pauline Tompkins, *American-Russian Relations in the Far East* (New York, 1949), also leans toward that theory. Betty Miller Unterberger, *America's Siberian Expedition, 1918–1920* (Durham, N.C., 1956); and Clarence A. Manning, *The Siberian Fiasco* (New York, 1952), are more critical of American policy. So is the memoir by General William S. Graves, commander of an expedition of which he disapproved, *America's Siberian Adventure* (New York, 1931). More specialized than any of these works are Ray W. McDuffee, "The Department of State and the Russian Revolutions, March–November 1917" (unpublished Ph.D. dissertation, Georgetown University, 1954), based exclusively on State Dept. sources; Claude E. Fike, "The Influence of the Creel Committee and the American Red Cross on Russian-American Relations, 1917–1919," *Journal of Modern History*, XXXI (June, 1959), 93–109, which greatly exaggerates the influence of those agencies; and George F. Kennan, "The Sisson Documents," *Journal of Modern History*, XXVIII (June, 1958), 130 ff., a detailed textual analysis. Kennan's "Soviet Historiography and America's Role in the Intervention," *American Historical Review*, LXV (Jan., 1960), 302–22, goes to great lengths to convict Soviet historians of bias in their treatment of the subject—something which one would suppose might have been self-evident.

Memoirs, Biographies, Collected Papers

By the time he reached the war years, Ray Stannard Baker in his *Woodrow Wilson: Life and Letters* (Garden City, 1927–1939), 8 vols., was reduced merely to arranging, without comment, the vast materials at his disposal. But his volumes, incoherent as they are, still constitute a useful source. Baker with William E. Dodd also edited *The Public Papers of Woodrow Wilson* (New York, 1927), 3 vols. Both works omit much valuable material which, until Wilson's papers have been published in definitive form, can be found only in the Wilson Papers. The same is true of Charles Seymour, *The Intimate Papers of Colonel House* (Boston, 1926–1928), 4 vols. Ella Winter and Granville Hicks, *The Letters of Lincoln Steffens* (New York, 1938), 2 vols., includes the better part of Steffens' outgoing correspondence; it may be supplemented with Steffens' *Autobiography* (New York, 1931). Oscar Cargill, "Lincoln Steffens: Pied Piper of the Kremlin," *Georgia Review*, V (winter, 1951), 430–44, is a rather shrill attack. Walter Johnson, ed., *Selected Letters of William Allen White* (New York, 1947), his *William Allen White's America* (New York, 1947); and White's own *Autobiography* (New York, 1946), pretty well exhaust that subject. White's biography of Wilson, *The Man, His Times, and His Task* (Boston, 1924), reveals more of the author than of the subject, as does David Lawrence, *The True Story of Woodrow Wilson* (New York, 1924).

Few of the autobiographies of the period equal those of Steffens and White in literary interest. Hutchins Hapgood, *A Victorian in the Modern World* (New York, 1939), is superb, but Norman Hapgood, *The Changing Years* (New York, 1930), is extremely pedestrian. Albert Jay Nock, *Memoirs of a Superfluous Man* (New York, 1941), is also disappointing. Robert Morss Lovett, *All Our Years* (New York, 1948), is informative and sometimes moving, and Frederic C. Howe, *Confessions of a Reformer* (New York, 1925), is even better. But Oswald Garrison Villard, *Fighting Years: Memoirs of a Liberal Editor* (New York, 1939); Morris Hillquit, *Loose Leaves from a Busy Life* (New York, 1934); Ray Stannard Baker, *American Chronicle* (New York, 1945); and Charles Edward Russell, *Bare Hands and Stone Walls: Some Recollections of a Side-Line Reformer* (New York, 1933), are uniformly uninspired. George Creel, *Rebel at Large* (New York, 1947), greatly exaggerates the author's rebelliousness. The memoirs of Samuel N. Harper, *The Russia I Believe In* (Chicago, 1945), confirm one's suspicion that Harper's gifts were social rather than literary. Those interested in Harper should also consult Bernard Pares, *My Russian Memoirs* (London, 1931).

Thomas W. Lamont, *Across World Frontiers* (New York, 1951), fills in some of the gaps left by Hermann Hagedorn's biography, *The Magnate: William Boyce Thompson and His Time* (New York, 1935). Raymond Robins left no memoirs, but he has been the subject of three pseudo-biographical studies. William Hard, *Raymond Robins' Own Story* (New York, 1920), is a panegyric, and William Appleman Williams, "Raymond Robins and Russian-American Relations, 1917–1938" (unpublished Ph.D. dissertation, University of Wisconsin, 1950), is scarcely less admiring. Sister Anne Vincent Meiburger, *Efforts of Raymond Robins toward the Recognition of Soviet Russia and the Outlawry of War, 1917–1933* (Washington, 1953), is a Catholic University doctoral thesis. It is not friendly to Robins or the Bolsheviks. Bruce Lockhart, *British Agent* (New York, 1933), throws additional light on the activities of Robins and his friends.

Norman Angell, *After All* (London, 1951), is useful, particularly in view of Angell's close connection with the *New Republic*. Of the *New Republic* editors, only Alvin Johnson, *Pioneer's Progress* (New York, 1952), wrote an autobiography. Francis Hackett, *I Chose Denmark* (New York, 1940), and Walter Weyl, *Tired Radicals* (New York, 1921), do not take the place of autobiographies. Ernest Poole and others edited a memorial volume, *Walter Weyl, An Appreciation* (New York, 1922), and Poole himself wrote an autobiography, *The Bridge: My Own Story* (New York, 1940). Lippmann has inspired a number of critiques, none of them very penetrating; the best is David E. Weingast, *Walter Lippmann* (New Brunswick, 1949). Croly still wants a biographer. The best study of the *New Republic* is Charles Budd Forcey, "Intellectuals in Crisis: Croly, Weyl, Lippmann and the New Republic" (unpublished Ph.D. dissertation, University of Wisconsin, 1954), now superseded by the same author's *The Crossroads of Liberalism: Croly, Weyl, Lippmann and the Progressive Era, 1900–1925* (New York, 1961). See also Forcey's "Walter Weyl and the Class War," in Harvey Goldberg ed., *American Radicals: Some Problems and Personalities* (New York, 1957), pp. 265–76.

OFFICIAL AND SEMI-OFFICIAL DOCUMENTS

Frank Alfred Golder, *Documents of Russian History, 1914–1917* (New York, 1927), is a useful compilation. On the question of German policy toward Russia see the collection of documents from the German foreign archives edited by Z. A. B. Zeman, *Germany and the Revolution in Russia, 1915–1918* (London, 1958). For the text of the secret treaties see F. Seymour Cocks, *The Secret Treaties and Understandings* (London, 1918). Russian-American relations are documented in C. K. Cumming and Walter W. Pettit, *Russian-American Relations, March, 1917–March, 1920* (New York, 1920), prepared under the auspices of the League of Free Nations Association and based in large part on the papers of Raymond Robins. See also U.S. Department of State, *Papers relating to the Foreign Relations of the United States, 1918, Russia* (Washington, 1931), 3 vols., and the same series for 1919, *Russia* (Washington, 1937). These should be supplemented by reference to the State Department files, especially file 861.00, in the National Archives. *Treaty of Peace with Germany*, Hearings before the Committee on Foreign Relations, U.S. Senate, 66th Cong., 1st sess. (1919), contains Bullitt's testimony, which B. W. Huebsch also issued as a pamphlet, *The Bullitt Mission to Russia* (New York, 1919).

The investigations of the Overman committee, which include the testimony of Robins, Louise Bryant, Bessie Beatty and others, are cited here as *Bolshevik Propaganda*, Hearings before the Subcommittee of the Committee on the Judiciary, U.S. Senate, 66th Cong., 1st sess. (1919). The Lusk Committee of the New York state legislature conducted hearings (1919) on the same subject and issued a lengthy report, *Revolutionary Radicalism: Its History, Purpose and Tactics*, Report of the Joint Legislative Committee Investigating Seditious Activities, New York State Senate (1920). Still another inquiry into Bolshevik propaganda, this one directed at the activities of Ludwig Martens' Soviet Bureau, is *Russian Propaganda*, Hearing before a Subcommittee of the Committee on Foreign Relations, U.S. Senate, 66th Cong., 2d sess. (1920). The subject comes up again, in rather broader form, in *Recognition of Russia*, Hearings before a Subcommittee of the Committee on Foreign Relations, 68th Cong., 1st sess. (1924). *Conditions in Russia*, Hearings before the Committee on Foreign Affairs, U.S. House of Representatives, 66th Cong., 3d sess. (1921) is concerned mainly with questions of trade.

Congressional Record, 65th Cong., 3d sess. (1919), includes the debate over the Johnson resolution for withdrawal from Siberia; the same publication, 68th Cong., 1st sess. (1923–1924), the debate over Borah's resolution for recognition of Soviet Russia.

Index